Praise for Why Great Leaders Don't Take Yes for an Answer

"*Why Great Leaders Don't Take Yes for an Answer* addresses a perennial and pernicious thorn in the leader's side—the yes-men in every organization. (And if you think your company is without them, you really need this book!) Leaders at all levels can use Mike Roberto's advice, to make better decisions and align their teams for results."

—Ken Blanchard, co-author of *The One Minute Manager*®
and *Customer Mania*

"Deciding how to decide: a powerful idea that all leaders should understand and put into practice. In doing so, they can become adept at stimulating candid dialogues, testing their company's core assumptions, and achieving alignment. Roberto's ideas have already begun to make a profound difference in the effectiveness of our management meetings. Our clients around the world would do well to adopt Roberto's straightforward recommendations."

—Ed Boswell, president and CEO, The Forum Corporation

"Too often leaders mistake silence for agreement. Roberto offers concrete advice on how to beat this trap. A must-read for leaders at all levels."

—Kathleen M. Eisenhardt, Stanford W. Ascherman M.D.
Professor, Stanford University and co-director,
Stanford Technology Ventures Program

"In his book *Why Great Leaders Don't Take Yes for an Answer*, Michael Roberto provides a unique and very enlightening look into the process of decision making. His thesis around 'critical consensus building' is worthwhile reading for any manager or entrepreneur that strives to be the most effective leader they can be."

—Jonathan Kraft, vice chairman, New England Patriots

"Unasked questions and undermined decisions are the two main reasons for corporate failure. To avoid these dangerous wrong turns, every executive should study Professor Roberto's clear road maps for making and implementing decisions."

—Wilbur L. Ross, Jr., chairman of the board,
International Steel Group

"*Why Great Leaders Don't Take Yes for an Answer* rises far and above the other books on encouraging openness and managing conflict. Instead of offering empty platitudes, Michael Roberto has delivered a thoughtful and well-researched book with clear, specific actions to make the lessons work in the real world. Anyone who supports the clear exchange of ideas can and should benefit from this excellent and thoroughly enjoyable book."

—Dr. David Sirota, chairman emeritus of Sirota Survey Intelligence and
author of *The Enthusiastic Employee: How Companies
Profit by Giving Workers What They Want*

"This is a book that should be on every manager's desk. Roberto writes in clear, easy-to-read language about why managing conflict and decision making in an explicit manner is so important to organizational success. He also gives practical examples of how to do it. The chapter on 'deciding how to decide' alone is worth the price of the book."

—Sue Annis Hammond, author of *The Thin Book of Appreciative Inquiry* and consultant, HRD Solutions

"One of the best compliments an author can get is for someone to begin reading a book and not put it down until it is finished. This was my experience with Roberto's great tome on leadership. The quotes at the beginning of each chapter are classic. Many of the examples helped me understand some of my best leadership decisions and also a few of my worst in running the specialized investment banking firm I have headed for the past 31 years. There are few really good books on leadership, at least few that I have read. Roberto's is the best."

—Matthew R. Simmons, author of *Twilight in the Desert: The Coming Saudi Oil Shock and the World Economy* and chairman, Simmons and Company International

"A great primer for all leaders on the art and science of decision making. Michael used examples ranging from the disastrous 1996 Everest climb to the Columbia disaster, the Bay of Pigs, and the Cuban missile crisis to thoughtfully outline best practices in the process of 'deciding how to decide!'"

—Lawrence N. Stevenson, CEO, PepBoys

"Every executive aspiring to be a good leader should read this book. First, Roberto crashes the myth that holds many back from being good leaders. That is, good leaders need to make the decisions. Instead, Roberto asserts that to be a good leader one must manage the decision-making process, not make the good decisions. But it is Roberto's insight into the decision-making process, or more importantly, the drivers of organizational performance, that is most valuable. All of us, no matter what level in the organization, need to embrace the need for cognitive conflict to produce the highest-quality decisions, while guarding against the ways in which affective conflict can greatly deteriorate the shared understanding and consensus necessary for effective implementation of these decisions. Roberto offers many tools and techniques for all of us to use to improve our ability to manage conflict and improve our organization's effectiveness and performance. While I believe that Constellation's success results from the fact that our operational model and its supporting culture and value reflect much of what Roberto describes, I also believe that we can use this model to ensure that managing conflict becomes an enduring part of Constellation's leadership culture."

—Richard Sands, chairman of the board and CEO, Constellation Brands, Inc.

"The premise of this book is music to my ears. For years I've been working with teams of people facing real challenges, both in the great outdoors with Outward Bound or in the midst of bringing my educational venture to life. Roberto has elegantly and eloquently put his finger on the very heart of the leadership dilemma. I look forward to putting the lessons to work at Shackleton Schools as we inspire and educate the next generation of leaders."

—Luke O'Neill, CEO and founder, Shackleton Schools

"Today, every CEO in the rapidly changing business environment cudgels his or her brains out on how to make and execute decisions effectively. This book is very much useful in that it shows extensively how to deal with such issues, together with abundant examples. Japanese business managers should read it to be exposed to such approaches that, I believe, are well applicable to consensus-driven Japanese companies."

—Shozo Hashimoto, former CEO, Nomura Research Institute, Ltd.

"Do you want to release the potential of your organization? If you have the ego and strength to hear contrary ideas, this is a fantastic read. Each paragraph, each sentence, is powerful, offering tools and suggestions to bring your organization to a higher level."

—Gerardine Ferlins, president and CEO, Cirtronics Corporation

"How we make decisions is what organizational leadership is all about, and with powerful accounts and compelling research, Michael Roberto brilliantly leads us to the essence of deciding how to decide when it really matters."

—Michael Useem, William and Jacalyn Egan professor of management, Wharton School of Business and author of *The Leadership Moment*

"Through the ages, many leaders have paid a price for not comprehending the need to balance conflict and consensus in the decision-making groups they head. Mike Roberto frames this tension exquisitely and provides tangible guidance for leaders who want variety, ferment, and constructive tension in their groups on the one hand, and unity in execution on the other. Based upon a wealth of rigorous academic research, and with loads of up-to-date and engaging examples, this book is a must for leaders at all levels."

—Donald C. Hambrick, Smeal chaired professor of management, Smeal College of Business Administration, The Pennsylvania State University

"Michael Roberto has written a soundly researched, yet easy-to-read, practical business book that can ensure that you will make better executive decisions. Read it and profit from its wisdom!"

—Dr. Drea Zigarmi, co-author of *The Leader Within and Leadership* and the *One Minute Manager*

"This book is an important contribution to managerial best practice. Roberto gives an impressive synthesis of original and prior research in writing that is rich, well-crafted, to the point, and studded with compelling case examples. Get this book and study it carefully as a tonic for decision processes in your own firm."

—Robert F. Bruner, distinguished professor of business administration, Darden Graduate School of Business Administration, University of Virginia

"Drawing on both decision-making scholarship in a number of academic disciplines and clinical research in organizations, Roberto develops a most useful way of thinking about decision making in complex organizations and provides a number of conceptual tools that executives can apply right away and that provide some new frontiers for scholars to study further."

—E. Ralph Biggadike, professor of professional practice, Columbia University Graduate School of Business

"Professor Roberto has provided a rigorous, research-based, and much-needed framework that allows executives to improve their decision making. Those managers who want to improve decision making—and results—need to read this book."

—Professor Morten Hansen, associate professor of entrepreneurship, INSEAD

"Far too often leaders squelch dissenting views and make it difficult for employees to deliver bad news. Others find it difficult to manage contentious debate and obtain closure on tough issues. Roberto provides practical advice for how leaders can encourage constructive disagreement, use this to achieve more creative solutions, and ultimately affect alignment and action."

—Jeff Weiss, director and founder, Vantage Partners

"While reading *Why Great Leaders Don't Take Yes for an Answer*, I kept thinking of the strategic decisions my team and I have made, and wished I had read the book 25 years ago. Focus on the decision-making process—not the decision itself—is the lesson of this book, and one that all executives need to learn."

—William C. Byham, Ph.D., chairman & CEO, Development Dimensions International and author of *Grow Your Own Leaders*

Why Great Leaders Don't Take Yes for an Answer

Ideas. Action. Impact.
**Wharton School
Publishing**

In the face of accelerating turbulence and change, business leaders and policy makers need new ways of thinking to sustain performance and growth.

Wharton School Publishing offers a trusted source for stimulating ideas from thought leaders who provide new mental models to address changes in strategy, management, and finance. We seek out authors from diverse disciplines with a profound understanding of change and its implications. We offer books and tools that help executives respond to the challenge of change.

Every book and management tool we publish meets quality standards set by The Wharton School of the University of Pennsylvania. Each title is reviewed by the Wharton School Publishing Editorial Board before being given Wharton's seal of approval. This ensures that Wharton publications are timely, relevant, important, conceptually sound or empirically based, and implementable.

To fit our readers' learning preferences, Wharton publications are available in multiple formats, including books, audio, and electronic.

To find out more about our books and management tools, visit us at whartonsp.com and Wharton's executive education site, exceed.wharton.upenn.edu.

Why Great Leaders Don't Take Yes for an Answer

Managing for Conflict and Consensus

Michael A. Roberto
Harvard Business School

Ideas. Action. Impact.
**Wharton School
Publishing**

Library of Congress Catalog Number: 2005920211

Vice President and Editor-in-Chief: Tim Moore
Acquisitions Editor: Paula Sinnott
Editorial Assistant: Kate E. Stephenson
Development Editor: Russ Hall
Marketing Manager: Martin Litkowski
International Marketing Manager: Tim Galligan
Cover Designer: Chuti Prasertsith
Managing Editor: Gina Kanouse
Copy Editor: Keith Cline
Indexer: Joy Dean Lee
Compositor: Jake McFarland
Manufacturing Buyer: Dan Uhrig

© 2005 by Pearson Education, Inc.
Publishing as Wharton School Publishing
Upper Saddle River, New Jersey 07458

Wharton School Publishing offers excellent discounts on this book when ordered in quantity for bulk purchases or special sales. For more information, please contact U.S. Corporate and Government Sales, 1-800-382-3419, corp-sales@pearsontechgroup.com. For sales outside the U.S., please contact International Sales at international@pearsoned.com.

Company and product names mentioned herein are the trademarks or registered trademarks of their respective owners.

Printed in the United States of America

First Printing June 2005

ISBN 0-13-145439-0

Pearson Education Ltd.
Pearson Education Australia Pty., Limited
Pearson Education South Asia Pte. Ltd.
Pearson Education Asia Ltd.
Pearson Education Canada, Ltd.
Pearson Educacion de Mexico, S.A. de C.V.
Pearson Education—Japan
Pearson Education Malaysia, Pte. Ltd.

Ideas. Action. Impact.
Wharton School Publishing

Bernard Baumohl
THE SECRETS OF ECONOMIC INDICATORS
Hidden Clues to Future Economic Trends and Investment Opportunities

Sayan Chatterjee
FAILSAFE STRATEGIES
Profit and Grow from Risks That Others Avoid

Sunil Gupta, Donald R. Lehmann
MANAGING CUSTOMERS AS INVESTMENTS
The Strategic Value of Customers in the Long Run

Stuart L. Hart
CAPITALISM AT THE CROSSROADS
The Unlimited Business Opportunities in Solving the World's Most Difficult Problems

Lawrence G. Hrebiniak
MAKING STRATEGY WORK
Leading Effective Execution and Change

Robert Mittelstaedt
WILL YOUR NEXT MISTAKE BE FATAL?
Avoiding the Chain of Mistakes That Can Destroy Your Organization

Mukul Pandya, Robbie Shell, Susan Warner, Sandeep Junnarkar, Jeffrey Brown
NIGHTLY BUSINESS REPORT PRESENTS LASTING LEADERSHIP
What You Can Learn from the Top 25 Business People of Our Times

C. K. Prahalad
THE FORTUNE AT THE BOTTOM OF THE PYRAMID
Eradicating Poverty Through Profits

Arthur Rubinfeld
BUILT FOR GROWTH
Expanding Your Business Around the Corner or Across the Globe

Scott A. Shane
FINDING FERTILE GROUND
Identifying Extraordinary Opportunities for New Ventures

Oded Shenkar
THE CHINESE CENTURY
The Rising Chinese Economy and Its Impact on the Global Economy, the Balance of Power, and Your Job

David Sirota, Louis A. Mischkind, and Michael Irwin Meltzer
THE ENTHUSIASTIC EMPLOYEE
How Companies Profit by Giving Workers What They Want

Thomas T. Stallkamp
SCORE!
A Better Way to Do Busine$$: Moving from Conflict to Collaboration

Yoram (Jerry)Wind, Colin Crook, with Robert Gunther
THE POWER OF IMPOSSIBLE THINKING
Transform the Business of Your Life and the Life of Your Business

To Grace, Celia, and Kristin

CONTENTS

Preface xiii

Acknoweldgments xxii

PART I   LEADING THE DECISION PROCESS

Chapter 1   The Leadership Challenge   3

Chapter 2   Deciding How to Decide   29

PART II   MANAGING CONFLICT

Chapter 3   An Absence of Candor   59

Chapter 4   Stimulating the Clash of Ideas   87

Chapter 5   Keeping Conflict Constructive   111

PART III   BUILDING CONSENSUS

Chapter 6   The Dynamics of Indecision   141

Chapter 7   Fair and Legitimate Process   165

Chapter 8   Reaching Closure   195

**PART IV   A NEW BREED OF TAKE-CHARGE
            LEADER**

Chapter 9   Leading with Restraint   223

Endnotes   237

Index   271

PREFACE

After 86 years of anguish and heartache, the Boston Red Sox finally won the World Series. Just two months later, the team's talented, young general manager, Theo Epstein, chose not to match the New York Mets' four-year $50+ million guaranteed contract offer to star pitcher Pedro Martinez. The decision received mixed reactions from the fans in Boston and New York. Red Sox fans recognized that the pitcher's skills had begun to erode, but still, they believed that it would be difficult to find someone of comparable ability to replace Martinez. Mets fans heralded the arrival of a new star to lead their beleaguered pitching staff, but they wondered whether Mets general manager Omar Minaya overpaid for an aging and injury-prone ballplayer. The debate rages on: Did Epstein and Minaya make good decisions?

At this moment, before any games have been played in 2005, no one knows for certain whether the leaders of these two teams made sound decisions. To judge them fairly, we must await the results of the upcoming season as well as several campaigns to follow. Then, with the benefit of hindsight, fans and sportswriters can evaluate the merits of choosing to sign or not sign Martinez to such a lucrative, long-term contract. We will hold the two general managers to account for the outcomes that the teams achieve, and people will debate how much these specific decisions affected the teams' performance.

In all types of organizations—from sports franchises to business enterprises to public institutions—leaders often must wait a long time to see the results of the decisions that they make. Should they judge all decisions simply based on the outcomes that their organizations achieve? In this book, I argue that leaders need not wait for the results to measure their decision-making effectiveness. Instead, leaders ought to take a hard look at the process that they are employing to make critical choices. Outcomes cannot be measured for months or perhaps years. The decision process can be evaluated in real time, as the choice is being made. Epstein and Minaya cannot control fully the outcomes that their teams achieve in the years ahead. Yet, in here and now, they can shape and influence the nature of the decision processes that their organizations employ. In so doing, the general managers can raise or lower the odds that they and their management teams can make sound choices.

Think for a moment about a decision that you and your team or organization is currently trying to make. Have you considered multiple alternatives? Have you surfaced and tested your assumptions carefully? Did dissenting views emerge during your deliberations, and have you given those ideas proper consideration? Are you building high levels of commitment and shared understanding among those who will be responsible for implementing the decision? The answers to these questions—and a number of others—help us to evaluate the quality of an organization's decision-making process. The core premise of this book is that a high-quality process tends to enhance the probability of achieving positive outcomes. Therefore, a leader can have an enormous impact through his management of an organization's decision-making processes. Good process does not simply mean sound analytics (i.e., the best use of the latest strategy framework or quantitative financial evaluation technique). Good process entails the astute management of the social, political, and emotional aspects of decision making as well. Decision making in complex organizations is far from a purely intellectual exercise, as most experienced managers know. Thus, an effective leader does not just produce positive results by weighing in on the content of critical choices in a wise and thoughtful manner; he also has a substantial impact by shaping and influencing how those decisions are made.

In this book, I make two fundamental arguments with regard to how leaders can enhance the quality of their decision-making processes. First, leaders must cultivate constructive conflict so as to enhance the level of critical and divergent thinking, while *simultaneously* building consensus so as to facilitate the timely and efficient implementation of the choices that they make. Managing the tension between conflict and consensus represents one of the most fundamental challenges of leadership. By consensus, I do not mean unanimity, like-mindedness, or even pervasive agreement. Instead, I define consensus to mean a high level of commitment *and* shared understanding among the people involved in the decision. Leaders can build buy-in and collective comprehension without appeasing everyone on their teams or making decisions by majority vote. This book explains how leaders can do that.

The second fundamental argument put forth in this book is that effective leaders can and should spend time "deciding how to decide." In short, creating high-quality decision-making processes necessitates a good deal of forethought. When faced with a complex and pressing issue, most of us want to dive right in to solve the problem. Given our expertise in a particular field, we have a strong desire to apply our knowledge and devise an optimal solution. However, leadership does not entail a single-minded focus on the content of the decisions that we face. It also involves some thought regarding how a group or organization should go about making a critical choice. Deciding how to decide involves an assessment of who should be involved in the deliberations, what type of interpersonal climate we would like to foster, how individuals should communicate with one another, and the extent and type of control that the leader will exert during the process. In this book, you see that leaders have a number of levers that they can employ to design more effective decision-making processes and to shape how they unfold over time. I argue that leaders should be directive when it comes to influencing the way in which decisions are made in their groups or organizations, without trying to dominate or micromanage the substance of the discussion and evaluation that takes place. Spending time deciding how to decide enhances the probability of managing conflict and consensus effectively.

This book offers practical guidance—grounded in extensive academic research—for leaders who want to improve the way that they make complex, high-stakes choices. One need not be a general manager or chief executive officer to benefit from the concepts described here. Any leader of a group of people—no matter the level in the organization—can apply the ideas examined in this book. Scholars and students too can benefit from this book, because it offers new conceptual frameworks about organizational decision making, integrates existing theory in novel ways, and introduces a set of rich case studies that illuminate interesting issues with relevance to both theory and practice.

The Research

The research for this book began in July 1996. It involved several major field research projects as well as the development of numerous case studies. The first major piece of research for this book involved a 2-year study of decision making in the aerospace/defense industry. I conducted an exhaustive examination of 10 strategic choices made by 3 subsidiaries of a leading firm in that market. The research involved well over 100 hours of interviews with managers in those businesses, 2 rounds of surveys, an extensive review of archival documents, and direct observations of meetings. By immersing myself in these organizations, I became intimately familiar with how these executives managed conflict and consensus more or less effectively. This book contains many examples from this body of research, although one should note that names of individuals and firms have been disguised for confidentiality reasons.

The second body of research for this book involved a survey of 78 business unit presidents across different firms listed in the April 2000 edition of the *Fortune 500*. Whereas the prior field research had enabled me to gather extensive amounts of qualitative data regarding a few senior management teams and a small set of strategic decision processes, this large sample survey-based study provided an opportunity to identify patterns in decision making across many firms.

The third major research project comprised in-depth interviews with 35 general managers of firms or business units in the Boston area across many different industries. In each interview, I asked the managers to compare two decisions that they had made—one that they considered successful and another that they did not. The study enabled me to focus very closely on how leaders thought about process choices that they had made as they were making critical decisions.

Finally, the research involved numerous case studies of particular decisions and organizations. A distinguishing feature of this research is that it includes cases from many disparate settings, not just business enterprises. I have examined decision making by mountain-climbing expeditions, firefighting teams, NASA managers and engineers, government policy makers, and various nonprofit institutions. The varied nature of these studies has enabled me to develop a rich understanding of how leaders and organizations make decisions in different settings and circumstances.

Two case studies deserve special mention here, because my colleagues and I spent an extraordinary amount of time examining those situations, using novel techniques both for gathering the data and presenting the ideas to students. David Garvin and I conducted an in-depth study of Paul Levy, the CEO of Beth Israel Deaconess Medical Center in Boston. The case, which we impart to students in multimedia format, proves distinctive because we tracked his turnaround of the organization in real time from the moment he took over as the chief executive. We interviewed him on video every two to four weeks during his first six months on the job, examined internal memos and e-mail communications between him and his staff, and tracked media coverage of the turnaround. This unique study gave us an up-close look at how a leader made decisions during a radical change effort, as well as how he altered the rather dysfunctional culture of decision making that existed in the hospital at the time.

The second case study that merits specific mention involves an examination of decision making at NASA as it pertains to the Columbia space shuttle accident in 2003. Amy Edmondson, Richard Bohmer, and I have studied this incident in detail, both through an exhaustive examination of the internal e-mails, meeting transcripts, memos, and presentations that were made public after the accident as well as through interviews with members of the Columbia Accident Investigation Board, a former shuttle astronaut, an ex-NASA engineer, and an expert on the 1986 Challenger accident. That study, which we also present to students in multimedia format, proves distinctive because we have documented critical events during the final mission from the perspective of six key managers and engineers. By trying to understand the decision making that took place from the vantage point of people at different levels and in disparate units of the organization, we have gained some unique insights into how and why certain choices were made.

Taken together, this extensive body of research provides the foundation for this book. This work employs a variety of research methodologies and draws upon several academic disciplines. Throughout this book, I also draw on existing theory developed by other scholars and cite the findings from empirical research conducted by others. Again, those theories and studies come in many different flavors; the book does not restrict itself to one particular academic domain in trying to explain how and why organizations and their leaders make decisions more or less effectively. This analysis aspires to be truly cross-disciplinary.

The Outline of This Book

This book is divided into four broad parts. Part I introduces a conceptual framework for thinking about how to diagnose, evaluate, and improve strategic decision-making processes. Chapter 1, "The Leadership Challenge," explains why leaders should cultivate conflict and consensus simultaneously as well as why they typically find it very difficult to achieve this objective. Chapter 2, "Deciding How to Decide," describes the implicit and explicit choices that leaders make to shape and influence how the decision process unfolds. Through these process choices, leaders can create the conditions that enable them to manage conflict and consensus in a constructive manner.

Part II—encompassing Chapter 3, "An Absence of Candor," Chapter 4, "Stimulating the Clash of Ideas," and Chapter 5, "Keeping Conflict Constructive"—focuses on the task of managing conflict. Chapter 3 describes the factors that inhibit candid dialogue and debate in organizations. It distinguishes between "hard" and "soft" barriers that block the discussion of dissenting views. "Hard" barriers consist of structural aspects of the organization such as the demographic composition of the senior management team, the complexity of reporting relationships, and ambiguity in job/role definitions. The "soft" barriers comprise things such as differences in status, the language system used to discuss failures in the organization, and certain taken-for-granted assumptions about how people should behave.

Chapter 4 explains how leaders can stimulate heightened levels of conflict in their firms. It describes a variety of mechanisms and practices that leaders can choose to employ, and it describes the strengths and weaknesses of each approach. Chapter 5 tackles the perplexing challenge of how leaders can encourage people to "disagree without being disagreeable." This chapter offers a useful set of tools and strategies for how leaders can keep conflict constructive.

Part III concentrates on how managers create consensus within their organizations without compromising the level of divergent and creative thinking. Chapter 6, "The Dynamics of Indecision," examines why some organizations become paralyzed by indecision. We learn why leaders often find it difficult to build commitment and shared understanding, or why sometimes they find themselves with a "false consensus" that unravels rather quickly when they try to execute a chosen course of action. Chapter 7, "Fair and Legitimate Process," focuses on two critical building blocks of consensus: procedural fairness and legitimacy. It explains how leaders can create processes in which people will cooperate effectively in the implementation effort even if they do not agree with the final decision. Chapter 8, "Reaching Closure," addresses how leaders can move to closure during a contentious set of deliberations. It describes how leaders manage the interplay between divergent and convergent thinking so as to bring a decision process to its conclusion in a timely fashion. Specifically, the chapter outlines a model of achieving closure through an approach of seeking "small wins" at various points during a complex and perhaps controversial decision-making process.

Part IV consists of Chapter 9, "Leading with Restraint," which reflects on how this book's philosophy of leadership and decision making differs from conventional views held by many managers. Specifically, I distinguish between two different approaches to "taking charge" when confronted with a difficult decision. The traditional approach puts the onus on leaders to provide the solutions to many of their organization's pressing problems. They need to "take charge" and act decisively. The alternative approach proposed here calls for leaders to take an active role shaping, influencing, and directing the process by which their organizations make high-stakes choices, without micromanaging the content of the decision. Effective leaders welcome others' input and acknowledge they do not have all the answers, but they still remain firmly in charge and retain the right and duty to make the final decision. However, they understand the importance of creating and leading an effective collective dialogue, in which others have a great deal of freedom to engage in a lively and vigorous debate about the issues and problems facing the organization. In short, this brand of take-charge leadership entails a disciplined focus on how choices are made, not simply what the organization should do.

At the conclusion of this book, detailed notes cite the research studies—mine and those of other scholars—that support the propositions and principles expounded in the main text. At times, the endnotes expand upon the ideas described in the main text, explain important caveats, or offer additional compelling examples of a particular phenomenon. My hope is that the endnotes offer useful guidance and direction for those scholars and practitioners who want to investigate certain topics in more depth.

Throughout this book, you will recognize a strong recurring theme—namely, that leaders must strive for a delicate balance of assertiveness and restraint. As you will see, the critical question for leaders becomes not *whether* they should be forceful and directive as they make strategic choices, but *how* they ought to exert their influence and control over the decision-making process. As you begin to read the pages that follow, I hope that you take time to reflect on past choices and to scrutinize the way in which you went about making those decisions. Moreover, I hope that you will consider experimenting with the techniques described here so as to not only enhance your probability of making sound choices, but also increase the likelihood that others will dedicate themselves enthusiastically to the execution of your plans.

ACKNOWLEDGMENTS

This book could not have been written without the cooperation of those individuals who provided me remarkable access to their organizations, participated in interviews, completed surveys, and permitted me to observe them at work. Hundreds of insightful practitioners spent countless hours with me over the past eight years, patiently and conscientiously answering each of my questions. They provided me a rich picture of the reality of organizational decision making—complete with all its challenges and pitfalls. I appreciate their candor and openness. These skilled and experienced practitioners taught me a great deal.

My students deserve a special acknowledgment as well. As they discussed many of the cases in this book, they offered distinctive insights based on their work and life experiences. They pushed my thinking and forced me to sharpen my ideas. I am grateful for the opportunity to have worked with so many talented participants in the MBA and Executive Education programs at Harvard Business School. These individuals remind me each and every day that a teacher cannot truly teach unless he strives to learn from, and with, his students.

I owe a tremendous debt to my colleagues with whom I have collaborated over the past few years on numerous articles and case studies. Many ideas in this book emerged from my work with talented scholars such as David Garvin, Amy Edmondson, Michael Watkins, Richard Bohmer, Lynne Levesque, and Anita Tucker. I have tried to give them proper credit throughout this book, as evidenced by the numerous citations in which their names appear. I want to especially thank David Garvin for serving as a mentor to me since my first days as a doctoral student at Harvard. He is a talented teacher and scholar with a deep understanding of management practice. Our collaborative endeavors have been a constant source of knowledge and insight for me. Amy Edmondson also has had a unique impact. She often points out how much she has learned from me. In reality, however, it is I who has done the lion's share of the learning in our work together.

Several other academic colleagues have been extremely helpful throughout the research process. Joe Bower, Jay Lorsch, Teresa Amabile, Ralph Biggadike, Jan Rivkin, David Ager, Mark Cotteleer, and Michael Raynor have influenced my thinking a great deal, provided me wise advice, and offered their support and encouragement over the years. Anne Smith and another anonymous reviewer read each chapter of the book carefully, and their comments strengthened the manuscript considerably. In addition, I am grateful to the Harvard Business School Division of Research for providing the funding for this research.

Faculty cannot produce case studies and research papers on their own; they need a great deal of help from many talented individuals. My research associates—Erika Ferlins, Gina Carioggia, and Laura Feldman—worked diligently to help me develop many of the case studies that are described here. Dave Habeeb, David Lieberman, Melissa Dailey, and Chris Lamothe contributed their extensive technological skill and expertise in the development of two innovative multimedia case studies that are cited throughout this book, and which have received widespread accolades from students and practitioners. Trudi Bostian has provided superb administrative support for the past five years, and Andi Truax transcribed more hours of taped interviews than I could possibly count as I conducted the field research.

My editors at Pearson Education have provided encouragement, feedback, and sage advice. I am grateful to Tim Moore for convincing me to embark on this project and for being so supportive along the way. Paula Sinnott and Russ Hall read each chapter with care and offered suggestions for improvement, and Gina Kanouse led the production team that copyedited the text and put the final product together.

Most importantly, I am indebted to my family. My parents, as well as my brother and his family, encouraged me to pursue my dreams here at Harvard. I am ever grateful that they helped me make the wise choice to pursue the vocation of teaching. My parents are the best decision makers that I know. They made a courageous and astute decision nearly 40 years ago when they left Italy and came to the United States, not knowing the language or precisely how they would earn a living. They sought opportunity for their children, and they sacrificed a great deal for us. *Non potete leggere o scrivere l'inglese, ma siete piuàstuti della maggior parte didi professore e dei eruditi, compreso me. Grazie con tutto il mio cuore per tutti che abbiate fatto per me.*

Finally, my children, Celia and Grace, remind me always that learning can be joyful, that curiosity leads to wonderful new discoveries, and that play stimulates our minds. Their hugs and infectious smiles erased any frustrations that emerged as I wrote this book. I made the best decision of my life when I chose to marry the kindest and most compassionate person whom I have ever met. I am grateful to Kristin for her patience, understanding, and encouragement throughout the process of writing this book. With the utmost gratitude to her, I close with the sentiments expressed by Nobel Prize winning author Pearl Buck, who once wrote: *The person who tries to live alone will not succeed as a human being. His heart withers if it does not answer another heart. His mind shrinks away if he hears only the echoes of his own thoughts and finds no other inspiration.*

PART I

LEADING THE DECISION PROCESS

1

THE LEADERSHIP CHALLENGE

"Diversity in counsel, unity in command."

—Cyrus the Great

In February 2003, the Columbia space shuttle disintegrated while re-entering the earth's atmosphere. In May 1996, Rob Hall and Scott Fischer, two of the world's most accomplished mountaineers, died on the slopes of Everest along with three of their clients during the deadliest day in the mountain's history. In April 1985, the Coca-Cola Company changed the formula of its flagship product and enraged its most loyal customers. In April 1961, a brigade of Cuban exiles invaded the Bay of Pigs with the support of the United States government, and Fidel Castro's military captured or killed nearly the entire rebel force. Catastrophe and failure, whether in business, politics, or other walks of life, always brings forth many troubling questions. Why did NASA managers decide not to undertake corrective action when they discovered that a potentially dangerous foam debris strike had occurred during the launch of the Columbia space shuttle? Why did Hall and Fischer choose to ignore their own safety rules and procedures and push forward toward the summit of Mount Everest despite knowing that they would be forced to conduct a very dangerous nighttime descent? Why did Roberto Goizueta and his management team fail to anticipate the overwhelmingly negative public reaction to New Coke? Why did President John F. Kennedy decide to support a rebel invasion despite the existence of information that suggested an extremely low probability of success?

We ask these questions because we hope to learn from others' mistakes, and we do not wish to repeat them. Often, however, a few misconceptions about the nature of organizational decision making cloud our judgment and make it difficult to draw the appropriate lessons from these failures. Many of us have an image of how these failures transpire. We envision a chief executive, or a management team, sitting in a room one day making a fateful decision. We rush to find fault with the analysis that they conducted, wonder about their business acumen, and perhaps even question their motives. When others falter, we often search for flaws in others' intellect or personality. Yet, differences in mental horsepower seldom distinguish success from failure when it comes to strategic decision making in complex organizations.

What do I mean by strategic decision making? Strategic choices occur when the stakes are high, ambiguity and novelty characterize the situation, and the decision represents a substantial commitment of financial, physical, and/or human resources. By definition, these choices occur rather infrequently, and they have a potentially significant impact on an organization's future performance. They differ from routine or tactical choices that managers make each and every day, in which the problem is well-defined, the alternatives are clear, and the impact on the overall organization is rather minimal.[1]

Strategic decision making in a business enterprise or public sector institution is a dynamic process that unfolds over time, moves in fits and starts, and flows across multiple levels of an organization.[2] Social, political, and emotional forces play an enormous role. Whereas the cognitive task of decision making may prove challenging for many leaders, the socio-emotional component often proves to be a manager's Achilles' heel. Moreover, leaders not only must select the appropriate course of action, they need to mobilize and motivate the organization to implement it effectively. As Noel Tichy and Dave Ulrich write, "CEOs tend to overlook the lesson Moses learned several thousand years ago—namely, getting the ten commandments written down and communicated is the easy part; getting them implemented is the challenge."[3] Thus, decision-making success is a function of both decision quality and implementation effectiveness. Decision quality means that managers choose the course of action that enables the organization to achieve its objectives more efficiently than all other plausible alternatives. Implementation effectiveness means that the organization successfully carries out the selected course of action, thereby meeting the objectives established during the decision-making process. A central premise of this book is that a leader's ability to navigate his or her way through the personality clashes, politics, and social pressures of the decision process often determines whether managers will select the appropriate alternative and implementation will proceed smoothly.

Many executives can run the numbers or analyze the economic structure of an industry; a precious few can master the social and political dynamic of decision making. Consider the nature and quality of dialogue within many organizations. Candor, conflict, and debate appear conspicuously absent during their decision-making processes. Managers feel uncomfortable expressing dissent, groups converge quickly on a particular solution, and individuals assume that unanimity exists when, in fact, it does not. As a result, critical assumptions remain untested, and creative alternatives do not surface or receive adequate attention. In all too many cases, the problem begins with the person directing the process, as their words and deeds discourage

a vigorous exchange of views. Powerful, popular, and highly successful leaders hear "yes" much too often, or they simply hear nothing
when people really mean "no." In those situations, organizations may
not only make poor choices, but they may find that unethical choices
remain unchallenged. As *Business Week* declared in its 2002 special
issue on corporate governance, "The best insurance against crossing
the ethical divide is a roomful of skeptics...By advocating dissent, top
executives can create a climate where wrongdoing will not go unchallenged."[4]

Of course, conflict alone does not lead to better decisions.
Leaders also need to build consensus in their organizations.
Consensus, as we define it here, does *not* mean unanimity, widespread agreement on all facets of a decision, or complete approval by
a majority of organization members. It does *not* mean that teams,
rather than leaders, make decisions. Consensus *does* mean that people have agreed to cooperate in the implementation of a decision.
They have accepted the final choice, even though they may not be
completely satisfied with it. Consensus has two critical components: a
high level of commitment to the chosen course of action and a strong,
shared understanding of the rationale for the decision.[5] Commitment
helps to prevent the implementation process from becoming derailed
by organizational units or individuals who object to the selected
course of action. Moreover, commitment may promote management
perseverance in the face of other kinds of implementation obstacles,
while encouraging individuals to think creatively and innovatively
about how to overcome those obstacles. Common understanding of
the decision rationale allows individuals to coordinate their actions
effectively, and it enhances the likelihood that everyone will act in a
manner that is "consistent with the spirit of the decision."[6] Naturally,
consensus does not ensure effective implementation, but it enhances
the likelihood that managers can work together effectively to overcome obstacles that arise during decision execution.

Commitment without deep understanding can amount to "blind
devotion" on the part of a group of managers. Individuals may accept

a call to action and dedicate themselves to the implementation of a particular plan, but they take action based on differing interpretations of the decision. Managers may find themselves working at cross-purposes, not because they want to derail the decision, but because they perceive goals and priorities differently than their colleagues. When leaders articulate a decision, they hope that subordinates understand the core intent of the decision, because people undoubtedly will encounter moments of ambiguity as they execute the plan of action. During these uncertain situations, managers need to make choices without taking the time to consult the leader or all other colleagues. Managers also may need to improvise a bit to solve problems or capitalize on opportunities that may arise during the implementation process. A leader cannot micromanage the execution of a decision; he needs people throughout the organization to be capable of making adjustments and trade-offs as obstacles arise; shared understanding promotes that type of coordinated, independent action.

Shared understanding without commitment leads to problems as well. Implementation performance suffers if managers comprehend goals and priorities clearly, but harbor doubts about the wisdom of the choice that has been made. Execution also lags if people do not engage and invest emotionally in the process. Managers need to not only comprehend their required contribution to the implementation effort, they must be willing to "go the extra mile" to solve difficult problems and overcome unexpected hurdles that arise.[7]

Unfortunately, if executives engage in vigorous debate during the decision process, people may walk away dissatisfied with the outcome, disgruntled with their colleagues, and not fully dedicated to the implementation effort. Conflict may diminish consensus, and thereby hinder the execution of a chosen course of action, as Figure 1-1 illustrates. Herein lies a fundamental dilemma for leaders: How does one foster conflict and dissent to enhance decision quality while simultaneously building the consensus required to implement decisions effectively? In short, how does one achieve "diversity in counsel, unity in command?" The purpose of this book is to help leaders tackle this daunting challenge.

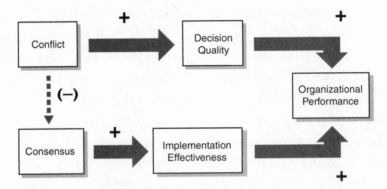

FIGURE 1-1: **The effects of conflict and consensus**

Decision-Making Myths

When we read about a CEO's failed strategy in *Business Week*, or analyze the actions of the manager profiled in a case study at Harvard Business School, we often ask ourselves: How could that individual make such a stupid decision? My students ask themselves this question on numerous occasions each semester as they read about companies that falter or fold. Perhaps we think of others' failures in these terms because of our hubris, or because we might need to convince ourselves that we can succeed when embarking upon similar endeavors fraught with ambiguity and risk. Jon Krakauer, a member of Rob Hall's 1996 Everest expedition, wrote, "If you can convince yourself that Rob Hall died because he made a string of stupid errors and that you are too clever to repeat those errors, it makes it easier for you to attempt Everest in the face of some rather compelling evidence that doing so is injudicious."[8]

Let's examine a few of our misconceptions about decision making in more detail and attempt to distinguish myth from reality. (See Table 1-1 for a summary of these common myths.) Can we, in fact, attribute the failure to a particular individual, namely the CEO, president, or expedition leader? Does the outcome truly suggest a lack of intelligence, industry expertise, or technical knowledge on the part of key participants? Did the failure originate with one particular flawed decision or should we examine a pattern of choices over time?

TABLE 1-1:   Myth Versus Reality in Strategic Decision Making

Myth	Reality
The chief executive decides.	Strategic decision making entails simultaneous activity by people at multiple levels of the organization.
Decisions are made in the room.	Much of the real work occurs "offline," in one-on-one conversations or small subgroups, not around a conference table.
Decisions are largely intellectual exercises.	Strategic decisions are complex social, emotional, and political processes.
Managers analyze and then decide.	Strategic decisions unfold in a nonlinear fashion, with solutions frequently arising before managers define problems or analyze alternatives.
Managers decide and then act.	Strategic decisions often evolve over time and proceed through an iterative process of choice and action.

Myth 1: The Chief Executive Decides

When Harry Truman served as president of the United States, he placed a sign on his desk in the Oval Office. It read *The Buck Stops Here*. The now-famous saying offers an important reminder for all leaders. The CEO bears ultimate responsibility for the actions of his or her firm, and the president must be accountable for the policies of his administration. However, when we examine the failures of large, complex organizations, we ought to be careful before we assume that poor decisions are the work of a single actor, even if that person serves as the powerful and authoritative chief executive of the institution.

A great deal of research dispels the notion that CEOs or presidents make most critical decisions on their own. Studies show that bargaining, negotiating, and coalition building among managers shape the decisions that an organization makes. The decision-making process often involves managers from multiple levels of the organization, and it does not proceed in a strictly "bottom-up" or "top-down" fashion. Instead, activity occurs simultaneously at multiple levels of the organization. The decision-making process becomes quite diffuse in some instances.[9] For example, in one study of foreign policy decision making, political scientist Graham Allison concluded that, "Large acts result from innumerable and often conflicting smaller actions by individuals at various levels of organization in the service of a variety of only partially compatible conceptions of national goals, organizational goals, and political objectives."[10] In short, the chief executive may make the ultimate call, but that decision often emerges from a process of intense interaction among individuals and subunits throughout the organization.

Myth 2: Decisions Are Made in the Room

Many scholars and consultants have argued that a firm's strategic choices emerge from deliberations among members of the "top management team." However, this concept of a senior team may be a bit misleading.[11] As management scholar Donald Hambrick wrote, "Many top management 'teams' may have little 'teamness' to them. If so, this is at odds with the implicit image...of an executive conference table where officers convene to discuss problems and make major judgments."[12]

In most organizations, strategic choices do not occur during the chief executive's staff meetings with his direct reports. In James Brian Quinn's research, he reported than an executive once told him, "When I was younger, I always conceived of a room where all these [strategic] concepts were worked out for the whole company. Later, I didn't find any such room."[13] In my research, I have found that crucial conversations occur "offline"—during one-on-one interactions and informal meetings of subgroups. People lobby their colleagues or superiors prior to meetings, and they bounce ideas off one another before presenting proposals to the entire management team. Managers garner commitment from key constituents prior to taking a public stance on an issue. Formal staff meetings often become an occasion for ratifying choices that have already been made, rather than a forum for real decision making.[14]

Myth 3: Decisions Are Largely Intellectual Exercises

Many people think of decision making as a largely cognitive endeavor. In school and at work, we learn that "smart" people think through issues carefully, gather data, conduct comprehensive analysis, and then choose a course of action. Perhaps they apply a bit of intuition and a few lessons from experience as well. Poor decisions must result from a lack of intelligence, insufficient expertise in a particular domain, or a failure to conduct rigorous analysis. Psychologists offer a slightly more forgiving explanation for faulty choices. They find that all of us—expert or novice, professor or student, leader or follower—suffer from certain cognitive biases. In other words, we make systematic errors in judgment, rooted in the cognitive, information processing limits of the human brain, that impair our decision making.[15] For instance, most human beings are susceptible to the "sunk-cost bias"—the tendency to escalate commitment to a flawed and risky course of action if one has made a substantial prior investment of time, money, and other resources. We fail to recognize that the sunk costs should be irrelevant when deciding whether to move forward, and therefore, we throw "good money after bad" in many instances.[16]

Cognition undoubtedly plays a major role in decision making. However, social pressures become a critical factor at times. People have a strong need to belong—a desire for interpersonal attachment. At times, we feel powerful pressures to conform to the expectations or behavior of others. Moreover, individuals compare themselves to others regularly, often in ways that reflect favorably on themselves. These social behaviors shape and influence the decisions that organizations make. Emotions also play a role. Individuals appraise how proposed courses of action might affect them, and these assessments arouse certain feelings. These emotions can energize and motivate individuals, or they can lead to resistance or paralysis. Finally, political behavior permeates many decision-making processes, and it can have positive or negative effects. At times, coalition building, lobbying, bargaining, and influence tactics enhance the quality of decisions that are ultimately made; in other instances, they lead to suboptimal outcomes.[17] Without a doubt, leaders ignore these social, emotional, and political forces at their own peril.

Myth 4: Managers Analyze and Then Decide

At one point or another, most of us have learned structured problem-solving techniques. A typical approach consists of five well-defined phases: 1) identify and define the problem, 2) gather information and data, 3) identify alternative solutions, 4) evaluate each of the options, 5) select a course of action. In short, we learn to analyze a situation in a systematic manner and then make a decision. Unfortunately, most strategic decision processes do not unfold in a linear fashion, passing neatly from one phase to the next.[18] Activities such as alternative evaluation, problem definition, and data collection often occur in parallel, rather than sequentially. Multiple process iterations take place, as managers circle back to redefine problems or gather more information even after a decision has seemingly been made. At times, solutions even arise in search of problems to solve.[19]

In my research, I have found that managers often select a preferred course of action, and *then* employ formal analytical techniques to evaluate various alternatives. What's going on here? Why does analysis follow choice in certain instances? Some managers arrive a decision intuitively, but they want to "check their gut" using a more systematic method of assessing the situation. Others use the analytics as a tool of persuasion when confronting skeptics or external constituencies, or because they must conform to cultural norms within the organization. Finally, many managers employ analytical frameworks for symbolic reasons. They want to signal that they have employed a thorough and logical decision-making process. By enhancing the perceived legitimacy of the process, they hope to gain support for the choice that they prefer.[20]

Consider the story of the Ford Mustang—one of the most remarkable and surprising new product launches in auto-industry history. Lee Iacocca's sales and product design instincts told him that the Mustang would be a smashing success in the mid-1960s, but much to his chagrin, he could not persuade senior executives to produce the car. Iacocca recognized that quantitative data analysis trumped intuition in the intensively numbers-driven culture created by former Ford executive Robert McNamara. Thus, Iacocca set out to marshal quantitative evidence, based on market research, which suggested that the Mustang would attract enough customers to justify the capital investment required to design and manufacture the car. Not surprisingly, Iacocca's analysis supported his initial position! Having produced data to support his intuition, Iacocca prevailed in his battle to launch the Mustang.[21]

The nonlinear nature of strategic decision making may seem dysfunctional at first glance. It contradicts so much of what we have learned or teach in schools of business and management. However, multiple iterations, feedback loops, and simultaneous activity need not be dysfunctional. A great deal of learning and improvement can occur as a decision process proceeds in fits and starts. Some nonlinear processes may be fraught with dysfunctional political behavior, but without a doubt, effective decision making involves a healthy dose of reflection, revision, and learning over time.

Myth 5: Managers Decide and Then Act

Consider the case of a firm apparently pursuing a diversification strategy. We might believe that executives made a choice at a specific point in time to enter new markets or seek growth opportunities beyond the core business. In reality, however, we may not find a clear starting or ending point for that decision process. Instead, the diversification decision may have evolved over time, as multiple parties investigated new technologies, grappled with declining growth in the core business, and considered how to invest excess cash flow. Executives might have witnessed certain actions taking place at various points in the organization and then engaged in a process of retrospective sense making, interpretation, and synthesis.[22] From this interplay between thought and action, a "decision" emerged.[23]

In my research, I studied an aerospace and defense firm's decision to invest more than $200 million in a new shipbuilding facility; the project completely transformed the organization's manufacturing process. When asked about the timing of the decision, one executive commented to me, "The decision to do this didn't come in November of 1996, it didn't come in February of 1997, it didn't come in May of 1997. You know, there was a concept, and the concept evolved." The implementation process did not follow neatly after a choice had been made. Instead, actions pertaining to the execution of the decision become intermingled with the deliberations regarding whether and how to proceed. The project gained momentum over time, and by the time the board of directors met to formally approve the project, everyone understood that the decision had already been made.

Managing Reality

When Jack Welch took over as CEO of General Electric, he exhorted his managers to "face reality…see the world the way it is, not the way you wish it were."[24] This advice certainly applies to the challenge of managing high-stakes decision-making processes in complex and dynamic organizations. Leaders need to understand how decisions actually unfold so that they can shape and influence the process to their advantage. To cultivate conflict and build consensus effectively, they must recognize that the decision process unfolds across multiple levels of the organization, not simply in the executive suite. They need to welcome divergent views, manage interpersonal disagreements, and build commitment across those levels. Leaders also need to recognize that they cannot remove politics completely from the decision process, somehow magically transforming it into the purely intellectual exercise that they wish it would become. As Joseph Bower wrote, "politics is not pathology; it is a fact of large organization."[25] Effective leaders use political mechanisms to help them build consensus among multiple constituencies. Moreover, leaders cannot ignore the fact that managers often perform analyses to justify a preferred solution, rather than proceeding sequentially from problem identification to alternative evaluation to choice. Leaders must identify when such methods of persuasion become dysfunctional, and then intervene appropriately to maintain the legitimacy of the process, if they hope to build widespread commitment to a chosen course of action. With this organizational reality in mind, let's turn to the first element of Cyrus the Great's wise advice for decision makers: namely, the challenge of cultivating constructive conflict.

The Absence of Dissent

How many of you have censored your views during a management meeting? Have you offered a polite nod of approval as your boss or a respected colleague puts forth a proposal, while privately harboring serious doubts? Have you immediately begun to devise ways to alter or reverse the decision at a later date?

If you have answered "yes" to these questions, be comforted by the fact that you are not alone. Many groups and organizations shy away from vigorous conflict and debate. For starters, managers often feel uncomfortable expressing dissent in the presence of a powerful, popular, and highly successful chief executive. It becomes difficult to be candid when the boss' presence dominates the room. We also find ourselves deferring to the technical experts in many instances, rather than challenging the pronouncements of company or industry veterans. Certain deeply held assumptions about customers, markets, and competition can become so in-grained in people's thought processes that an entire industry finds itself blindly accepting the prevailing conventional wisdom. Pressures for conformity also arise because cohesive, relatively homogenous groups of like-minded people have worked with one another for a long time.[26] Finally, some leaders engage in conflict avoidance because they do not feel comfortable with confrontation in a public setting. Whatever the reasons—and they are bountiful—the absence of healthy debate and dissent frequently leads to faulty decisions. Let's turn to a tragic example to see this dynamic in action.[27]

Tragedy on Everest

In 1996, Rob Hall and Scott Fischer each led a commercial expedition team attempting to climb Mount Everest. Each group consisted of the leader, several guides, and eight paying clients. Although many team members reached the summit on May 10, they encountered grave dangers during their descent. Five individuals, including the two highly talented leaders, perished as they tried to climb down the mountain during a stormy night.

Many survivors and mountaineering experts have pointed out that the two leaders made a number of poor decisions during this tragedy. Perhaps most importantly, the groups ignored a critical decision rule created to protect against the dangers of descending after nightfall. Climbers typically begin their final push to the summit from a camp located at an altitude of about 26,000 feet (7,900 meters). They climb through the night, hoping to reach the summit by midday. Then, they scramble back down to camp, striving to reach the safety of their tents before sunset. This tight 18-hour schedule leaves little room for error. If climbers fall behind during the ascent, they face an extremely perilous nighttime descent. Hall and Fischer recognized these dangers. Moreover, they understood that individuals would find it difficult to abandon their summit attempt after coming so tantalizingly close to achieving their goal. They knew that climbers, as they near the summit, are particularly susceptible to the "sunk-cost bias." Thus, they advocated strict adherence to a predetermined decision rule. Fischer described it as the "two o'clock rule,"—i.e., when it became clear that a climber could not reach the top by two o'clock in the afternoon, that individual should abandon his summit bid and head back to the safety of the camp. If he failed to do so, the leaders and/or the guides should order the climbers to turn around. One team member recalled, "Rob had lectured us repeatedly about the importance of having a predetermined turnaround time on summit day...and abiding by it no matter how close we were to the top."[28]

Unfortunately, the leaders, guides, and most clients ignored the turnaround rule during the ascent. Nearly all the team members, including the two leaders, arrived at the summit after two o'clock. As a result, many climbers found themselves descending in darkness, well past midnight, as a ferocious blizzard enveloped the mountain. Not only did five people die, many others barely escaped with their lives.

Why did the climbers ignore the two o'clock rule? Many team members recognized quite explicitly the perils associated with violating the turnaround rule, but they chose not to question the leaders' judgment. The groups never engaged in an open and candid dialogue regarding the choice to push ahead. Neil Beidleman, a guide on Fischer's team, had serious reservations about climbing well past midday. However, he did not feel comfortable telling Fischer that the group should turn around. Perceptions of his relative status within the group affected Beidleman's behavior. He was "quite conscious of his place in the expedition pecking order," and consequently, he chose not to voice his concerns.[29] He reflected back, "I was definitely considered the third guide...so I tried not to be too pushy. As a consequence, I didn't always speak up when maybe I should have, and now I kick myself for it."[30] Similarly, Jon Krakauer, a journalist climbing as a member of Hall's team, began to sense the emergence of a "guide-client protocol" that shaped the climbers' behavior. Krakauer remarked, "On this expedition, he (Andy Harris—one of Rob Hall's guides) had been cast in the role of invincible guide, there to look after me and the other clients; we had been specifically indoctrinated not to question our guides' judgment."[31]

The climbers on these expedition teams also did not know one another very well. Many of them had not met their colleagues prior to arriving in Nepal. They found it difficult to develop mutual respect and trust during their short time together. Not knowing how others might react to their questions or comments, many climbers remained hesitant when doubts surfaced in their minds. Russian guide Anatoli Boukreev, who did not have a strong command of the English language, found it especially difficult to build relationships with his teammates. Consequently, he did not express his concerns about key aspects of the leaders' plans, for fear of how others might react to his opinions. Regretfully, he later wrote, "I tried not to be too argumentative, choosing instead to downplay my intuitions."[32]

Hall also made it clear to his team during the early days of the expedition that he would not welcome disagreement and debate during the ascent. He believed that others should defer to him because of his vast mountain-climbing expertise and remarkable track record of guiding clients to the summit of Everest. After all, Hall had guided a total of 39 clients to the top during 4 prior expeditions. He offered a stern pronouncement during the early days of the climb: "I will tolerate no dissension up there. My word will be absolute law, beyond appeal."[33] Hall made the statement because he wanted to preempt pushback from clients who might resist turning around if he instructed them to do so. Ironically, Hall fell behind schedule on summit day and should have turned back, but the clients did not challenge his decision to push ahead. Because of Hall's early declaration of authority, Krakauer concluded that, "Passivity on the part of the clients had thus been encouraged throughout our expedition."[34]

Before long, deference to the "experts" became a routine behavior for the team members. When the experts began to violate their own procedures or make other crucial mistakes, that pattern of deference persisted. Less-experienced team members remained hesitant to raise questions or concerns. Fischer's situation proved especially tragic. His physical condition deteriorated badly during the final summit push, and his difficulties became apparent to everyone including the relative novices. He struggled to put one foot in front of the other, yet "nobody discussed Fischer's exhausted appearance" or suggested that he should retreat down the slopes.[35]

Unfortunately, the experience of these teams on the slopes of Everest mirrors the group dynamic within many executive suites and corporate boardrooms in businesses around the world. The factors suppressing debate and dissent within these expedition teams also affect managers as they make business decisions. People often find themselves standing in Neil Beidleman's shoes—lower in status than other decision makers and unsure of the consequences of challenging those positioned on a higher rung in the organizational pecking order. Many leaders boast of remarkable track records, like Rob Hall, and employ an autocratic leadership style. Inexperienced individuals find themselves demonstrating excessive deference to those with apparent expertise in the subject at hand. Plenty of teams lack the atmosphere of mutual trust and respect that facilitates and encourages candid dialogue. Fortunately, most business decisions are not a matter of life or death.[36]

The Perils of Conflict and Dissent

Of course, dissent does not always prove to be productive; cultivating conflict has its risks. To understand the perils, we must distinguish between two forms of conflict. Suppose that you ask your management team to compare and contrast two alternative courses of action. Individuals may engage in substantive debate over issues and ideas, which we refer to as cognitive, or task-oriented, conflict. This form of disagreement exposes each proposal's risks and weaknesses, challenges the validity of key assumptions, and even might encourage people to define the problem or opportunity confronting the firm in an entirely different light. For these reasons, cognitive conflict tends to enhance the quality of the solutions that groups produce. As former Intel CEO Andrew Grove once wrote, "Debates are like the process through which a photographer sharpens the contrast when developing a print. The clearer images that result permit management to make a more informed—and more likely correct—call."[37]

Unfortunately, when differences of opinion emerge during a discussion, managers may find it difficult to reconcile divergent views. At times, people become wedded to their ideas, and they begin to react defensively to criticism. Deliberations become heated, emotions flare, and disagreements become personal. Scholars refer to these types of personality clashes and personal friction as affective conflict. When it surfaces, decision processes often derail. Unfortunately, most leaders find it difficult to foster cognitive conflict without also stimulating interpersonal friction. The inability to disentangle the two forms of conflict has pernicious consequences. Affective conflict diminishes commitment to the choices that are made, and it disrupts the development of shared understanding. It also leads to costly delays in the decision process, meaning that organizations fail to make timely decisions, and they provide competitors with an opportunity to capture advantages in the marketplace.[38] Figure 1-2 depicts how cognitive and affective conflict shape decision-making outcomes.[39]

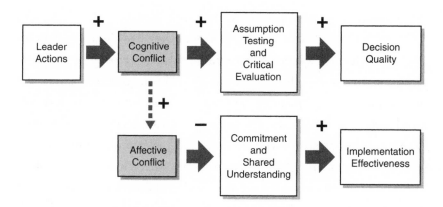

FIGURE 1-2: Cognitive and affective conflict

Consider the case of a defense electronics firm examining how to restructure a particular line of business. The chief executive wanted to take a hard look at the unit because it had become unprofitable. Multiple options emerged, and managers conducted a great deal of quantitative analysis to compare and contrast each possible course of action. A lively set of deliberations ensued. The chief financial officer played a particularly important role. He scrutinized all the proposals closely, treating each with equal skepticism. One manager remarked that, "He would be able to articulate the black and white logical reasons why things made sense, or why they didn't make sense...He was incredibly objective...like Spock on *Star Trek*." Unfortunately, not everyone could remain as objective. Some managers took criticism very personally during the deliberations, and working relationships became strained. Discussions became heated as individuals defended their proposals in which they had invested a great deal of time and energy. Some differences of opinion centered on a substantive issue; in other cases, people disagreed with one another simply because they did not want others to "win" the dispute. As one executive commented, "We could have put the legitimate roadblocks on the table, and separated those from the emotional roadblocks. We would have been much better off. But, we put them all in the same pot and had trouble sorting out which were real and which weren't." Ultimately, the organization made a decision regarding how to restructure, and looking back, nearly everyone agreed that they had discovered a creative and effective solution to the unit's problems. However, the organization struggled mightily to execute its chosen course of action in a timely and efficient manner. The entire implementation effort suffered from a lack of buy-in among people at various levels of the organization. Management overcame these obstacles and, eventually, the business became much more profitable. Nevertheless, the failure to develop a high level of consensus during the decision process cost the organization precious time and resources. Figure 1-3 depicts how conflict and consensus can come together to lead to positive outcomes rather than poor choices and flawed implementation efforts.

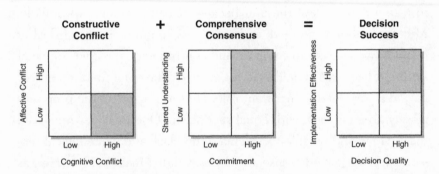

FIGURE 1-3:   The path to decision success

Why Is This So Difficult?

Why is managing conflict and building consensus so challenging? The roots of the problem may reside in one's style of leadership. Often, however, the difficulty reflects persistent patterns of dysfunction within groups and organizations. Let's try to understand a few sources of difficulty that leaders must overcome as they shape and direct decision processes.

Leadership Style

Leaders may have certain personal preferences and attributes that make it difficult to cultivate constructive conflict and/or build consensus within their organizations. For instance, some executives may be uncomfortable with confrontation, and therefore, they tend to avoid vigorous debates at all costs. They shy away from cognitive conflict because loud voices and sharp criticism simply make them uneasy. Others may be highly introverted, and consequently, they may discover that their employees find it difficult to discern their intentions as well as the rationale that they have employed to make decisions.

Some executives prefer to manage by fear and intimidation, and they enjoy imposing their will on organizations. That leadership style also squelches dissenting voices, and it can leave employees feeling unenthusiastic about a proposed plan of action that they did not help to formulate. Of course, a few extraordinary leaders foster enormous levels of commitment while employing this approach. Consider, for instance, the management style of Bill Parcells, the famous professional football coach. He has dramatically turned around four very unsuccessful franchises over the past two decades, and his teams have won two world championships. He thrives on confrontation, instills a great deal of fear in his players, and makes decisions in a highly autocratic fashion. Yet, players put forth an incredible effort for Parcells, and they frequently express an intense desire to please him, despite the fact that he makes their lives difficult at times. In general, however, success often proves difficult to sustain over the long haul for those who employ this leadership pattern. Perhaps that explains why Parcells has chosen to shift frequently from one team to another during his coaching career.[40]

Cognitive Biases

A few mental traps also stand in the way as leaders try to manage conflict and consensus. For instance, most individuals search for information in a biased manner. They tend to downplay data that contradicts their existing views and beliefs, while emphasizing the information that supports their original conclusions. This confirmation bias explains why leaders may not aggressively seek to surface dissenting views, or why they may not listen carefully to those voices. Naturally, managers become frustrated if they perceive that leaders are processing information in a biased manner, and that disappointment can diminish buy-in.[41] Overconfidence bias becomes a factor in many situations as well. Most of us tend to overestimate our own capabilities. Consequently, we may not recognize when we need to solicit input and advice from others, or we downplay the doubts that others display regarding our judgments and decisions.[42]

Threat Rigidity

In many cases, strategic decision making occurs in the context of a threatening situation—the organization must deal with poor financial performance, deteriorating competitive position, and/or a dramatic shift in customer requirements. When faced with a threatening context, the psychological stress and anxiety may induce a rigid cognitive response on the part of individuals. People tend to draw upon deeply ingrained mental models of the environment that served them well in the past. Individuals also constrict their information gathering efforts, and they revert to the comfort of well-learned practices and routines. This cognitive rigidity impairs a leader's ability to surface and discuss a wide range of dissenting views. To make matters worse, factors at the group and organizational level complement and reinforce this inflexible and dysfunctional response to threatening problems. Consequently, organizational decision processes become characterized by restricted information processing, a constrained search for solutions, a reduction in the breadth of participants, and increased reliance on formal communication procedures.[43]

In-Groups Versus Out-Groups

As people work together throughout the decision process, they have a natural tendency to categorize other members of the groups in which they interact. They classify some people as similar to them (the in-group) and others as quite different based on a few salient demographic characteristics or professional attributes (the out-group). For instance, an engineer may distinguish those group members with similar functional backgrounds from individuals who have spent their careers working in finance or marketing. In general, people tend to perceive in-group members in a positive light and out-group members in a negative light. These perceptions shape the way that individuals interact with one another. Highly divisive categorization processes—those circumstances in which people draw sharp distinctions between in-groups and out-groups—can diminish social interaction among group members, impede information flows, and foster interpersonal tensions.

Individuals also appraise other group members in terms of personal attributes such as intelligence, integrity, and conscientiousness. Unfortunately, a person's self-appraisal often does not match the view that others have. An individual may see himself as highly trustworthy, whereas others have serious doubts about whether he is reliable and dependable. When individuals tend to see themselves in a manner consistent with others' views and perceptions, groups perform more effectively. If many perceptual disconnects exist within a group, people find it difficult to interact constructively. It becomes difficult to manage disputes and lead deliberations smoothly.[44]

Organizational Defensive Routines

Organizations often develop mechanisms to bypass or minimize the embarrassment or threat that individuals might experience. Managers employ these "defensive routines" to preserve morale, make "bad news" a bit more palatable, and soften the impact of negative feedback. They want people to remain upbeat and positive about the organization's mission as well as their own situation. For instance, in many firms, we witness the existence of an implicit understanding of the need to employ a routine for helping employees to "save face" when they have failed. Unfortunately, such behaviors depress the level of candor within the organization, and they make certain issues "undiscussable." Over time, these defensive practices become deeply ingrained in the organizational culture. They do not occur because a specific individual wants to avoid embarrassing a colleague, but rather because all managers understand that this is "the way things are done around here." Leaders often find it extremely difficult to dismantle these deeply embedded barriers to open and honest dialogue.[45]

A Deeper Explanation

All the factors described previously certainly make it difficult to manage conflict and consensus effectively. The core contention of this book, however, is that many leaders fail to make and implement decisions successfully for a more fundamental reason—that is, they tend to focus first and foremost on finding the "right" solution when a problem arises, rather than stepping back to determine the "right" process that should be employed to make the decision. They fixate on the question, "What decision should I make?" rather than asking "How should I go about making the decision?" Answering this "how" question correctly often has a profound impact on a leader's decision-making effectiveness. It enables leaders to create the conditions and mechanisms that will lead to healthy debate and dissent as well as a comprehensive and enduring consensus.

Naturally, leaders also must address the content of critical high-stakes decisions, not simply the processes of deliberation and analysis. They have to take a stand on the issues, and they must make difficult trade-offs in many cases. Moreover, creating and leading an effective decision-making process does *not* guarantee a successful choice and smooth implementation. However, developing and managing a high-quality decision-making process does greatly enhance the *probability* of successful choices and results.[46]

Throughout this book, I argue that leaders should stay attuned constantly to the social, emotional, and political processes of decision. However, they need to do more than this. They must not simply react passively to the personality clashes and backroom maneuvering that emerges during a decision-making process. Instead, they should actively shape and influence the conditions under which people will interact and deliberate. They must make choices about the type of process that they want to employ and the roles that they want various people to play. In short, leaders must "decide how to decide" as they confront complex and ambiguous situations, rather than fixating solely on the intellectual challenge of finding the optimal solution to the organization's perplexing problems. With this broad theme in mind, let's begin to tackle the marvelous challenge of discovering how leaders can cultivate "diversity in counsel, unity in command."

2

DECIDING HOW TO
DECIDE

"Chance favors the prepared mind."

—Louis Pasteur

In April 1961, President John F. Kennedy made the decision to authorize U.S. government assistance for the Bay of Pigs invasion— an attempt by 1,400 Cuban exiles to overthrow the Castro regime. Three days after the brigade of rebels landed on the coast of Cuba, nearly all of them had been killed or captured by Castro's troops. The invasion was a complete disaster, both in terms of the loss of life and the political damage for the new president. Nations around the world condemned the Kennedy administration's actions. As the president recognized the dreadful consequences of his decision to support the invasion, he asked his advisers, "How could I have been so stupid to let them go ahead?"[1]

The president and his advisers certainly did not lack intelligence; David Halberstam once described them as "the best and the brightest" of their generation.[2] Nevertheless, the Bay of Pigs decision-making process had many flaws.[3] Veteran officials from the Central Intelligence Agency (CIA) advocated forcefully for the invasion, and they filtered the information and analysis presented to Kennedy. The proponents of the invasion also excluded lower-level State Department officials from the deliberations for fear that they might expose their plan's weaknesses and risks. Throughout the discussions, the president and his Cabinet members often deferred to the CIA officials, who appeared to be the experts on this matter, and they chose to downplay their reservations about the invasion. Kennedy did not seek out unbiased experts to counsel him. Arthur Schlesinger, a historian serving as an adviser to the president at the time, later wrote that the discussions about the CIA's plan seemed to take place amidst "a curious atmosphere of assumed consensus."[4] In the absence of vigorous dissent and debate, many critical assumptions remained unchallenged. For instance, the CIA officials argued repeatedly that Cuban citizens would rise up against the Castro government as soon as the exiles landed at the Bay of Pigs, thereby weakening the Communist dictator's ability to repel the invading force. No such domestic uprising ever took place. Proponents also contended that the exiles could retreat rather easily to the mountains nearby if they encountered stiff opposition upon landing on the shore. However, the invading force would need to travel over rough terrain for nearly 80 miles to reach the safety of those mountains.[5]

After the botched invasion, President Kennedy evaluated his foreign policy decision-making process, and he instituted several key improvements. In October 1962, when Kennedy learned that the Soviets had placed nuclear missiles in Cuba, he assembled a group of advisers to help him decide how to proceed, and he put these process improvements into action.[6] This group, known as Ex Comm (an abbreviation for Executive Committee of the National Security Council), met repeatedly throughout the Cuban missile crisis.[7]

What process changes did Kennedy enact? First, the president directed the group to abandon the usual rules of protocol and deference to rank during meetings. When he did not attend meetings, the group operated without an official chairman. He did not want status differences or rigid procedures to stifle candid discussion. Second, Kennedy urged each adviser not to participate in the deliberations as a spokesman for his department; instead, he wanted each person to take on role of a "skeptical generalist." Kennedy directed each adviser to consider the "policy problem as a whole, rather than approaching the issues in the traditional bureaucratic way whereby each man confines his remarks to the special aspects in which he considers himself to be an expert and avoids arguing about issues on which others present are supposedly more expert than he."[8] Third, the president invited lower-level officials and outside experts to join the deliberations occasionally to ensure access to fresh points of view and unfiltered information and analysis. Fourth, members of Ex Comm split into subgroups to develop the arguments for two alternative courses of action. One subgroup drafted a paper outlining the plan for a military air strike, while the other articulated the strategy for a blockade. The subgroups exchanged memos and developed detailed critiques of one another's proposals. This back-and-forth continued until each subgroup was prepared to present its arguments to the president. Fifth, Robert Kennedy and Theodore Sorensen, two of the president's closest confidants, were assigned to play the role of devil's advocates during the decision-making process. Kennedy wanted them to surface and challenge every important assumption as well as to identify the weaknesses and risks associated with each proposal. Sixth, the president deliberately chose not to attend many of the preliminary meetings that took place, so as to encourage people to air their views openly and honestly. Finally, Kennedy did not try to make the decision based upon a single recommendation put forth after his advisers had discussed and evaluated the situation. Instead, he asked that his advisers present him with arguments for alternative strategies, and then he assumed the responsibility for selecting the appropriate course of action.[9] For a summary of the differences between the two decision-making processes, see Table 2-1.

TABLE 2-1: Bay of Pigs Versus Cuban Missile Crisis

Process Characteristics	Bay of Pigs	Cuban Missile Crisis
Role of President Kennedy	Present at all critical meetings	Deliberately absent from preliminary meetings
Role of participants	Spokesmen/advocates for particular departments and agencies	Skeptical generalists examining the "policy problem as a whole"
Group norms	Deference to experts Adherence to rules of protocol	Minimization of status/rank differences Freedom from rules of protocol
Participation and involvement	Extreme secrecy—very small group kept "in the know" Exclusion of lower-level aides and outsiders with fresh points of view	Direct communication between Kennedy and lower-level officials with relevant knowledge and expertise Periodic involvement of outside experts and fresh voices
Use of subgroups	One small subgroup, driving the process "The same men, in short, both planned the operation and judged its chances of success."[10]	Two subgroups of equal size, power, and expertise Repeated exchange of position papers and vigorous critique and debate
Consideration of alternatives	Rapid convergence upon a single alternative No competing plans presented to the president	Balanced consideration of two alternatives Arguments for both options presented to the president
Institutionalization of dissent	No individual designated to occupy the special role of devil's advocate	Two confidants of the president playing the role of "intellectual watchdog"— probing for the flaws in every argument

This case demonstrates how leaders can learn from failures and then change the process of decision that they employ in the future. Here, we see President Kennedy identifying the flaws in the processes employed in the Bay of Pigs, and then *deciding how to decide* in critical foreign policy situations going forward. Kennedy recognized that the Bay of Pigs deliberations lacked sufficient debate and dissent, and that he had incorrectly presumed that a great deal of consensus existed, when in fact, latent discontent festered within the group. Perhaps more importantly, Kennedy understood that he had not given much thought to how the Bay of Pigs decision should be made before plunging into deliberations. Consequently, ardent advocates of the invasion took control of the process and drove it to their preferred conclusion. By making key process design choices at the outset of the Cuban missile crisis, Kennedy shaped and influenced how that decision process unfolded, and in so doing, he enhanced the quality of the solution that he and his team developed. This chapter takes a closer look at the managerial levers that leaders can use to set the stage for an effective decision-making process and introduces a conceptual framework to help leaders think about the impact of those levers (see Figures 2-1 and 2-2).

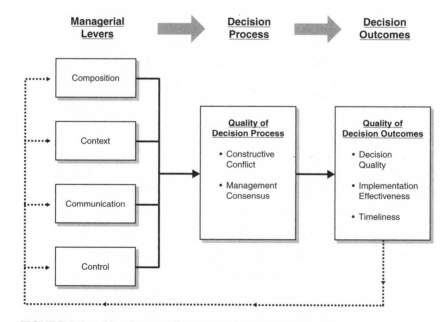

FIGURE 2-1: Shaping quality processes and outcomes

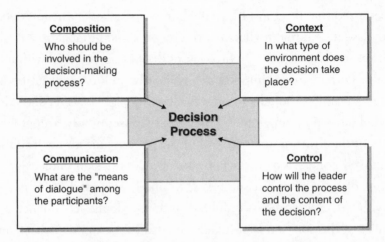

FIGURE 2-2:   Setting the stage: four critical sets of choices

Managerial Levers

The leader makes four important sets of choices that affect his ability to cultivate constructive conflict and build enduring consensus. First, the leader determines the *composition* of the decision-making body. Who should have an opportunity to participate in the process? What should drive those choices? Second, he shapes the *context* in which deliberations will take place. What norms and ground rules will govern the discussions? Third, the leader determines how *communication* will take place among the participants. How will people exchange ideas and information, as well as generate and evaluate alternatives? Finally, the leader must determine the extent and manner in which he will *control* the process and content of the decision. What role will the leader play during discussions, and how will he direct the process? As we shall see, Kennedy's process improvements after the Bay of Pigs entailed changes in each of these four areas.

Composition

When making strategic choices, most executives do not simply consult with the set of direct reports with whom they meet on a regular basis, nor should they expect that this particular group is well-suited to make all high-stakes decisions. Like President Kennedy, one should assemble a decision-making body based upon an assessment of the needs of the situation at hand. For instance, Ex Comm included many, but not all, members of the president's Cabinet. It also contained individuals who did not report directly to the president, and who did not participate regularly in Cabinet meetings. In most instances, leaders need to be willing to draw upon people at multiple levels of the organization as the decision process unfolds. Naturally, a leader must act with care when bypassing senior staff members to speak with individuals at lower levels. Being open and transparent about such communications is a must.

Job titles, positions in the organizational hierarchy, and considerations of status and power within the firm should not be the primary determinants of participation in a complex high-stakes decision-making process. Instead, the leader should consider four other factors—access to expertise, implementation needs, the role of personal confidants, and the effects of demographic differences—when selecting who should become involved in a set of deliberations.[11]

First, people should participate if they have knowledge and expertise that is relevant to the situation at hand. When scanning potential participants, the leader ought to ask himself: Can a particular individual provide data or information that others do not possess? Beyond that, one should consider whether an individual might be useful to offer a fresh point of view during deliberations, or perhaps to counter the conventional wisdom that prevails among most of the apparent experts on the matter. In the Bay of Pigs, President Kennedy failed to ensure that key players from the State Department, with deep knowledge of the Cuban government and society, participated in the Cabinet-level discussions regarding the

CIA's invasion plan. In contrast, Kennedy reached down below the level of his direct reports during the Cuban missile crisis to ensure that he had access to unfiltered information from people with knowledge pertinent to the situation.

Leaders need to be willing to communicate directly with people several levels down in an organization when making critical decisions. Otherwise, they will be relying on data and analysis that often has been summarized and packaged for presentation in a way that distorts the true picture of the situation. Information often becomes massaged and filtered on its way up the hierarchy. Consequently, leaders often find themselves confronted with a set of analyses that downplays important risks, fails to acknowledge conflicting interpretations of the data among lower-level officials, and offers a slanted argument in defense of a particular proposal.[12]

In the Columbia space shuttle tragedy, we see a vivid example of how executives can fail to assess a dangerous threat accurately, because they have not been presented with all the information required to make a sound decision. After the foam strike during the launch of Columbia, some lower-level engineers became extremely concerned about the possibility of catastrophe upon re-entry into the earth's atmosphere. As we now know, these engineers exchanged an extensive series of e-mails questioning the judgment, put forth by respected technical experts and managers, that the foam strike did not present a "safety of flight" issue. However, senior executives at NASA did not become aware of these concerns, nor of the extensive disagreement among lower-level officials, until after the tragedy took place. NASA managers relied too much on job titles and the rules of protocol to dictate patterns of involvement and participation in the decision process. They should have actively solicited the views of knowledgeable individuals at lower levels of the hierarchy, and they should have probed further to ensure that they understood the uncertainties, presumptions, and conflicting interpretations associated with the analysis of the debris strike that occurred during launch.[13]

Of course, expertise alone should not dictate participation in a strategic decision-making process. Leaders also need to consider how the decision will be implemented across the organization. If managers know that someone will play a critical role during the implementation process, it may make sense to solicit that person's advice during the decision process. The involvement of key implementers has two obvious advantages. First, it enables senior executives to incorporate into their decision process detailed information about the costs and challenges of carrying out each alternative course of action. As a middle manager at one aerospace firm told me, he became involved in a high-level business restructuring decision because, as someone who would be ultimately responsible for enacting critical facets of the decision, he could "work a straw man implementation plan that we could cost to come up with what investment would be required to execute particular alternatives." Second, executives build commitment and shared understanding throughout the organization by involving key implementers in the decision-making process. Individuals often become disenchanted if they are asked to carry out a plan for which they have had little or no opportunity to provide input. Giving implementers a voice in the decision process enables executives to build a sense of collective ownership of the plan. When individuals feel that it is "their decision" as opposed to "management's decision," they are more likely to go the extra mile during the implementation process.[14]

Personal relationships also can and should shape the composition of the decision-making body that a leader assembles when faced with the need to make an important strategic choice. No, one should not rely on cronies or sycophants when making key decisions. However, leaders can benefit by drawing on people with whom they have a strong personal bond, characterized by mutual trust and respect, to help them think through complex issues. In fact, in an insightful study of top management teams in the computer industry, Stanford University professor Kathleen Eisenhardt found that the more successful chief executives consistently utilized a few close confidants as sounding boards on strategic issues.[15] She described these individuals as "experienced counselors" who met with the leader privately, listened to his doubts and concerns, and offered candid advice. Whereas Eisenhardt's study showed that the "oldest and most experienced executives filled the counselor role,"[16] my own research across many different types of organizations shows that leaders tend to select confidants not according to seniority, but because they admire the personal character, intelligence, and integrity of the individuals, and they have a strong prior working relationship with them. The president of a defense contractor explained, "He and I tend to go offline with each other. At 7:30 in the morning or 6:00 in the evening, we compare notes and do sanity checks with one another. He and I have worked together and known each other for a long time, and we have a great mutual respect for each other."[17]

These confidants play a particularly important role when managers operate in turbulent and ambiguous environments, because most leaders face a few critical moments of indecision and doubt prior to making high-stakes choices.[18] Eisenhardt's research shows that confidants not only offer solid advice and a fresh point of view to leaders, they also help them overcome last-minute misgivings and protect against the pernicious tendency toward indecisiveness, delay, and procrastination that often prevails in organizations faced with high environmental ambiguity and turbulence.[19]

Leaders also can draw upon close personal confidants to play special roles in decision-making processes. For example, President Kennedy asked Ted Sorensen and his brother, Robert, to play the role of the devil's advocate during the Cuban missile crisis. At first glance, it may seem odd that the attorney general and a speechwriter were involved at all in such a momentous foreign policy decision. Their positions in the bureaucracy certainly did not dictate their involvement in the process. However, the president trusted these two men a great deal and valued their judgment. Kennedy knew that others would not be quick to dismiss critiques offered by these two individuals because of the well-known personal bond between them and the president. In addition, Kennedy recognized that these two men would be more comfortable than most other advisers when it came to challenging his own views and opinions.

Finally, as leaders select people with whom to advise and consult, they should consider how demographic similarities and differences among participants shape the nature and quality of decision-making processes. Does one want to bring together a highly diverse group of people, or should a leader surround himself with people of similar backgrounds? The answer may seem obvious, but before we accept the conventional wisdom, we ought to examine the research findings on this issue.

A long stream of research on top management teams has explored the question of whether demographic heterogeneity enhances team and organizational performance. By demographic heterogeneity, researchers mean differences among team members in age, gender, team and organizational tenure, functional background, and the like. Many scholars have argued that heterogeneous groups should outperform more homogenous ones, because the former ought to exhibit greater cognitive diversity. In other words, groups benefit from give-and-take among people with different perspectives, expertise, talents, and approaches to problem solving. However, empirical studies have produced conflicting results regarding the impact of demographic heterogeneity on senior team and organizational performance. How do we explain these contradictory findings? Diverse groups tend to generate higher levels of cognitive conflict, but as argued in Chapter 1, "The Leadership Challenge," intense debates often lead to affective conflict. Moreover, high levels of heterogeneity sometimes can be associated with less-frequent communication among members, lower levels of cohesiveness, weaker identification with the group, and enhanced coordination challenges. Consequently, diverse groups may find it difficult to keep conflict constructive and build management consensus.[20]

Leaders should not conclude from this analysis that they should refrain from building diverse teams. Instead, as they assemble groups of advisers, they need to be aware of the needs of their situation. If the decision at hand requires a great deal of novel and creative thinking, and if the leader's usual group of advisers occasionally falls in the trap of thinking alike, he may want to strive for increased heterogeneity. In contrast, if the decision implementation necessitates frequent communication and intense coordination, and the usual set of advisers has encountered difficulty reconciling starkly contrasting views of the world, the leader may lean toward a bit more homogeneity. Perhaps more important than trying to achieve the optimal the level of diversity, leaders should begin each decision process by surveying the demographic similarities/differences among key participants, and then seek measures to counterbalance the pitfalls associated with high levels of either homogeneity or heterogeneity.[21]

Context

Ensuring that the appropriate mix of individuals becomes involved in an issue represents just a small portion of the challenge for managers trying to develop a high-quality decision process. They also have an opportunity to shape and influence the context in which that process takes place. Context affects behavior in very powerful ways, and it has two distinct dimensions. Structural context consists of the organization's reporting relationships, monitoring and control mechanisms, and reward and punishment systems.[22] The psychological context consists of the behavioral norms and situational pressures that underlie the decision-making process.

Structural context remains relatively stable over time, although seemingly subtle changes can have a profound impact on managerial behavior. Leaders typically do not change incentive schemes or alter the organization chart on a frequent basis. They certainly would not want to modify the structural context for each high-stakes decision that comes along. In that sense, it does not represent a lever that managers can change easily a means of influencing how a particular decision-making process will unfold. However, leaders need to mindful of how the structural context will shape individual and collective behavior during the process of problem solving and negotiation.

Psychological context can be more fluid. Situational pressures certainly vary across decisions. One might assume that variables such as time pressure and the sense of urgency remain outside an executive's control. However, leaders typically have the opportunity to make time pressure more or less salient for their subordinates, perhaps by stressing the first-mover advantages that a competitor has achieved or even by establishing deadlines and milestones for the decision process. Leaders often heighten the sense of urgency within their organizations as a means of stimulating change.[23] Naturally, accentuating these types of situational pressures can be risky. Stress, anxiety, and arousal can diminish the cognitive performance of decision makers.[24] In particular, research on firefighters suggests that less-experienced individuals may be particularly susceptible to the negative effects of stress.[25] Leaders must consider these risks as they accentuate situational pressures as a means of pushing for faster and higher performance.

Shared norms also may exhibit fluidity. They may differ across groups or units within the organization, and they can be altered explicitly as well as implicitly based on a leader's behavior at the outset of a decision process. For instance, President Kennedy made a clear and explicit attempt to recast the behavioral norms that governed the actions of his advisers during the Cuban missile crisis.

What types of behavioral norms should a leader try to foster among participants in a decision-making process? As psychologist Richard Hackman has pointed out, many groups establish ground rules that seek to ensure smooth and harmonious interaction among participants. However, he stresses that being polite and courteous to one another—not interrupting others, for example—certainly does not ensure successful performance![26]

What, then, should leaders strive to achieve when shaping the psychological context in which decisions are made? My colleague, Amy Edmondson, has shown how the creation of a climate of psychological safety stimulates collective problem solving and learning within organizations. She defines psychological safety as the "shared belief that a group is safe for interpersonal risk-taking."[27] It means that individuals feel comfortable that others will not rebuke, marginalize, or penalize them based upon what they say during a group discussion. When this shared belief exists, people will take a variety of interpersonal risks. They will share private information, admit mistakes, request assistance or additional data, surface previously undiscussable topics, and express dissenting views.[28]

It can be difficult to enhance psychological safety, particularly in hierarchical organizations characterized by substantial status differences among individuals. However, leaders can take steps to change the climate within their decision-making bodies. For instance, they can lead by example, acknowledging their own fallibility and admitting prior errors as a means of encouraging people to take interpersonal risks of their own. In an award-winning article titled "The Failure-Tolerant Leader," Richard Farson and Ralph Keyes offer a plethora of examples of leaders who successfully broke down communication barriers and encouraged more divergent thinking in their organizations by openly talking about their own mistakes. For instance, they write that, "The late Roberto Goizueta got years of one-liners from the New Coke fiasco that he sponsored. Admitting his mistake conveyed to his employees better than a hundred speeches or a thousand memos that 'learning failures,' even on a grand scale, were tolerated."[29]

Leaders also can alter the language system typically employed within an organization. At times, commonly used words can attach a stigma to important learning behaviors, such as the admission of a mistake. For instance, Julie Morath, chief operating officer at Children's Hospital and Clinics in Minneapolis, recognized that the language system in her organization attached a stigma to those who surfaced and discussed medical errors. Consequently, the organization could not improve patient safety, because many accidents or near-miss situations remained unidentified. Therefore, she created a list of "words to work by"—explicit do's and don'ts regarding language—as a means of encouraging people to talk more openly about patient safety failures. Many employees noted that this effort helped to create a different atmosphere within the hospital and made people more willing to discuss and learn from failures.[30]

Communication

Communication mechanisms represent the third major lever that leaders can employ to enhance the quality of decision-making processes. Managers face a choice regarding the means of dialogue that they want to employ. In other words, they can determine how ideas and information are exchanged, as well as how alternatives are discussed and evaluated. To put it simply, leaders can choose between two distinct approaches to shaping the avenues of dialogue and communication. They can adopt a structured approach, dictating quite specifically the procedures by which participants should offer viewpoints, compare and contrast alternatives, and reach a set of conclusions. Alternatively, leaders can employ a largely unstructured approach, whereby they encourage managers to discuss their ideas freely and openly without adherence to well-defined procedures for how the deliberations should take place.

In the typical unstructured discussion, leaders guide the deliberations with a light touch. They encourage participants to engage in a free exchange of ideas and opinions, while insuring that each person has an adequate opportunity to express their views. They encourage individuals to support their recommendations with sound logic and compelling data, and to try to convince others of the merits of their proposals while recognizing and respecting other perspectives. Ultimately, leaders encourage participants to reconcile opposing views and find common ground. Scholars have dubbed this approach the "consensus method" because of its emphasis on reaching a solution that all members can accept, and because it does tend to foster high levels of commitment and group harmony.[31] See Table 2-2 for a summary of the strengths and weaknesses of this approach to decision making.

TABLE 2-2:   Strengths and Weaknesses of the Free Exchange Approach

Benefits	Costs
Most managers use this "free exchange" approach regularly and feel somewhat comfortable with it.	May lead to premature agreement or convergence on a single alternative.
Entails lower opportunity costs for participants: time, experience, training.	Sometimes leads to the suppression of dissent, especially as a majority opinion emerges.
Generates greater group harmony, which may have a beneficial impact on implementation and other future group interaction.	Generates lower levels of critical evaluation.
May be more appropriate for situations characterized by sufficient data and clear alternatives.	Does not uncover as many new alternatives, assumptions, and perspectives.

Too much convergent thinking, of course, can be a dangerous thing. Left to their own devices, groups all too often find themselves prematurely honing in on a single alternative. Therefore, leaders may need to introduce structured procedures to foster more creative and divergent thinking, as well as enhanced conflict and debate. Scholars and consultants have developed numerous mechanisms for organizing a discussion so as to promote a combination of imaginative and critical thinking. For instance, Edward de Bono invented a procedure called "Six Thinking Hats" to help groups consider a problem from multiple perspectives (see Table 2-3). With this technique, participants examine a decision using a variety of thinking styles. For instance, when "wearing the white hat," individuals must employ an objective, data-driven approach to the decision. In contrast, those donning the "red hat" use intuition and emotion to examine the situation. Many groups find this technique useful as a way of pushing individuals to move beyond their usual problem-solving habits and routines, while encouraging everyone to think "outside the box."[32]

TABLE 2-3   Six Thinking Hats

Hat Color	Problem-Solving Style
White	Rational, objective, data-driven
Red	Intuitive and emotional
Black	Focused on all that could go wrong
Yellow	Upbeat and optimistic mindset
Green	Imaginative and freewheeling perspective
Blue	Process facilitator/chairperson mindset

In the Cuban missile crisis, we see variants of two longstanding, very effective procedures for fostering divergent thinking and vigorous debate. Scholars have termed these approaches the "Dialectical Inquiry" and "Devil's Advocacy" methods. Although the names may frighten you, for fear that they imply rather complex and arcane procedures, there is no reason to be alarmed. These approaches, in fact, represent simple mechanisms for nurturing cognitive conflict. Each entails dividing a decision-making entity into two subgroups. In the Dialectical Inquiry method, one subgroup develops a detailed proposal and presents it to the others, preferably in written as well as oral form. They, in turn, generate an alternative plan of action. The two subgroups then debate the competing proposals, and they seek agreement on a common set of facts and assumptions before trying to select a course of action. Ultimately, the subgroups focus on reconciling divergent viewpoints and selecting a course of action consistent with the agreed-upon set of facts and assumptions. During this final stage of the process, the subgroups often generate new options as a means of moving beyond the original points of contention between the competing camps.

The Devil's Advocacy approach works in a similar fashion. One subgroup develops a comprehensive plan of action and describes it to the others. However, they do not attempt to generate competing options. Instead, they build a detailed critique of the first subgroup's proposal. Again, both subgroups should strive to present their arguments in written and oral form for maximum effectiveness. The first subgroup then returns to the drawing board, modifying their plan, or perhaps inventing a new option, as a means of addressing the criticisms and feedback that they have received. An iterative process of revision and critique then takes place until the two subgroups feel comfortable agreeing, at a minimum, on a common set of facts and assumptions. After reaching agreement on these issues, the subgroups work together to craft a plan of action that each side can accept.

These two structured decision-making procedures have many advantages (see Table 2-4).[33] They tend to generate a great deal of cognitive conflict, and they stimulate the generation of multiple alternatives. Moreover, they help decision makers identify the flaws and weaknesses inherent in any plan, and they focus explicit attention on the underlying assumptions held by various participants. Naturally, one could achieve some of these same benefits by designating an individual to occupy a special role, either as the devil's advocate or as the person responsible for inventing creative options. However, by directing people to work in subgroups, these procedures make it easier for an individual with dissenting views to put forth his ideas. After all, it tends to be quite difficult for one person, standing in opposition to the majority, to avoid the pressures for conformity that often emerge within groups.[34] One should note, for instance, that Kennedy assigned two people to serve as devil's advocates in the Cuban missile crisis, perhaps recognizing that a single critic/dissenter would find it quite difficult to confront the other members of Ex Comm.

TABLE 2-4:   Strengths and Weaknesses of Structured Approaches

Benefits	Costs
Leads to considerable critical evaluation.	May adversely impact group harmony, decision acceptance, and implementation.
Explicitly outlines the supporting argument for a particular alternative (assumptions, facts).	Entails opportunity costs for participants: time experience, training.
Generates multiple alternatives.	Subgroups may generate "safe" alternatives knowing that others will closely scrutinize their proposals.
Avoids early convergence on a single alternative.	DI: Synthesis of opposing alternatives may lead to mediocre compromise.
Fosters a high level of individual understanding of the final decision.	DA: Process may focus too much on destroying a particular alternative, rather than constructing other viable courses of action.
Does not force individuals to stand alone as dissenters/critical evaluators.	

Although these procedures offer many benefits for leaders interested in cultivating creative thinking and vigorous debate, they do not come without risks. Naturally, affective conflict can emerge. Subgroups may become so entrenched in their competing positions that they cannot reconcile divergent views and find common ground. Polarization of opinion may even occur, imperiling a leader's ability to build commitment and shared understanding. Critics can become so effective at dissecting every proposal put forth by others that the decision makers become convinced that no identifiable course of action will meet the organization's needs, resulting in a frustrating period of indecision. Alternatively, subgroups may adopt seriously flawed compromise solutions when faced with an impasse.

Faced with these potential problems, leaders must use these procedures with great care, and they ought to assess whether the situation warrants taking such risks. Consider, for instance, a situation in which a leader knows that a strong coalition of managers supports a particular course of action, and he fears that they may stream roll the others into accepting this plan. Such a circumstance appears suitable for the application of one of the structured procedures outlined here. Similarly, a leader may be wary of how cohesive and seemingly like-minded his relatively homogenous group of subordinates have become. That particular state of affairs also may warrant the use of a structured mechanism for stimulating dissent and debate. In sum, leaders need not enter each decision process with the intent of empowering subordinates to shape and determine the means of dialogue, nor should they impose procedures in a top-down fashion regardless of the circumstances. They should strive to match the process of communication with the needs created by the situation at hand.[35]

Control

When shaping how strategic choices are made, the final lever at the leader's disposal concerns the crafting of his distinctive position in the decision process. The leader must decide the extent to which he intends to control both the process and the content of the decision. Specifically, the leader has choices to make along four dimensions. First, he must decide how and when to introduce his own views into the deliberations. Second, he needs to consider the extent and manner in which he will intervene actively to direct discussion and debate. Third, the leader has an opportunity to play a special role during the decision process. For instance, he might consistently occupy the position of the "futurist," looking far beyond the time horizon considered by his advisers. Alternatively, he might personally adopt the responsibility for playing the devil's advocate. Finally, the leader must determine how he will attempt to bring closure to the process and reach a final decision.

Leaders must choose whether to reveal their views at the start of a decision process. When a leader begins by arguing for a particular course of action, he shapes the way that others define the problem at hand, search for alternatives, and express their ideas and opinions. In some cases, it creates a perception that the leader has already made up his mind, and therefore, that the team members do not have a genuine opportunity to influence the final decision. In fact, the early declaration of the leader's position may have several adverse effects on the decision-making process (see Table 2-5).[36]

The leader may create the impression that the decision has already been made, and that he is unlikely to change his mind. In this case, team members may become frustrated if they believe that the leader simply wants to create the *appearance* of a consultative process. In addition, he may frame the issue in a manner that constricts the range of alternatives that are generated by participants. Decision frames are "mental structures people create to simplify and organize the world."[37] Frames shape the way that people think about a problem. They can be useful because they enable individuals to cope with complexity. However, frames also constrain the range of options that are considered, and distort the how people interpret data. When a leader announces his position in the early stages of a decision process, he imposes a particular frame, and consequently, may inhibit the group from exploring other ways of thinking about the problem. Finally, announcing an initial position may discourage individuals from expressing dissent and offering minority views. As pointed out earlier, when the leader states his opinion forcefully, it can be difficult for others to disagree with him publicly.

The leader can avoid these detrimental effects by choosing not to reveal his preferred solution during the early stages of the group discussions. Alternatively, the leader may offer a tentative proposal, but emphasize that he is quite open to differing views and willing to modify his position if superior solutions emerge during the discussion. In either case, the leader should stress that he will try to keep an open mind as he listens to each person's ideas and recommendations. This approach will foster a belief that participants have the potential to influence the final decision in a substantial way.

TABLE 2-5: Announcing an Initial Position

Type of Impact	Pitfalls and Dangers
Legitimacy effect	Creating the impression that the decision has already been made
	Fostering a belief that the decision process is simply a "charade of consultation"[38]
Framing effect	Trapping the group into one way of thinking about the problem or issue
	Constraining the range of options developed and evaluated by others
Conformity effect	Discouraging the surfacing of minority viewpoints
	Encouraging people to misrepresent their views or downplay reservations in an attempt to curry favor with the leader

In some crisis situations, however, a leader faces a compelling rationale for declaring his views at the outset of a decision process. Consider the case of President Bush's response to the terrorist attacks of September 11, 2001. He framed the situation very clearly for his advisers (and for the nation as a whole) during his initial reaction to the attacks: "They had declared war on us, and I made up my mind at that moment that we were going to war."[39] By using the language of war, he provided a lens through which he and his advisers have examined the terrorist problem to this day. One could argue that he constrained future discussions and squelched subsequent opportunities for debate by framing the situation as he did. The evidence suggests that his actions may have, at least to some extent, had this effect. However, consider for a moment how the nation would have reacted if he had *not* acted in this manner. If Bush did not offer a clear and rapid response, the American people would have doubted his leadership capabilities and questioned whether he had the mettle to handle the crisis. Witness the negative reaction to the decision not to return immediately to Washington, D.C., on that day. A tentative or ambiguous response at the time of the attacks may have made it difficult for Bush to sell his subsequent policy decisions to the American public.[40] In sum, during crises, leaders must be at least a bit more willing to accept the potential negative consequences associated with a forceful statement of their initial position.

When the deliberations begin, the leader may or may not intervene actively to direct the pattern of participation and involvement. In research with my colleagues, Amy Edmondson and Michael Watkins, we have distinguished between an activist model of process facilitation/intervention and a more laissez-faire approach.[41] In the interventionist model, leaders guide the timing and extent of participation by various individuals involved in the deliberations. They invite specific participants to offer their views, and they inquire repeatedly as to where individuals stand on specific topics. They pose follow-up questions for clarification purposes and play back people's statements to ensure that they have been interpreted correctly. Moreover, they emphasize points that they deem important, but which perhaps have been a bit misunderstood or marginalized. The contrasting leadership mode calls for a much less directive approach to discussion facilitation. Leaders allow participants to enter and exit the deliberations more freely, and they do not try to control where people focus their attention.

The activist mode functions quite effectively when participants in a decision process possess a great deal of private information (i.e., data to which others do not have access and about whose existence they may not even be aware). Why is this so? Group members tend to discuss commonly shared information a great deal during decision-making processes, while paying less attention to privately held data.[42] The failure to surface this private information can lead to suboptimal, or even fundamentally flawed, decisions. By intervening actively, leaders can ensure that people have an ample opportunity to disclose unshared information, and that participants have an adequate chance to recognize the revelation of important private information.[43]

Because the activist mode can create discomfort among some participants and perhaps slant the discussion in unforeseen ways, leaders should be cautious about its utilization. For those reasons, leaders should adopt a much less interventionist approach when all participants share a common pool of pertinent information and expertise.

In addition to deciding how to facilitate the decision process, leaders must determine whether they want to occupy a special role during the deliberations. Kathleen Eisenhardt's research suggests that a useful technique for nurturing healthy debate is "cultivation of a symphony of distinct roles."[44] She found that effective senior management teams tend to fall into habitual patterns of behavior in which certain members occupy informal, yet commonly understood, roles on a rather consistent basis. Leaders not only can encourage subordinates to take on certain roles, they can also occupy those positions themselves if necessary.

Eisenhardt and her colleagues found that a number of management teams have an individual who serves as the "futurist"—that person tends to be the visionary who pushes the team to examine long-term strategic trends and market developments when they get bogged down in short-term operational issues. Others serve repeatedly as "steadying forces" who temper overconfidence and remind people not to get caught up in circumstances of "irrational exuberance." Leaders can occupy two other roles as well. They may serve as a devil's advocate, and they can be the person pushing frequently for an "action orientation"—challenging inertia and indecisiveness while reminding people constantly of the recent moves that competitors have made to establish a market advantage. Although Eisenhardt's work stresses the permanence of role structures within some teams, leaders need not always occupy the same role in every process to be effective decision makers. They may find it useful to shift roles over time as different threats and opportunities emerge.

Perhaps the most important dimension of control concerns how the leader intends to bring closure to the decision-making process.

Edmonson, Watkins, and I identify two distinct approaches to selecting a course of action along with a group of advisers. On the one hand, the leader may serve as a mediator, "trying to bring team members with different views together to arrive at a mutually acceptable solution."[45] The leader does not impose his will on the group in this mode, but rather he facilitates deliberations in an effort to find common ground among multiple parties. The leader may weigh in on the matter with his own views, but he does not use his power and rank to dictate the outcome. In contrast, the leader may adopt an arbitrator orientation, "listening to competing arguments and selecting the course of action that he believes is best for the organization."[46] President Kennedy operated in this mode during the Cuban missile crisis. He made it clear that he wanted to hear the opposing sides present their proposals to him, and then he would go off on his own to evaluate the arguments and make a final decision. President Bush employed a similar approach when deciding to attack Afghanistan after the terrorist attacks of September 11, 2001.

Naturally, leaders may begin by trying to serve as a mediator among players with competing goals and interests, and then shift to the arbitrator orientation if the group cannot reach an agreement on a mutually acceptable course of action. Indeed, Eisenhardt's research suggests that many effective leaders employ just such a blended approach. She described the phenomenon as "consensus with qualification." In this mode, leaders try to bring people along until they can find a solution that everyone finds satisfactory. If time runs short, tempers flare repeatedly, or the parties simply cannot reach common ground, then the leader can take sole responsibility for selecting a course of action.[47]

When deciding how to operate in a particular situation, executives must consider a number of factors including their personal leadership style, the extent to which time pressure exists, the personalities of the parties involved, and the extent to which the interests of various players are diametrically opposed. Perhaps more important than selecting the optimal mode for a given situation, the leader needs to be very clear about how he intends to behave when disagreements emerge and a decision must be made. Individuals can become readily disenchanted if the leader's approach to reaching closure does not conform to their prior expectations. Providing a clear process roadmap in this regard serves the leader well if he hopes to build commitment among all parties involved.

The Power to Learn

President Kennedy demonstrated during the Cuban missile crisis that a leader has many levers available to affect the quality of a high-stakes decision-making process. Moreover, he showed that leaders have the opportunity to learn from prior failures and use those lessons to modify the process choices that they make in the future. Of course, it takes a certain mindset to acknowledge one's failures and invite others to provide advice regarding how to change going forward. The culture in many organizations also inhibits productive learning. As organizational learning expert David Garvin has noted, many firms have a culture that regards learning as an activity that distracts resources and attention from the "real work" that needs to be done.[48]

President Kennedy's actions demonstrate another important distinction regarding the learning process that takes place after critical choices are made. When decision failures occur, many executives focus on the issues involved, and they seek to identify the mistaken judgments and flawed assumptions that they made. However, many leaders do not push further to investigate *why* they made these errors. Too many of them engage only in *content-centric learning*. By that, I mean that they search for lessons about how they will make a *different decision* when faced with a similar business situation in the future. For instance, an apparel executive reported to me about a decision to move into a new product category. When the decision proved to be a failure, he reflected back and concluded that the firm did not have the skills and capabilities to succeed in a fashion-driven market segment. He resolved to never invest in a fashion-oriented business again.

Kennedy adopted a different learning orientation. He engaged in *process-centric learning*, meaning that he thought carefully about *why* the Bay of Pigs decision-making procedures led to mistaken judgments and flawed assumptions. He did not simply draw a series of conclusions about how to handle future choices regarding U.S. policy toward Cuba or the support of rebel movements in other countries. He searched for lessons about how to employ a *different process* when faced with tough choices in the future.[49]

The power of process-centric learning can be remarkable. Consider that apparel executive once again. His conclusion about fashion-driven product categories proved to be a solid example of productive content-centric learning. Yet, he did not rest having derived those lessons from the failure. Reflecting back, that manager also concluded that he had become too emotionally attached to his original idea, and consequently he discounted a series of warning signs, focused on confirmatory information, and failed to listen to dissenting voices. How many times did that apparel executive apply the lesson regarding fashion-driven product categories? The answer: much less than the number of occasions on which that same executive benefited by adopting a different approach to the collection and interpretation of information during a high-stakes decision-making process.

The Prepared Mind

Louis Pasteur once said, "Chance favors the prepared mind." Indeed, the prepared mind of an effective leader thinks carefully about the type of decision-making process that they want to employ, before they immerse themselves in the weeds of a particular business problem. Moreover, the prepared mind searches constantly for the opportunity to learn from past successes and failures, and then improve the way that they go about making crucial choices in the future.

PART II
MANAGING CONFLICT

3

AN ABSENCE OF
CANDOR

**"Don't be afraid of opposition. Remember, a kite rises
against, not with the wind."**

—Hamilton Wright Mabie

When Jack Welch became CEO of General Electric in April 1981, he
found that the company had become incredibly bureaucratic and
hierarchical. In some instances, 12 layers of management separated
workers on the factory floor from the office of the CEO. Many managers, particularly those serving on the large corporate office staff,
spent considerable amounts of time reviewing and approving plans,
reports, and memos in a relatively passive manner.

The focal point of many strategy review sessions became GE's
infamous, incredibly thick, planning books. Chock full of forecasts
and calculations, these books passed through many layers of the hierarchy for review, but they rarely became the basis for an open and

frank dialogue between the CEO and the person leading a particular business unit. Welch soon became frustrated that strategic planning sessions had become "dog and pony shows" rather than candid discussions about the future direction of each business. Everyone spoke politely, refrained from ruffling any feathers, and generally played it "close to the vest" rather than openly confronting controversial issues.

Welch described the atmosphere in these sessions as one of "superficial congeniality." By that, he meant that the climate seemed "pleasant on the surface, with distrust and savagery roiling beneath it." As he put it, "The phrase seems to sum up how bureaucrats typically behave, smiling in front of you but always looking for a 'gotcha' behind your back."[1] Candor and constructive conflict simply did not characterize most communications within the General Electric organization.

Think for a moment about your own organization. Do you have an atmosphere of candid communication? Are people engaging in "superficial congeniality" during meetings? Do people say "yes" when they really mean "no"? Are people comfortable speaking up when they have concerns or dissenting views? Do you find yourself taking silence to mean consent? Before reading on, review the list of warning signs, found in Table 3-1, that might suggest the existence of a serious communication problem within your organization—namely, a lack of cognitive, or task-oriented, conflict.

TABLE 3-1:   Signals That Insufficient Candor Exists Within Your Organization

Warning Signs

Do management meetings seem more like hushed, polite games of golf or fast-paced, physical games of ice hockey?[2]

Do subordinates wait to take their verbal and visual cues from you before commenting on controversial issues?

Are planning and strategy sessions largely about the preparation of hefty binders and fancy presentations, or are they primarily about a lively, open dialogue?

Do the same people tend to dominate management team meetings?

Warning Signs

Is it rare for you to hear concerns or feedback directly from those several levels below you in the organization?

Have senior management meetings become "rubber stamp" sessions in which executives simply ratify decisions that have already been made through other channels?

Are people highly concerned about following rules of protocol when communicating with people across horizontal levels or vertical units of the organization?

Do you rarely hear from someone who is concerned about the level of criticism and opposition that they encountered when offering a proposal during a management team meeting?

After answering the questions in Table 3-1, you may conclude that your organization has a different problem than the one Welch discovered when he took over at General Electric—namely, the existence of too much cognitive conflict. In short, people may argue a great deal, but so much so that the organization finds it difficult to reach a final decision.[3] The later chapters of this book examine this problem in more detail. Specifically, later chapters address how leaders can foster constructive conflict, while also reaching closure in a timely manner. For many of you, however, conflict and candor may be woefully inadequate in your organizations. The remainder of this chapter focuses on understanding that particular problem.

As you consider Welch's description of GE in 1981 (or the assessment that you just completed of your organization), you might conclude that the firms simply need a change in personnel. Remove some of those GE bureaucrats, and the nature of the dialogue within these planning sessions would change. Sounds reasonable, does it not? Perhaps many of the bureaucrats simply did not have the courage to express their opinions on thorny issues, or they had become too comfortable and complacent in their jobs, preferring not to question the status quo to which they had grown so accustomed. Maybe GE had hired a number of managers who did not have the personality to engage in constructive conflict and debate with highly talented peers and superiors. Alternatively, one might argue that these managers refrained from engaging in candid give-and-take during planning sessions because they did not have the capability and expertise to offer informed judgments. Better managers, with greater experience and a deeper understanding of the firm's businesses, might be more willing to engage in frank dialogue and lively debate.

Unfortunately, when it comes to encouraging more candor and constructive dissent within organizations, changing the players often does *not* change the outcome of the game. In most instances, the unwillingness to speak up, to express dissent, and to challenge prevailing opinions is not simply about the existence of personality flaws or skill deficiencies among key people within the organization. The problem typically runs much deeper; it has *structural* and *cultural* roots that have grown over time and become difficult to change. In short, the problem is *systemic* (see Table 3-2). New people, put in the same situations, might very well behave in a similar manner.[4]

TABLE 3-2:   Two Perspectives on the Failure to Speak Up

	Individualistic Perspective	Systemic Perspective
Focal points during the examination of communication failures	Individual behavior during the discussions or deliberations Specific judgments made during the current situation	Organizational and historical factors that shaped individual behavior Typical patterns of communication and decision making over long periods of time
Causal explanations given for communication failures	Skill deficiencies Insufficient expertise Lack of courage/conviction Personality preferences	Hierarchical structures Status differences Rules of protocol Cultural norms Cognitive beliefs/mental models
Responses to communication failures	Assign blame Administer punishment/discipline Alter compensation Change personnel	Simplify/alter the organization structure Change reward system Enhance training and development Create new forums for communication Alter the language system Establish new ground rules for decision-making meetings and processes

To understand the systemic nature of this problem, let's take a closer look at how NASA managers and engineers behaved during the Columbia space shuttle's catastrophic final flight.

Columbia's Final Mission

When NASA engineers learned of the foam strike that occurred during the launch of Columbia on January 16, 2003, some of them became concerned because of the apparent size of the debris that had impacted the shuttle. Rodney Rocha, a NASA engineer with expertise in this area, recalls that he "gasped audibly" when he viewed photos of the foam strike on the day after the launch.[5] Soon, an ad-hoc group formed to investigate the issue. The engineers called themselves the Debris Assessment Team, and they elected Rocha as the co-chair of the group (along with Pam Madera, an engineering manager from NASA's prime contractor on the shuttle program).[6]

On Flight Day 5, Linda Ham chaired a regular meeting of the Mission Management Team, the group responsible for overseeing the Columbia's mission and resolving outstanding problems that occurred during the flight.[7] When the foam strike issue surfaced, she reminded everyone that debris strikes had occurred often on previous missions. Indeed, foam had impacted the shuttle on almost every mission stretching back to the first flight in 1981. Although the original design specifications indicated that no foam shedding should occur, engineers and managers gradually became accustomed to the debris hits, and they grew comfortable with the notion that these foam strikes could not endanger the shuttle. Instead, they simply represented a maintenance problem that would lengthen the turnaround time between missions. During this meeting, Ham also remarked that foam was "not really a factor during the flight because there is not much we can do about it."[8] By that, she meant that, even if the foam strike constituted a "safety of flight" risk, she did not believe that

NASA could engage in any action during the mission to ensure the shuttle's safe re-entry into the earth's atmosphere.

Meanwhile, the Debris Assessment Team concluded that it needed additional data to make an accurate assessment of the damage imposed by the foam strike. The team decided to petition superiors within the engineering chain of command for additional imagery of the shuttle, a request that required NASA to seek assistance from the Department of Defense, which could employ its spy satellites to take photos of the shuttle in space. Interestingly, they chose not to petition Ham directly, apparently because of concerns that such an action may have contradicted the usual rules of protocol.

In any event, shuttle management chose not to seek additional imagery from defense officials. Rocha became incensed, and he wrote a scathing e-mail detailing how he felt about management's failure to approve the imagery request. He shared the e-mail with his colleagues in his unit, but he chose not to send the e-mail to superiors or to senior shuttle program managers.[9] Later, he explained, "Engineers were often told not to send messages much higher than their own rung in the ladder."[10] Here, we have a clear instance in which Rocha did not engage in candid communication, and he felt reluctant to express his dissenting views.

Several days later, the foam strike issue resurfaced at a regular meeting of the Mission Management Team. Rocha attended along with a number of others, including Shuttle Program Manager Ron Dittemore. Ham received an update on the Debris Assessment Team's work from a manager who had obtained an update from Rocha and his group. That manager emphasized that the Debris Assessment Team had concluded that the foam strike was not a safety of flight issue based upon computer modeling, but he did not mention the desire for additional imagery or the fact that the computer models were not designed to analyze this type of debris strike. Ham quickly affirmed the conclusion that this was not a safety of flight issue, and she repeatedly emphasized this finding to her team. She asserted forcefully that the foam hit represented a turnaround issue. Despite his deeply held reservations and doubts, Rocha did not speak up during the meeting.

Later, when asked to comment on the fact that engineers did not speak up more forcefully to express their grave concerns, Flight Director Leroy Cain admonished the engineers, saying, "You are duty bound as a member of this team to voice your concerns, particularly as they relate to safety of flight. You wouldn't have to holler. You stand up and say, 'Here's my concern, and this is why I'm uncomfortable.'"[11] Rocha disagreed, indicating that it was not nearly that easy to express a dissenting view. He remarked, "I couldn't do it (speak up more forcefully)...I'm too low down...and she's (Ham) way up here."[12]

When we look at this tragic situation, one can ask: Would things have transpired differently if other people occupied the positions held by Ham and Rocha? Perhaps, but a close look at the situation suggests that this may not necessarily be the case. As the Columbia Accident Investigation Board examined the incident, they found that the behavior of many of the managers and engineers during the Columbia tragedy reflected cultural norms and deeply ingrained patterns of behavior that had existed for years at NASA. The organization had operated according to hierarchical procedures and strict rules of protocol for as long as the shuttles had been flying. Communications often followed a strict chain of command, and engineers rarely interacted directly with senior managers who were several levels higher in the organization. Status differences had stifled dialogue for years. Deeply held assumptions about the lack of danger associated with foam strikes had minimized thoughtful debate and critical technical analysis of the issue for a long period of time. Because the shuttle kept returning safely despite debris hits, managers and engineers developed confidence that foam strikes did not represent a safety of flight risk. Ham's behavior did not simply represent an isolated case of bad judgment; it reflected a deeply held mental model that had developed gradually over two decades as well as a set of behavioral norms that had long governed how managers and engineers interacted at NASA.

In fact, the problems that plagued the communications leading up to the Columbia disaster stretched back to the Challenger catastrophe 17 years earlier. Commenting on the parallels to Challenger, former astronaut Sally Ride, a member of the commissions that investigated each shuttle catastrophe, remarked that, "I think I'm hearing an echo here."[13] By that, she meant that, although the technical causes may have been different, the organizational causes seemed remarkably similar. NASA had not solved the systemic problems that had inhibited candid dialogue and debate about technical concerns 17 years earlier. Diane Vaughan, a sociologist who has studied both shuttle disasters, explains why NASA did not have a constructive internal debate about the dangers that ultimately led to each catastrophe:

At a meeting that I attended at NASA, somebody pointed out that both Rodney Rocha and Roger Beaujolais (the engineer who had concerns about the O-Rings prior to the Challenger disaster) were people who were defined as worriers in the organization. The boy who called wolf. So that they didn't have a lot of credibility. And the person's thinking was, 'Isn't it possible that we can just change personnel?' The thought was that this was a personality problem. This was no personality problem. This was a structural and a cultural problem. And if you just change the cast of characters, the next person who comes in is going to be met with the same structure, the same culture, and they're going to be impelled to act in the same way.[14]

Vaughan may take this argument a bit too far here. One might conclude from these comments (erroneously, in my view) that she believes that the problem lies solely in terms of structure and culture, and that she does not acknowledge the leadership deficiencies of any shuttle program managers. Regardless of how we interpret her statement, an important point remains: To adhere to the systemic view does not necessarily mean that one must absolve individuals of all personal responsibility for discouraging open dialogue and debate.[15]

Hard Versus Soft Barriers

When people feel uncomfortable speaking up, we typically can trace the causes of the problem to a combination of "hard" and "soft" barriers to candid communication (see Table 3-3). The hard barriers are structural in nature, whereas the soft barriers constitute cultural inhibitors to frank dialogue and debate.[16] Common hard barriers include the complexity of the organizational structure, the clarity of job/role definitions, the presence of information filtering mechanisms, and the composition of decision-making bodies. Typical soft barriers include perceptions of status, the language system used to talk about problems and mistakes, the mental models and cognitive frames that become deeply embedded in the culture over time and shape the way people think about particular issues, and the often "taken-for-granted" assumptions about how people ought to communicate with one another. As you can imagine, the structural factors tend to represent managerial levers that can be more easily modified, whereas the soft barriers often remain more difficult and time-consuming to dismantle or change.

TABLE 3-3:   Hard and Soft Barriers

Hard Barriers	Soft Barriers
Structural complexity	Status differences
Ambiguous job/role definitions	Language system
Information filtering mechanisms	Issue framing
Decision-making group composition	Taken-for-granted assumptions

Hard Barriers

Structural Complexity

Take a moment and try to sketch out an organization chart for your firm. How difficult is this exercise? How many dotted-line relationships exist? Do you have a matrix organization? Are some reporting relationships unclear? What type of ad-hoc or informal groups exist within the organization, and how do they fit into the hierarchy? For most of you in large organizations, this exercise will prove rather frustrating. You will become confused at times as you try to draw the chart, or you will find yourself dismayed by the dizzying array of boxes, arrows, solid lines, and dotted lines on the page.

Structural complexity serves as a powerful inhibitor to candid communication and constructive debate. Simplified structures facilitate the efficient flow of information, enhance coordination across multiple units, and increase the likelihood that important messages will not be lost in a maze of dotted-line relationships, ad-hoc committees, and stodgy bureaucracies. Welch uses several evocative metaphors to describe how the many layers in the old hierarchy at GE inhibited constructive dialogue:

> **Sweaters are like [organizational] layers. They are insulators. When you go outside and you wear four sweaters, it's difficult to know how cold it is...Another effective analogy was comparing an organization to a house. Floors represent layers and the walls functional barriers. To get the best out of an organization, these floors and walls must be blown away, creating an open space where ideas flow freely, independent of rank or function.**[17]

During his tenure at GE, Welch reduced the number of layers in the hierarchy, and he sought constantly to simplify the organization structure. In most cases, only 6 layers of management separated the

CEO from the shop floor, as opposed to as many as 12 prior to Welch's tenure, and the typical manager had twice as many direct reports as compared to the situation in the 1970s. In making these changes, Welch sought to foster "simple, straightforward communication" on any topic by anyone throughout the organization.[18]

In the case of Columbia, NASA had a complex matrix organization structure. The shuttle program not only involved thousands of NASA employees, but also people who worked for private contractors that had longstanding relationships with the space agency. People working on the shuttle program also were not co-located; instead, they worked at field centers in Texas, Florida, Alabama, and elsewhere. Many interactions took place via conference calls and e-mails rather than through face-to-face communication. Finally, ad-hoc committees, such as the Debris Assessment Team, often formed to work on specific problems. However, it was not always clear how they fit within the formal hierarchy. Sheila Widnall, former secretary of the Air Force and a member of the Columbia Accident Investigation Board, remarked on the confusion regarding the Debris Assessment Team: "I thought their charter was very vague. It wasn't really clear to whom they reported. It wasn't even clear who the chairman was. And I think they probably were unsure as to how to make their requests to get additional data."[19]

Role Ambiguity

Speaking candidly and expressing dissenting views becomes extremely difficult if an individual does not have a clear understanding of his or her role and responsibilities within the organization. Take, for example, the case of the 1994 friendly fire incident in northern Iraq, in which two United States F-15 fighter jet pilots mistakenly shot down two U.S. Black Hawk helicopters traveling in the "no fly zone" that had been established to protect the Kurdish people from the Saddam Hussein regime.[20] Captain Eric Wickson and Lieutenant Colonel Randy May flew the two F-15 jets involved in this incident.

Colonel May served as Wickson's squadron commander. Therefore, in normal day-to-day interactions, May occupied the role of the superior, with Wickson as his subordinate. However, during this particular mission, the roles were temporarily reversed. Captain Wickson served as the flight lead, and Colonel May was his wingman. That arrangement put Wickson in charge while the two pilots were in the air.

How did role ambiguity inhibit candid dialogue and contribute to the tragedy that occurred on that day? Wickson made the initial identification of the aircraft, mistakenly concluding that they were Russian-made Iraqi Hind helicopters. According to protocol, May, as the wingman, should have confirmed that identification. In reality, he stopped short of doing so. When Wickson asked his wingman for confirmation, May responded by saying, "Tally two," meaning that he had indeed seen two helicopters. However, he did not say "Confirm Hinds," indicating that he also believed that they were enemy aircraft. Confronted with an ambiguous response, Wickson took the absence of any clear objection to mean confirmation of his identification. The two men went on to shoot down the helicopters, with May never raising any questions or concerns. Why did May remain silent if he was unsure about the identification? Why did Wickson not request a clearer confirmation? The ambiguity of their reporting relationship appears to have suppressed candid dialogue at this critical moment. Scott Snook, who wrote a fascinating book about this incident, describes the dynamic:

> **In addition to subtly encouraging Tiger 01 [Wickson] to be more decisive than he otherwise might have been, the inversion [subordinate as flight lead] may also have encouraged him to be less risk averse, to take a great chance with his call, confident that if his call was indeed wrong, surely his more experienced flight commander would catch his mistake...Ironically, we find Tiger 02 [May] similarly seduced into a dangerous**

mindset...the expectations built into the situation by this unique dyadic relationship with his junior lead induced a surprisingly high degree of mindlessness and conformity...Apparently, there is such a strong norm in the Air Force that, without too much difficulty, we can imagine the wingman, even though he is senior in rank, easily slipping into the role of an obedient subordinate.[21]

If role ambiguity can take place in a hierarchical organization such as the military, with a clear chain of command, it can certainly happen in business organizations with less formal structures and reporting relationships. People may find themselves leading an ad-hoc team that includes people who have more senior positions in the formal organizational hierarchy. Alternatively, it may not even be clear who is in charge of certain informal committees or groups, or matrix organizational structures may cause some confusion regarding accountability and leadership responsibilities. Over the past year, I have taught the friendly fire case to many of the senior managers at a large global financial services firm. Each time I teach the case, I ask whether any of the managers have encountered the type of role ambiguity experienced by May and Wickson, and if so, whether it inhibited communication. Without hesitation, most of the managers confirm that they have found themselves in this predicament on more than one occasion.

Information-Filtering Mechanisms

In many organizations, structural mechanisms exist that constrain the flow of information. Perhaps most commonly, many business leaders choose to hire someone as a chief operating officer or "number two." That person often becomes the channel by which other managers convey information and ideas to the leader, as well as the mechanism by which the leader communicates many decisions to his subordinates.[22]

In some cases, leaders may not have a COO type, but they do assign someone, either formally or informally, as their "chief of staff." Much like the White House chief of staff, this person often keeps the leader's schedule, controls subordinates' access to the leader, facilitates meetings, and serves as an intermediary who gathers information from various executives and presents it to the leader in a concise manner.

In both cases, the structure may inhibit candid dialogue and the free expression of dissent. These intermediaries may constrict the flow of information to the leader, though they may not mean any harm. They strive simply to ensure the efficient use of the leader's time; however, their very presence often discourages subordinates from making the effort to express their concerns or dissenting views directly to the leader. They become a buffer between the leader and those doing the actual work, perhaps making the leader insensitive or unaware of the concerns of those on the front lines.

In his study of the decision-making approaches employed by many twentieth-century American presidents, political scientist Alexander George found that the relatively formal use of a chief of staff as an information-filtering mechanism could make it difficult for some presidents to hear for themselves a wide-ranging set of opinions on key issues. George worried that a president could become "unaware or disinterested in the important preliminaries of information processing" as he increasingly used the chief of staff as a "buffer between himself and cabinet heads."[23]

Recognizing these risks, Secretary of Defense Donald Rumsfeld, in his infamous rules for serving in the White House, offers the following advice for someone playing this intermediary role:

**A president needs multiple sources of information.
Avoid excessively restricting the flow of paper, people,
or ideas to the president, though you must watch his**

time. If you overcontrol, it will be your "regulator" that controls, not his. Only by opening the spigot fairly wide, risking that some of his time may be wasted, can his "regulator" take control.[24]

Unfortunately, it can difficult to manage the tension between the need for efficiency and the need for a broad array of information sources. The very presence of a person or persons operating as a filtering mechanism often sends the wrong signals to the organization and discourages the type of open communication that a leader desires, particularly the upward communication of bad news.

Composition of Decision-Making Bodies

The structure and composition of decision-making groups certainly shapes the level and nature of dissent and debate. As noted in the previous chapter, demographic homogeneity affects team dynamics, particularly the level of cognitive conflict. Bringing people together of similar gender and race, as well as functional and educational backgrounds, tends to reduce the cognitive diversity within a group, and therefore makes it less likely that divergent views will emerge. While demographic diversity brings challenges as well, it often helps to spark more divergent thinking and dissenting views.

However, similarity of group member tenure may have a slightly different, more complex effect on team dynamics. Consider, for instance, a team that has recently formed, consisting of people who have not interacted previously as a group. Presumably, in the absence of strong, effective leadership at the outset, they will exhibit low levels of interpersonal trust and psychological safety, much like the members of the Everest expeditions in 1996. Consequently, the new team may not engage in a high level of conflict and dissent, because people are not comfortable speaking up in front of relative strangers. As the team begins to feel more comfortable with one another, the level of candor and debate may rise considerably. Many observers have pointed out, for instance, that the Bay of Pigs fiasco occurred during the very early days of the Kennedy administration, when the president's foreign policy team had only recently been formed. By the time of the Cuban missile crisis, the same group of people had been working together for nearly two years, and the level of interpersonal trust had grown considerably. For that reason, it may have been easier for the group to engage in a candid and vigorous debate about how to handle the crisis.

Long-term collective tenure, however, may become problematic. A group may find itself becoming too like-minded and perhaps a bit complacent. Members may begin to adopt such strongly held shared mental models that they do not engage in much divergent thinking. Assumptions about how the world works may become taken for granted and difficult to surface and challenge. Many observers have pointed out that the senior management teams at once-great companies that stumbled badly—such as IBM, Xerox, and Digital Equipment Corporation—included many executives who had worked together for a long time.[25] Richard Foster, a senior partner at McKinsey, found that many of these firms that lost their once formidable competitive advantage actually experienced what he called "cultural lock-in," or an inability to adapt their mental models as the external environment changed dramatically.[26] In sum, the relationship between the shared tenure of a group and the level of dissent and debate may be curvilinear (see Figure 3-1). Groups may encounter the most challenging communication hurdles either early in their tenure, or at the point where many members have been working together for a long period of time.[27]

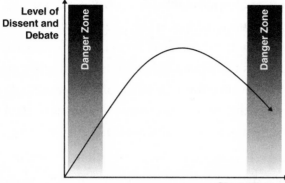

FIGURE 3-1:   The relationship between shared tenure and dissent in many firms

Soft Barriers

Status Differences

As we saw in the Everest case, status differences certainly can dampen people's willingness to share opinions and concerns freely. Status plays a major role in many types of organizations. For instance, in their studies of cardiac surgery teams, my colleagues Amy Edmondson, Richard Bohmer, and Gary Pisano found that the status difference between surgeons and nurses made it difficult for the latter group to voice its concerns or offer sound suggestions during complex medical procedures. Perhaps more importantly, they found that the more effective teams included surgeons who took great care to downplay the status differential and to welcome input from the nurses and other medical professionals on the cardiac surgery teams.[28] In short, status differences do not doom organizations to experience serious problems of speaking up; effective leadership can dismantle this barrier to candid communication.

One must remember, however, that status need not correlate with position in the formal organizational hierarchy. A startling example of this phenomenon took place during the friendly fire incident in northern Iraq. On that tragic day, air-force personnel working in an

AWACS plane had responsibility for controlling the skies in the no fly zone. They were supposed to warn the fighter pilots about any enemy threats or friendly aircraft in that region. They did not do so. They remained silent as the fighter pilots shot down the two Black Hawk helicopters, not even uttering a word of caution or asking a quick question, despite the fact that they had been tracking the friendly aircraft in that region just a few minutes earlier.

When asked why they remained silent, Captain Jim Wang remarked that AWACS personnel were trained to "shut up and be quiet" during this type of mission.[29] Of course, their training instructed them to do no such thing; it directed them to "warn and control" in these situations. Why then did Wang interpret his mandate in such a starkly different manner? Many observers have pointed to the status difference between AWACS personnel and fighter pilots. The latter commanded a great deal of respect and awe for their ability to take out the enemy while flying at remarkable speeds through perilous combat situations. Think Tom Cruise as "Maverick" in the classic movie *Top Gun*. In contrast, the AWACS officers spent their time watching radar screens and interpreting computer data. Think the administrative and support functions at a Wall Street investment bank, as opposed to the superstar traders, who rake in huge profits for the firm, wear the designer suits, and drive the super-luxury Italian sports cars.[30]

One of the senior officers on the AWACS plane described his reaction to the visual identification by the flight lead, Captain Wickson: "My initial reaction was—I said—Wow, this guy is good— he knows his aircraft."[31] Amazingly, despite the fact that radar screens suggested the possibility of friendly aircraft in the area, the AWACS officers deferred to the fighter pilots who were trying to perform a very challenging visual identification while traveling at 500 miles per hour through a narrow valley with the helicopters between 500 and 1,000 feet away.

Interestingly, the senior AWACS officer involved in the incident held the same rank as the wingman, Lt. Colonel May, and a higher rank than the flight lead who was making the visual identification. In fact, the two other most senior AWACS officers also held ranks that were superior to that of the flight lead, Captain Wickson. Status, then, overwhelmed formal rank in the organizational hierarchy in this case. More senior officers remained silent, in part because they allowed status differences to shape their behavior.

Similar dynamics occur within many business organizations, often with dysfunctional results. For instance, at Enron in the late 1990s, three separate organizations—Wholesale Trading, Gas Pipeline, and International—competed with one another for resources and talent. The wholesale trading unit became the high-status organization within Enron, despite the fact that the old pipeline business continued to generate the strongest cash-flow margins. Nevertheless, trading represented the future, and with Jeffrey Skilling as its leader, it became the darling of senior management and Wall Street analysts. The wholesale trading business became the place to be, and the people who built that business became legends within the firm. One cannot help but to ask whether the status differences that emerged within Enron inhibited candid dialogue about many of the business practices being employed in the late 1990s.[32]

Language System

Organizations develop their own language systems over time, complete with a whole host of unique terms and acronyms. Language systems, particularly as they relate to the characterization and discussion of problems and concerns, can become a powerful barrier to candid discussion and critical questioning of existing views and practices.

At NASA, for instance, a language system gradually emerged for labeling and categorizing problems associated with the space shuttle. Rather than sticking to the very formal system of declaring an unexpected issue an "anomaly," they began to distinguish between "in-family" and "out-of-family" events. *In-family* described those problems that they had seen before, and *out-of-family* characterized the incidents that did not fit within their experience base.

Unfortunately, as time passed, managers and engineers began to treat "out-of-family" events as if they were "in-family." Sheila Widnall found this slippery slide rather disturbing, and she offered a word of caution about the language system that had developed at NASA. She felt that the term *family* sounded "very comfy and cozy" and made it easier for NASA officials to begin believing that "everything will be okay" even though the issue was quite serious. [33]

The United States Forest Service (USFS) experienced a similar language problem during the tragic Storm King Mountain fire of 1994, in which 12 wildland firefighters perished in Colorado. In that incident, investigators concluded that the firefighters had not adhered to standard procedures. However, the language system employed by the USFS suggests room for a slippery slide similar to the one experienced at NASA. In 1957, the USFS developed a list of "Standard Orders" for wildland firefighters. Shortly thereafter, it constructed a list of "18 Situations That Shout Watch Out." Note the interesting difference in language. The latter term does not necessarily imply a hard-and-fast rule that must always be obeyed. Instead, it conveys the notion of a cautionary guideline rather than a strict procedure that must always be followed.[34]

Of course, we also wrote in an earlier chapter about the language system at Children's Hospital in Minnesota. In that case, the terminology often used at the hospital when discussing medical accidents conveyed a culture of "accusing, blaming, and criticizing" individuals. When Morath took charge at Children's, she created a new set of terms for discussing accidents, with the words chosen carefully so as to stress a systemic view of the causes of medical accidents as well as an emphasis on learning from mistakes. The language shift helped to raise people's willingness to discuss medical errors, and in fact, during Morath's first year at the hospital, official reports of medical accidents rose considerably. The evidence clearly indicated that people were not making more errors, but instead, they had become more comfortable talking about problems in an open, frank manner.[35]

Issue Framing

Chapter 2, "Deciding How to Decide," discussed how leaders frame issues when they take an initial position on a problem, and how these frames may constrain the range of alternative solutions discussed by the organization. However, issue framing occurs at a much broader level as well—not only at the decision level but at the level of a multi-year project or initiative. When broad corporate programs and initiatives begin, leaders often strive to provide ways for people to think about the events that will follow. In short, they provide a frame—a lens by which people can interpret upcoming actions. These broad frames can have much more wide-ranging and long-lasting effects than the frames that may be created by taking a position on a specific problem at a point in time.[36]

At NASA, when the shuttle program began, the agency justified the huge investment by arguing that the vehicle would eventually pay for itself by carrying commercial and defense payloads into space on a regular basis. When he announced the start-up of the program, President Nixon stated that the shuttle would "revolutionize transportation into near space, by routinizing it."[37] Note here the particular use of language and how it helped to establish a very specific and powerful frame for the program. The space vehicle was a "shuttle" that would embark on "routine" travel beyond the earth's atmosphere.

With that, NASA had framed the shuttle as an operational program rather than as a research and development initiative.[38] Diane Vaughan explains:

The program was framed within the concept of routine space flight. The shuttle was supposed to operate like a bus: transporting things, objects, people back and forth

into space on a regular basis. And in that sense, that whole definition that this program was going to be an operational system was the beginning of the downfall, because they were really operating an experimental technology, but there was pressure to make it look routine to attract customers for payloads.[39]

As a result of this framing of the shuttle as a routine operational program, people began to behave differently when problems surfaced. Schedule pressures rose considerably, as did the burden of proof required for an engineer who had a concern or a dissenting view about a safety issue that might require a delay in the schedule. Roger Tetrault, the former CEO of McDermott International and a member of the Columbia Accident Investigation Board, remarked that people began to "underemphasize the risks in order to get funding...but nobody in the aircraft industry who builds a new plane who would say after 100 flights or even 50 flights that that plane was operational. Yet, the shuttle was declared an operational aircraft, if you will, after substantially less than 100 flights."[40] In sum, the initial framing of the program established an atmosphere in which engineers found it increasingly difficult to speak up or express dissenting views when they had safety concerns.

The most effective leaders take great care, when they launch new initiatives, to anticipate the unintended consequences of a particular frame. For instance, in early 2002, when Craig Coy became CEO of Massport—the agency responsible for operating aviation facilities and shipping ports in the Boston area—he created three business units, and he directed three executives to manage these units as profit centers. In the past, these operating unit managers had some control over expense budgets, but they had no authority over the revenue-generation activities. Now, each business unit leader became accountable for the revenues, costs, and cash flows generated by his or her area.

This change represented a major shock to the culture at the agency. Of course, Coy recognized up front that this new way of looking at the business might encourage managers to compromise on security issues to bolster profits and cash flow. Such actions would be highly damaging for the institution in the wake of the September 11 attacks, particularly due to the role that Boston's Logan Airport played in that tragedy. Therefore, he took quick action to ensure that this would not take place, beginning with a very large commitment of capital to make Logan Airport the first commercial aviation facility in the nation to electronically screen all checked baggage. Coy made the commitment without resorting to the usual return on investment type analysis that he had begun advocating for nonsecurity projects. This early move, although substantively important, also served as an important signal and symbol to the operating unit managers that they should not allow the "profit center" mentality to cloud their judgments about security priorities.[41]

Taken-for-Granted Assumptions

The final, commonly experienced soft barrier involves assumptions about how people should interact with others in the organization, particularly those at different horizontal levels or in different vertical units. Every organization culture develops these presumptions over time; they become the consensus view of "the way that we work around here." Gradually, these assumptions become taken for granted by most members of the firm. As Edgar Schein notes, many of these cultural norms begin to take root when the founder establishes the organization, and they get propagated through the continuous retelling of stories and myths about the early days of the firm. As new members enter the organization, they gradually become indoctrinated into these informal, yet widespread and commonly understand "ways of working." Naturally, some of these cultural norms change over time, particularly as firms become larger and more bureaucratic.[42]

At NASA, the evidence from the investigation suggests that adherence to procedure and rules of protocol had become a strong cultural norm by the 1990s. People did not typically communicate with people that were more than one level up in the organization. Deference to seniority and experience also became accepted practice. As one former engineer explained to me, "Everything at NASA reverts back to the most senior person at the table...if they don't buy in, then your idea is just that—an idea."[43] Each of these norms tended to stifle open communication at the space agency.

At a large specialty retailer that I studied, senior managers took for granted that contentious debates should be resolved during off-line conversations rather than large meetings of the entire leadership team. This had become routine practice at the firm, and as new members joined the executive team, they soon learned how to act within this set of cultural norms and boundaries. Each person that I interviewed offered a response similar to this one: "The meeting is not a forum where we engage in debate. If there is disagreement, then we quickly tend to agree to take it offline."[44]

Unfortunately, although many of the new members learned to "play the game," they did not find this practice to be productive. They become increasingly frustrated at the lack of open debate during staff meetings. One senior executive mentioned that he had grown accustomed to the norms at his prior employer, where "real calls were made in the room...there was healthy give-and-take." In this case, people often did not have an opportunity to rebut the ideas and proposals offered by colleagues, because those arguments were put forth in private, offline meetings with the president as opposed to wider group forums.

Of course, not all taken-for-granted assumptions about interpersonal behavior and collective decision-making reflect dysfunctional behavior, but they can develop into a problem because the behaviors do become so deeply embedded in the organizational culture over time. Moreover, because they are often taken for granted, people do not regularly question why they are behaving in this manner. They simply find themselves conforming to time-honored practice at the institution.

Leadership Matters

Systemic factors—both structural and cultural—clearly inhibit candid dialogue and debate within organizations. This chapter has offered a glimpse of some of the most common "hard" and "soft" barriers that arise within organizations. Many more surely do exist. I have argued that these systemic factors often shape people's behavior within firms, both the actions of those who may appear to be suppressing dissent as well as the behavior of those who are failing to speak up. For instance, military culture and history shaped how the AWACS officers interacted with the F-15 pilots during the tragedy in northern Iraq in 1994. We cannot understand the AWACS officers' behavior by viewing it in isolation. We must examine the system in which these individuals worked and made decisions on a daily basis. Similarly, we cannot understand the past behavior of nurses at Children's Hospital in Minnesota, and particularly their reluctance to speak up about accidents or near-miss situations, without recognizing the prevailing cultural norms and status relationships prevalent not just within that hospital, but also within the broader medical profession at that time.

Having said that, one cannot discount the critical role that a particular leader's style and personality can play in encouraging or discouraging candid dialogue within an organization. Leadership does matter. Make no mistake about that. When Rob Hall tells his team that he will not tolerate dissent, he cannot send any more powerful message to his team. Systemic factors do not appear to be shaping his behavior; rather, it seems to reflect his own preferences for how to lead an expedition. Similarly, at the specialty retailer, the president chose to rely heavily on offline conversations largely due to his own nonconfrontational style and aversion to conflict in large group settings.

Even when systemic factors play a more substantial role, such as in the case of the Columbia disaster, one should not absolve the individuals of all personal accountability. Structural and cultural factors certainly shaped the way that shuttle program managers led the decision-making processes that took place during the mission. However, one can easily imagine how reasonably minor changes in the way that leaders gathered information, asked questions, and conducted meetings could have made a significant difference in the level of open dialogue and debate about the foam strikes.

Perhaps most importantly, leaders cannot wait for dissent to come to them; they must actively *go seek it out* in their organizations. If leaders offer personal invitations to others, requesting their opinions, ideas, and alternative viewpoints, they will find people becoming much more willing to speak freely and openly. The *mere existence of passive leadership* constitutes a substantial barrier to candid dialogue and debate within organizations. As the Columbia Accident Investigation Board concluded, "Managers' claims that they didn't hear engineers' concerns were due in part to their not asking or listening."[45] Journalist William Langewiesche, in an article about the Columbia accident published in *Altantic Monthly*, reported an exchange between one investigator and Linda Ham. The content of that conversation captures the very essence of what I mean by passive leadership as the ultimate barrier to candid dialogue and debate.

> *Investigator*: As a manager, how do you seek out dissenting opinions?
>
> *Ham*: Well, when I hear about them.
>
> *Investigator*: Linda, by their very nature, you may not hear about them.

Ham: Well, when somebody comes forward and tells me about them.

Investigator: But, Linda what techniques do you use to *get* them?

Apparently, Ham did not have an answer to this final question.[46]

4

STIMULATING THE CLASH OF IDEAS

"Truth springs from argument amongst friends."

—David Hume

If an organization has become saddled with a culture of polite talk, superficial congeniality, and low psychological safety, how can a leader spark a heightened level of candor? What specific tools can leaders employ to ignite a lively, yet constructive scuffle? To answer this question, let us begin by examining the story of how one chief executive created a decision process that was "confrontational by design."[1]

In early 1997, Steven Caufield, the CEO of a leading shipbuilding firm, began to consider the formation of a strategic alliance that would strengthen his firm's ability to win the intense competition to design and build a new generation of vessels for the U.S. Navy. He wanted to move quickly, having learned his lessons from a bidding war several years earlier. His firm had been "left at the altar" during that competition, when industry teams formed rather quickly, leaving him with few choices for strategic partners. As Caufield and his management team began to discuss potential alliances this time, he became concerned that everyone seemed to be focusing quite narrowly on two options. Moreover, people's biases, prior allegiances, and emotional feelings about various firms seemed to be taking the place of careful critical thinking. Caufield decided to create a forum for thoughtful deliberation and debate; in short, he set out to start a good fight.

As it turns out, a modest degree of forethought regarding the decision process provided the fuel that ignited a vigorous and thoughtful debate. After spirited deliberations, Caufield struck boldly and quickly to form a powerful three-firm alliance—a move that caught rivals by surprise. The partners went on to win several key contracts. Caufield reflected on how he set the stage for some productive wrangling:

> **We did a lot of hard work before the key offsite meetings. That was the key. I think my colleagues and I really had some strong brainstorming sessions in which we discussed who the participants should be, what should their roles be, who would facilitate, what process we would use, and what my role would be during the meetings. Going into those meetings, we had a clear understanding of the roles that we were going to be playing, and we knew the process that we were going to follow.**

Caufield's Story

Because a few early signals suggested that the U.S. Navy soon would launch a competition for the design and construction of a new warship, Caufield began to work with several colleagues to design a process for choosing alliance partners. The group decided to invite a select set of company managers as well as outside consultants and aerospace industry experts to a series of offsite meetings. They chose participants carefully to bring together a range of relevant expertise, ensure a diversity of opinions and perspectives, and create a healthy blend of personalities. The group elected two people to serve as facilitators during the offsite sessions, while determining that Caufield should absent himself from the early sessions for fear of inhibiting candid discussion. Caufield wanted the participants to evaluate a range of options and present him with a ranking of the top three potential alliances. He intended to critique the group's work, ask probing questions, and test their assumptions. Then, he hoped to work together with the participants to refine their recommendations and come to a consensus regarding which firm or firms to approach regarding a partnership. Caufield explained his role:

I like to challenge my team to brainstorm in a free and open session, and sometimes when the boss is there, it's not as free and open as it can be. Then, I can come in and review the process that they went through very quickly and examine their recommendations. I'm now challenging their thought process, and in turn, I'm inviting them to challenge mine.

Having defined people's roles, Caufield and his colleagues set out to develop a wide-ranging list of alternatives that should be discussed at the meeting, knowing that earlier discussions had been overly constrained. After consultation with people throughout the organization, the group came up with nine possible combinations, including a few that appeared rather unlikely to succeed, at least at first glance. The facilitators also developed a list of criteria for evaluating each alternative. Caufield clearly wanted multiple criteria to be evaluated simultaneously at the offsite sessions. He had become frustrated with earlier discussions in which each executive tended to focus on a single issue of importance to him, and therefore, would jump quickly to an option that performed well along that narrow dimension. In the end, the group agreed on a list of six key evaluation criteria. For instance, the delivery criterion focused on a potential partner's track record in delivering products on schedule and under budget, and the "impact to other work" criterion examined how each potential alliance might affect the firm's relationships with partners and subcontractors on other programs.

As for how to debate the options, Caufield and his colleagues made a decision to create two subgroups, although these teams operated a bit differently than those in the Kennedy case. The first subgroup evaluated all nine alternatives along three specific criteria, whereas the second examined the options based on the other three factors. By designing the process in this way, Caufield and his colleagues hoped that the two teams would bring different information and perspectives to a final debate. Moreover, they wanted each subgroup to listen to how the other side had evaluated each alternative before becoming wedded to a particular course of action. After the teams had narrowed the field to a few preferred options, Caufield joined the participants to listen, probe, and question all conclusions. He explained the rationale for selecting this approach:

We selected the individuals on the two groups to give a spread of expertise and viewpoints, so that we wouldn't get a pre-ordained answer [out of either subgroup]... The mission was to try to remove as much of the bias and emotion as we could...By forcing people to take each of these criteria and discuss them, we felt that we could at least force people to render an honest perspective, to engage in an honest debate. But in order to get everybody on the same baseline, we decided that we had to define each one of these factors or criteria.

Indeed, at the outset of the meetings, the facilitators distributed detailed definitions of each criterion to all the participants, and they established a simple 1 to 5 rating system for evaluating the options along each dimension. These actions constituted a concerted effort to ensure that people spoke a common language, rather than "talking past one another."

Perhaps most importantly, the facilitators laid out a process roadmap at the outset (see Figure 4-1), including a set of ground rules to guide behavior. They encouraged people to listen carefully, "pull no punches" during the debates, offer unvarnished opinions to Caufield, and stick to fact-based arguments with concrete supporting evidence. Caufield initially set the tone by asking everyone not to try to anticipate what he wanted to hear. He reminded participants that they were asked to participate because he valued their expertise and judgment. He wanted all the risks and weaknesses on the table before making a decision. Caufield's rallying cry: "I want everything on the table. No idea is a stupid idea. Every idea is a good idea."

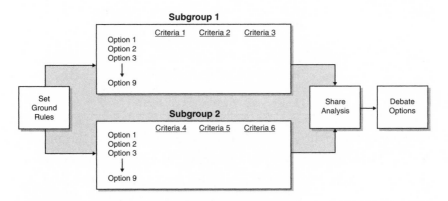

FIGURE 4-1: Mapping the decision process

Pulling All the Right Levers

This story demonstrates how a leader can use each of the four Cs— composition, context, communication, and control—to sew the seeds for a fruitful debate and an effective decision-making process (see Table 4-1). With regard to composition, Caufield took great care selecting the participants, even working with the facilitators to think about whom to assign to each subgroup. Caufield did not limit membership to his direct reports. Moreover, he did not define diversity in terms of demographic differences; instead, he thought carefully about the proper balance of insiders versus outsiders, the range of expertise upon which to draw, and the mix of personalities around the table. Caufield sought true diversity of cognitive style and perspective, not simply a heterogeneous set of resumés and biographies.[2]

TABLE 4-1:   Process Design: The Making of a Strategic Alliance Decision

Managerial Lever	Specific Action
Composition	Selecting participants Inviting outsiders Choosing subgroup assignments
Context	Establishing ground rules Setting the tone with initial statements Moving offsite
Communication	Outlining the options and decision criteria Devising a system for subgroups to exchange information and analyses
Control	Absenting himself from early sessions Developing a process roadmap Playing the role of devil's advocate personally Designating others as facilitators

Setting the right context became a critical part of the process design. Moving offsite helped eliminate distractions and create an open atmosphere. By not attending the early sessions, Caufield signaled his desire to foster a candid discussion. His initial statements—"no idea is a bad idea"—further emphasized his willingness to hear unconventional or unpopular views. The ground rules reminded participants what was expected of them during the process.

By creating subgroups, outlining the options, and defining the evaluation criteria, Caufield and his colleagues determined how participants should communicate with one another. Their process choices spurred a great deal of divergent thinking in the early stages.

In many cases, managers foster conflict so as to ensure the generation of multiple alternatives. Interestingly, in this situation, that dynamic functioned in reverse; Caufield put a wide range of options on the table and asked participants to consider each one carefully so as to spur a greater divergence of thought and perspectives than had occurred in earlier discussions. By asking the group to even consider some options that seemed highly unlikely, Caufield hoped to move people outside of their comfort zone and encourage the generation of some altogether new options—an event that did transpire during the deliberations. The criteria definitions facilitated smooth communication during the oft-heated debates by ensuring that everyone was "speaking the same language" and "comparing apples to apples" when arguing about the alternatives.

Finally, Caufield chose to take control of how the debate should take place, but he did not constrain the content of the deliberations a great deal. He welcomed a great deal of input regarding the list of options and evaluation criteria, and at the outset, he chose not to express his own views as to how to proceed. Moreover, Caufield defined his own role very clearly. He set the tone early, and then absented himself for awhile before returning to play the devil's advocate. By designating two facilitators, he ensured that others would be drawing out comments from those who might be more reluctant to offer dissenting views, while not putting himself in a highly interventionist role. Finally, Caufield made it clear that he would seek consensus within the group, but that ultimately, he would make the call if people could not reach agreement.

Here then, we have a vivid example of how a leader can develop a clear roadmap for a decision process in a manner that encourages vigorous debate rather than making people feel as though he aspires to reach a predetermined outcome. One should note that Caufield did not perform this critical design work alone. He gathered input from many people and gave the facilitators the freedom to guide the debate. Perhaps most importantly, all participants understood the goals and stages of the process, as well as how they were expected to behave.

The Leader's Toolkit

Setting the stage for a vigorous debate requires leaders to take a holistic view—pulling multiple levers simultaneously to shape an effective process. Having said that, we have seen that specific tools and techniques—such as Dialectical Inquiry or Devil's Advocacy—can play a particularly important role in helping to foster conflict and debate. Often, leaders begin by deciding on a particular technique that they wish to employ, and then they build the rest of the process around that creative mechanism for sparking divergent thinking.

What, then, are some of the techniques that leaders may employ? In general, leaders may draw upon four types of tools to encourage divergent thinking, which often naturally leads to more conflict and dissent (see Figure 4-2). First, they can use role-play methods to ask managers to put themselves in others' shoes. Second, leaders may employ mental simulation techniques, in which they encourage people to imagine the future and think through how events may unfold in different ways over time. One can ask people to examine an issue using a diverse set of conceptual models and frameworks. Finally, leaders may create a point-counterpoint dynamic of some kind, much like Kennedy and Caufield chose to do. As leaders employ these techniques, they must remember that some methods will work better than others in particular settings and with specific individuals. They must evaluate the situation and the group with whom they are working, and then select the techniques that they believe will work best in those circumstances.[3]

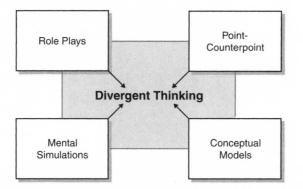

FIGURE 4-2:   Stimulating divergent thinking: the leader's toolkit

Role-Play Methods

In professional football, teams put themselves in their rivals' shoes all the time. During a typical week of practice, the players in the starting lineup practice against a "scout team" consisting of second stringers who simulate the plays and schemes typically utilized by the upcoming opponent. As practice takes place, the coaches often gain a better understanding of what works and does not work against that rival. They invent improved strategies, scrap certain plays, and think of new ways to surprise the opponent during the game. Coaches and players often marvel at the benefits of having someone who can imitate a rival to near perfection. For instance, after the New England Patriots defeated the Indianapolis Colts in a critical 2004 playoff game, the winning coach, Bill Belichick, praised a team member who never stepped on the field that day; he singled out backup quarterback Damon Huard, who simulated the behavior of Colts' star quarterback Peyton Manning during the entire week of practice. With Huard's help, the coaches devised some "new wrinkles" on defense that confused Manning during the game.[4]

Business executives can role play their competitors as well. My research suggests that these exercises often lead to new ways of thinking about the firm's competitive strategy and a much richer debate.[5] For instance, when one of the country's leading armored combat

vehicle manufacturers began thinking about the formation of an
international joint venture, a group of executives tried to simulate the
actions of a set of firms who might form a competing alliance. The
exercise sparked new debate, shed light on their own venture's weaknesses, and generated new insights about rival behavior. One manager even made the analogy to the scout team in professional football:

**We actually had someone role play the other alliance
that was forming, and they did a competitive assessment
of us, just like a football team. You know, you scrimmage
using the other guy's plays. The results portrayed the
other alliance's view of us, and it was very revealing.**

Role-play exercises need not focus strictly on the notion of stepping into a rival's shoes; often, it helps to imagine someone moving
into your office and taking your job. In the early 1980s, Intel experienced a substantial decrease of market share in the memory-chip
business; soon, the financial losses began to mount. However, senior
executives remained highly committed to the product line; they had
cut their teeth in that business as Intel became a leader in the industry. Memory chips represented a core aspect of the firm's identity, and
to some extent, the identity of the managers who built that business.
As the losses escalated, company President Andrew Grove sat in his
office with Chairman and CEO Gordon Moore. Grove looked out at
a Ferris wheel in a nearby amusement park, and he asked Moore: "If
we got kicked out and the board brought in a new CEO, what do you
think he would do?"[6] Soon, the two men realized that they were
throwing good money after bad in the memory-chip business. They
had become overly committed to a product line in which they had
invested a great deal of money as well as much of their own time and
personal reputation. Grove and Moore decided to exit the memory-
chip business. Grove explained how the simple role-play exercise

encouraged them to think differently, question many of their assumptions, and explore new strategic alternatives:

New managers come unencumbered by such emotional involvement...They see things much more objectively than their predecessors did. If existing management want to keep their jobs when the basics of the business are undergoing profound change, they must adopt an outsider's intellectual objectivity...That's what Gordon and I had to do when we figuratively went out the door, stomped out our cigarettes, and returned to do the job.[7]

Mental Simulation

Psychologist Gary Klein has found that many people simulate future scenarios rapidly in their mind as they make critical decisions. For instance, he found that firefighters often do not have the time to compare and contrast multiple alternatives while in the midst of battling a raging blaze. However, they often identify a plausible course of action, and then mentally simulate how events will unfold if they pursue that strategy for fighting the fire. If the simulation yields a favorable result, they take action; if not, they search for a new alternative.[8]

It turns out that asking people to imagine different future states, and to discuss those mental pictures with one another, can be a powerful tool for sparking debate within organizations. Many managers have heard about scenario planning, a formal strategic planning technique practiced and refined for years by firms such as Royal/Dutch Shell. It involves a structured method for thinking about how industry conditions might unfold in very different ways in the future, and then considering how a variety of strategic alternatives might play out under those contrasting conditions. At Royal/Dutch Shell, it meant conceiving divergent paths for global energy markets, and then thinking about how those changes would affect oil prices, consumption patterns, and rival behavior.[9] Stanford Professor Kathleen Eisenhardt has argued that scenario thinking fosters constructive conflict within top management teams. She explains that "scenario thinking forces executives to start with the future and think backward to the present. This reversal of normal linear thinking provides an alternative lens and yields an unusual and unexpected perspective on strategic issues."[10] University of Virginia Professors Leslie Grayson and James Glawson acknowledge that scenario building may not tell managers which strategy to pursue, but it does spark new debate and causes people to surface and reexamine many basic assumptions.[11]

Klein has taken a different, but equally effective, approach to using mental simulation as a mechanism for encouraging divergent thinking within organizations. He advocates the use of a simple "pre-mortem" exercise to help people test one another's beliefs regarding the risks and obstacles that may occur if the firm chooses a particular course of action. Here's how it works. You begin by picturing what complete failure would look like. Then, you imagine the different paths that may lead to that total failure and consider the probability that each of these scenarios might actually take place. This discussion should generate a prioritized list of the most substantial concerns and risks associated with the decision. Finally, the group must determine whether these pitfalls can be avoided, or whether the organization should choose an entirely different course of action.[12] Like Klein, I have found that this simple, structured exercise often makes people feel more comfortable critiquing their colleagues' ideas and plans, particularly if a firm adopts this approach on a routine basis. For more on how to perform a pre-mortem, see Table 4-2.

TABLE 4-2: Conducting a Pre-Mortem

Step 1	Identify the participants in the exercise and establish norms and ground rules for the discussion.
Step 2	Make certain that all participants have a strong shared understanding of the decision under consideration.
Step 3	Imagine a complete failure that transpires as a result of this decision.

Step 4	Brainstorm the different paths or scenarios that may lead to that failure.
Step 5	Identify the probability and the severity of each of those scenarios (no need for detailed quantitative analysis).
Step 6	Determine the scenarios that warrant the most attention (i.e., those that are both likely and severe).
Step 7	Should we make a different decision? Or can we enhance our approach to implementation as a means of avoiding failure?
Step 8	If you choose to proceed with this decision, work on an implementation plan to prevent the bad scenario(s) from unfolding, or devise a plan to deal with the bad scenario if and when it transpires so as to minimize the damage.
Step 9	Summarize your learnings from the exercise and communicate them to everyone involved in the decision-making process.
Step 10	When the decision is finally implemented, conduct a post-mortem, and go back during that process to revisit the conclusions from the pre-mortem. Identify ways that the pre-mortem process can be improved.

Conceptual Models

Occasionally, leaders may find it useful to introduce a simple set of models or frameworks that may be applied to a particular business problem, and then designate people to use these different lenses during the decision-making process. The objective is to induce each person to launch his inquiry from a different vantage point. When people come together to share their ideas and analysis, they often discover that they have arrived at different conclusions regarding how the firm should proceed.

Kevin Dougherty, the head of Sun Life's Canadian Group Insurance subsidiary, adopted a version of this technique several years ago. At the time, Sun Life executives worried a great deal about how the Internet might revolutionize the way that consumers procured insurance and other financial-management products. Unfortunately, he and his management team did not have a great deal of expertise in the area of e-commerce. Most managers seemed to think of the Web as a useful tool for making business processes more

efficient, but they had not considered how it might lead to fundamentally different business models in the financial-services industry.

Dougherty asked a consultant to provide his management team
with a broad overview of e-commerce trends. Then, the consultant
described four e-commerce business models. For example, he
explained the auction models employed successfully by firms such as
eBay and Priceline.com. Then, Dougherty divided everyone into four
teams, and he assigned each group to consider how one particular
model might apply to the insurance business. He also asked them to
investigate how that model might present a strategic opportunity or
threat for Sun Life. Based upon what they learned from this evaluation, each team had to develop a proposal for a new venture, product,
or service. Bruce Kassner, assistant vice president of underwriting,
explained his experience with the process: "Forcing me to stay within
a specific model made me think a bit differently than I would have
otherwise. It made me see some value in a model that I wouldn't have
seen value in, had I been free to generate any type of business idea."[13]

Some managers see this technique as overly directive, because it
ties them to a particular conceptual lens. Thus, leaders may try a vari-
ation of this technique, in which they ask people to apply a variety of
conceptual lenses to an issue, without constraining each individual to
one specific problem-solving approach.[14] While some may still feel
that this approach channels people's thinking too much, it may be
necessary in cases where managers need some help getting started
with their analysis, or where everyone seems to be thinking in lock
step with one another at the outset. Moreover, leaders need to
remember that this technique provides a useful way to jumpstart
debate, but they need not remain wedded to the approach throughout the process.

Point-Counterpoint

In the Kennedy and Caufield examples, we have seen the power of
employing variants of the Dialectical Inquiry and Devil's Advocacy

methods described in detail in Chapter 2. (For details on how to employ these two techniques, see Table 4-3.) Indeed, many successful leaders have adopted similar techniques, because they provide a very direct way to induce conflict. For instance, at Polycom, CEO Robert Hagerty occasionally has employed "red teams" and "blue teams" to scrutinize a potential acquisition. As Hagerty says, "I assign a red team to come up with the reasons why we shouldn't do the deal. The blue team presents the argument for the acquisition. It is an effective way to institutionalize naysayers."[15]

TABLE 4-3: Guidelines for Leading Dialectical Inquiry and Devil's Advocacy Processes[16]

Dialectical Inquiry	Devil's Advocacy
The team divides into two subgroups.	The team divides into two subgroups.
Subgroup 1 develops a proposal, fleshing out the recommendation, key assumptions, and supporting data.	Subgroup 1 develops a proposal, fleshing out the recommendation, key assumptions, and supporting data.
Subgroup 1 presents the proposal to Subgroup 2 in written and oral forms.	Subgroup 1 presents the proposal to Subgroup 2 in written and oral forms.
Subgroup 2 generates one or more alternative courses of action.	Subgroup 2 develops a detailed critique of these assumptions and recommendations. It presents this critique in written and oral forms. Subgroup 1 revises its proposal based on the feedback.
The two subgroups come together to debate the proposals and seek agreement on a common set of assumptions.	The subgroups continue in this revision-critique-revision cycle until they converge on a common set of assumptions.
Based on those assumptions, the subgroups continue to debate various options and strive to agree on a common set of recommendations.	Based on those assumptions, the subgroups work together to develop a common set of recommendations.

In some organizations, leaders have chosen to institutionalize the point-counterpoint approach. They have built it in to the organizational structure so that a natural tension exists between people who occupy different positions within the firm. Consider, for example, how Electronic Arts, the market-share leader in the video-game industry, manages the product development process. Most of its rivals appoint one person with total responsibility for overseeing the design of a new game. Electronic Arts has created two separate leadership roles. Each person maintains distinct areas of accountability. The producer focuses on product quality, building a creative game that can be enjoyable for consumers to play. The development director tries to come in under budget and on schedule. Paul Lee, chief operating officer of Worldwide Studios at the firm, describes the purpose of this unique organizational structure:

> **We have created a system of checks and balances or creative conflict. The producer focuses on ensuring that the game design is the best...The development director focuses on project management, budget, schedule, on-time delivery, etc. And they clash. We force that conflict and that discussion so that the team will push the envelope.[17]**

Electronic Arts did not invent the concept of designing conflict into the organization, nor is the technique confined to business enterprises. In fact, President Franklin Roosevelt took the practice to quite an extreme in the 1930s. He often provided subordinates with overlapping assignments and jurisdictions so as to induce competition and conflict. Moreover, he intentionally provided cabinet heads and advisers with ambiguous definitions of their roles in his administration. Political scientist Alexander George has written that this organizational model sparked some very creative debates within the Roosevelt administration, but it also fostered an environment that appeared chaotic at times.[18] For that reason, leaders should mimic Roosevelt's extreme approach at their own peril. Only someone with Roosevelt's masterful political skills could manage such a complex set of relationships. Nevertheless, the core concept of building tension into the design of job responsibilities merits close attention.

"Watch Out" Situations

As leaders strive to create a process characterized by vigorous debate, they undoubtedly encounter a number of pitfalls—situations that seem to scream "watch out!" In many instances, leaders take some care to "decide how to decide" before trying to tackle the problem. They even employ many of the techniques that we have discussed for stimulating divergent thinking. However, despite good intentions in many cases, leaders manage to send the wrong signals to their advisers, and they fail to realize the full potential of the techniques they have chosen to employ. Worse yet, they may handle the situation so poorly that they squelch dissent going forward. Let's take a look at a few of these common mistakes that leaders make (see Table 4-4).

TABLE 4-4: Common Pitfalls and Mistakes

Intention	Result	Description
Employ devil's advocates	Domesticating dissenters	Token, ritualized use of devil's advocates; self-congratulatory attitude
Facilitate the dialogue	Creating a hub-and-spoke communication system	Creating a series of leader-member exchanges rather than open dialogue and wide-ranging discussion among everyone
Maximize time efficiency	Crowding out response time	Packing the agenda; moving quickly from topic to topic without providing time for dissenting views to emerge
Provide time for dialectical inquiry	Encouraging entrenchment and polarization	Letting people become entrenched in subgroups so that they cannot approach the debate with an open mind
Make data-driven decisions	Striving for false precision	Focusing on the minutiae of the quantitative analysis rather than testing assumptions/logic

Domesticating the Dissenters

In James Thomson's insightful analysis of President Lyndon Johnson's escalation of the war in Vietnam, he argues that several key advisers played the role of devil's advocates, but they became "domesticated" over time. For instance, Johnson used to refer to Thomson, who served in the administration, as his "favorite dove." Over time, Johnson's warm and humorous treatment of Thomson's strongly held views neutralized his effectiveness as an ardent critic of the administration's policy. Johnson gave several dissenters—George Ball, Bill Moyers, and Thomson—the opportunity to speak their minds on a regular basis, but he seemed to treat them as "token" dissenters. Turning to the devil's advocate became an empty ritual during meetings. Johnson seemed to enjoy having them occupy the designated role of a devil's advocate, as if it made him and other proponents feel good to have created an institutionalized mechanism for the expression of dissent.[19] As Irving Janis has written, it was as if Johnson and his supporters could "pat themselves on the back for being so democratic about tolerating open dissent."[20] The use of devil's advocates enhanced the legitimacy of their decision process, even though it was not contributing to better quality decisions.

Learning from this tragic situation, leaders need to be mindful of the ritual use of devil's advocates, particularly if the same person occupies that role over time. It can become a routine exercise to satisfy a procedural requirement, rather than a legitimate attempt to hear dissenting views. Janis has suggested that leaders may avoid this pitfall by rotating the role of devil's advocate within an executive team.[21] Alternatively, the leader may occupy the role at times as Caufield did in the strategic alliance decision.

Creating a Hub-and-Spoke System

When leaders do spark debate within their management team, they need to be mindful of how they position themselves within the flow of dialogue. Leaders can choose a "hub-and-spoke" model of communication, in which people aim their arguments at the leader during a debate, trying primarily to persuade him of the merits of their positions. Managers do not actually engage in give-and-take; instead, the dialogue becomes a series of leader-member conversations. The debate becomes a fragmented series of one-on-one dialogues. Subordinates begin to frame their comments in anticipation of what the leader wants to hear, or they become silent if they worry excessively about having to engage in a direct exchange with their boss.

Alternatively, a leader can employ a "point-to-point" system of communication, in which he encourages advisers to interact repeatedly with one another rather than routing their arguments through him. The latter system often creates a much more creative exchange of ideas, and it enables the leader to step back, hear the give-and-take among advisers, and compare and contrast the arguments with some objectivity. Subordinates tend to listen more carefully to one another, and they improve their own proposals based upon the critiques posed by others. The debate moves more quickly, and people tend to build off each other's ideas quite effectively. During the Cuban missile crisis, Kennedy fostered a great deal of point-to-point communication among his staff members. Contrast that with Lyndon Johnson's approach to decision-making about Vietnam, in which advisers often focused nearly all their attention on the president, seeking to persuade him to adopt their point of view.

Crowding Out Response Time

Leaders often find themselves trying to run meetings as efficiently as possible, given their hectic schedules and the multitude of topics that need to be covered at each gathering. Unfortunately, agenda overload, coupled with the quest for efficiency, often works against a leader's best efforts to stimulate debate.[22] Efficiency goals must be balanced with the objectives of making a high-quality decision and building commitment to the chosen course of action.

Why does efficiency crowd out debate? For some dissenters, it takes some time to gather the courage to express their views or to determine precisely how they would like to articulate their point. For others, they may want to listen to others and gain a better understanding of the issues before offering their views. The rapid pace of the discussion may become discouraging to those who are not comfortable "shooting from the hip" as soon as a new topic opens.

The Columbia space shuttle incident provides a vivid example of this phenomenon. The Mission Management Team meetings moved quickly from one topic to another during Columbia's final mission. Each meeting had a packed agenda. The leader asked for input, but often coupled that with a statement of her beliefs on the subject, while not waiting more than a few moments to allow people raise questions or concerns.[23] Brigadier General Duane Deal, a member of the Columbia Accident Investigation Board, has noted that the pace and tone of the meetings became intimidating to employees who had some concerns, but were struggling to process confusing and ambiguous information.[24]

Encouraging Entrenchment and Polarization

Some leaders overcompensate when it comes to the efficiency of the decision process. When employing competing teams in a Dialectical Inquiry type process, they often make the mistake of allowing managers to spend too long in their subgroups prior to bringing everyone together to debate all the options. The leaders mean well; they simply want to provide participants ample opportunity to investigate a particular alternative and to consider its pros and cons thoroughly. Unfortunately, over time, people become heavily invested, cognitively and emotionally, in the option that they have been examining.[25] Naturally, they find themselves less willing to entertain other options, or to hear criticism of their proposals. Furthermore, as people work closely together over time, they may begin to associate more closely with their subgroups as opposed to the full team. They may start to perceive subgroup members in a very positive light, while taking a more critical view of those colleagues who are members of the other subgroup. Those distinctions can impede communication and make it difficult for people to reach compromises. Debates can become highly contentious.[26]

Striving for False Precision

Many organizations perform a great deal of formal analysis during critical decision-making processes. If possible, managers try to quantify as many of the costs and benefits associated with alternative courses of action. Quantitative data can certainly facilitate the comparison of various options, and they can help ensure that debates remain fact based and logical, rather than degenerating into purely emotional confrontations. Moreover, quantitative analysis tends to lend an air of legitimacy to the decision-making process; it helps convince others inside and outside the organization that managers went through a thoughtful analysis prior to choosing a course of action.[27]

Unfortunately, the strong desire to quantify as many aspects of the decision as possible occasionally distracts people from the real issues. Managers begin to argue about minor differences of opinion regarding the numbers, rather than addressing fundamental problems associated with one or more alternatives. People's time becomes consumed with attempting to generate as precise a number as possible. However, the high degree of uncertainty about future events makes such efforts at precision rather futile and perhaps even counterproductive.

Think for a moment about a typical acquisition decision. Managers often spend an inordinate amount of time trying to perfect the financial model that forecasts the cash flow in the years ahead. However, as Polycom Chief Financial Officer Mike Kourey has said, "At the end of the day, many discounted cash-flow models turn out to be bogus. With the right assumptions, any deal can appear promising. That is why we test the assumptions carefully."[28] Unfortunately, many firms tinker endlessly with the financial model, without probing the underlying strategic and operational premises that lie behind the cash-flow forecasts. As attention focuses on minor variations of a financial forecast, those who may have questions regarding the strategic logic behind the acquisition may not feel comfortable raising those questions. They may conclude that the decision has been made to go forward, and managers are now simply trying to determine the right price to pay for the target firm.[29]

Practice Makes Perfect

Encouraging conflict can indeed be a tricky endeavor; as we have seen, leaders often inadvertently discourage dissent and diminish the effectiveness of a debate. Fortunately, practice does make perfect—or at least substantial improvement—when it comes to managing conflict. Researchers David Schweiger, William Sandberg, and Paula Rechner have examined how groups perform as they employ the Devil's Advocacy and Dialectical Inquiry techniques repeatedly over time. As you may expect, groups benefited from experience in this experimental study. As teams utilized the techniques more often, they engaged in higher levels of critical evaluation and made better-quality decisions (as measured by a panel of expert judges). The time required to reach a decision diminished with experience. Furthermore, people expressed a higher level of satisfaction with the processes, fellow team members, and final decisions as they gained more experience with these techniques.[30]

Several very successful business leaders, such as Jack Welch and Chuck Knight, have demonstrated how important it is to make vigorous debate the norm, rather than the exception, within an organization. As people engage in debate on a regular basis, in a wide range of settings within the firm, they become more comfortable with conflict. At General Electric, everyone quickly came to understand the type of dialogue that Welch intended to foster, and they learned how to engage in a heated, yet productive, debate with him. Colleagues recognized that "Jack will chase you around the room, throwing objections and arguments at you," and that, "If you win [an argument], you never know if you've convinced him or if he agreed with you all along and he was just making you strut your stuff."[31] Welch reinforced these impressions by declaring "constructive conflict" one of GE's core values, something about which he talked early, loudly, and often.[32]

Chuck Knight, Emerson Electric's long-time CEO, designed confrontation into the company's infamous strategic planning process. The planning conferences represented the focal point of this process. At a series of one or two-day meetings, Knight and several other corporate officers met with the managers of each division at the firm. During those conferences, Knight pushed people very hard to defend their strategies. Over time, the combative mood of these conferences became part of company folklore. Knight even coined a phrase to describe the process that he often used to stimulate divergent thinking. The "logic of illogic" referred to how Knight asked unconventional, even illogical, questions to test the assumptions and the logic behind every strategic plan. Over Knight's nearly 30-year tenure as chief executive, the confrontational mood of the planning conferences became part of the culture. That is, it became one of the "taken-for-granted" assumptions about "how we do things around here"—not simply in planning conferences, but in all forums for dialogue and deliberation. Knight maintains that managers became more comfortable with the confrontational nature of the planning process as they gained experience with it. They learned how to prepare for the meetings, how to respond to critiques of their plans, and how to handle contentious situations. They learned how to use conflict to make better decisions.[33]

Knight and Welch made conflict a way of life in their organizations. Unfortunately, some leaders try to draw upon techniques for stimulating divergent thinking on a few special occasions, perhaps when the stakes are unusually high. In most other instances, they run fairly low-key, polite meetings in which their employees feel quite comfortable. When they try to ignite a vigorous debate, without much personal or organizational experience in this area, they either fail to generate conflict as they intended to do, or the dispute becomes highly dysfunctional.

Great organizations and great leaders practice the use of conflict on a regular basis. They exhibit patience and persistence in applying many of the techniques described here. They work diligently to make certain that conflict becomes embedded in the processes and values of the firm. Their experiences demonstrate what Aristotle taught us so many years ago when he said, "We are what we repeatedly do. Excellence, then, is not an act, but a habit."

5

KEEPING CONFLICT
CONSTRUCTIVE

**"Anybody can become angry, that is easy; but to
be angry with the right person, and to the right
degree, and at the right time, and for the right
purpose, and in the right way, that is not within
everybody's power. That is not easy."**
—Aristotle

In the 1950s, comedian Sid Caesar starred in one of the most popular
programs on television—*Your Show of Shows*. The program's success
may be credited to the remarkable team of comedy writers that collaborated to write each week's script. Many of the team members
became comedic legends in their own right—Mel Brooks, Larry
Gelbart, Neil Simon, Woody Allen, and Carl Reiner, to name just a
few. They spent day and night together in the "Writers' Room"—a
place where the ideas flowed freely, people competed fiercely
with one another, and creative genius emerged from contentious
disagreement.[1]

Producer Max Liebman often stressed that "from a polite confer-ence comes a polite movie."[2] The young writers certainly took his advice to heart. In his autobiography, Sid Caesar recalled the mighty struggles that took place in the Writers' Room: "Chunks of plaster were knocked out of walls; the draperies were ripped to shreds; Mel Brooks frequently was hanged in effigy by the others."[3] Nevertheless, the writers produced legendary skits week after week, worked effec-tively together for years, and remained friends and collaborators for decades. Somehow, the heated arguments represented what writer Mel Tolkin described as "good creative anger."[4]

Imagine, however, if a stranger walked into the Writers' Room one day, not knowing anything about the team's history, and he wit-nessed the madness that Caesar and others have described. Naturally, one might have a hard time believing that this group could produce such a spectacular show or that the members would enjoy working together for years. Tomorrow, if you tried to emulate this pattern of behavior with your management team, you might very well have a disaster on your hands. However, in the Writer's Room, the heated nature of the conflict did not become a liability for the group. With astute leadership over a long period of time, Caesar had created an atmosphere, as well as a creative decision-making process, in which the writers could argue in a passionate, yet productive fashion. He had created a context in which hanging a team member in effigy did not represent aberrant or dysfunctional behavior, but rather a healthy and "normal" way of coping with cognitive conflict. This chapter examines how leaders can act before, during, and after a decision-making process to ensure that conflict within their management teams remains vigorous yet constructive. This chapter does not advo-cate direct emulation of the antics of Caesar and friends, but we will try to develop a set of principles that applies in settings ranging from the Writers' Room to the boardroom.

Diagnosing the Debate

In many organizations, debates become dysfunctional before the leader recognizes the warning signs. Diagnosing these situations as they unfold represents a critical leadership capability. How does a leader discern whether a passionate debate among his advisers and subordinates stands on the verge of becoming dysfunctional? Imagine two scenarios. In one instance, individuals continue to raise interesting questions that provoke novel lines of collective discovery. People try to understand others' positions, and they remain open to new ideas. The search for creative new options persists. In another scenario, people repeat the same worn-out arguments, opposing camps have dug in their heels, and the loudest voices dominate the discussion. People stop trying to comprehend one another; they simply strive to persuade. Conflict proves constructive as long as it propels a process of collective problem-solving and exploration. It serves little purpose if people simply want to *prove* their point, rather than *discover* solutions collectively.[5]

As debates drag on, leaders must be aware that their well-intentioned efforts to maintain a constructive dialogue between people with entrenched positions may do more harm than good. For instance, many leaders believe that they can reach a compromise between opposing camps if they simply keep the debate focused on the facts, while ensuring that everyone has equal access to relevant information. Indeed, my research, as well as a number of studies by Kathleen Eisenhardt and her colleagues, shows that the tactic of focusing on facts tends to be helpful during contentious debates.[6] However, unintended consequences may arise when two groups with opposing views attempt to interpret a common set of information.

One fascinating experimental study highlights the hidden dangers of "fact-based problem solving." Psychologists Charles Lord, Lee Ross, and Mark Lepper once asked a group of death-penalty supporters to examine two empirical studies regarding the deterrent efficacy of capital punishment. One study confirmed their existing beliefs, whereas the other offered disconfirming data. The researchers also presented the two studies to a group of death-penalty opponents. After each side analyzed identical sets of data, their views on capital punishment did not converge. In fact, increased polarization of opinion occurred! What happened? People assimilated the data in a biased manner, placing more weight on the evidence that supported their initial position. As the researchers commented, it seems that people "are apt to accept confirming evidence at face value while subjecting disconfirming evidence to critical evaluation."[7]

The lesson for leaders is clear: Focusing on the facts does not always yield the intended results. Polarization can occur even when a group appears to be pursuing an "objective and rational" decision-making process. Not surprisingly, a number of warning signs often appear as debates begin to become dysfunctional. By asking themselves a set of simple questions, such as those found in Table 5-1, leaders can monitor the "health" of a debate and intervene before too much damage is done.

TABLE 5-1:   Warning Signs

1	Have people stopped asking questions intended to gain a better understanding of others' views?
2	Has the group stopped searching for new information?
3	Have individuals stopped revising their proposals based on the feedback and critiques offered by others?
4	Have people stopped asking for help with the interpretation of ambiguous data?
5	Have people begun to repeat the same arguments, only more stridently and loudly over time?
6	Have people stopped admitting concerns about their own proposals recently?
7	Have less outspoken individuals begun to withdraw from the discussions?

Affective Conflict

The most glaring sign of trouble during a debate may be the emergence of affective, or interpersonal, conflict. It often goes hand in hand with the emergence of dueling camps and the polarization of views. People may cross the line from issue evaluation to personal criticism in these situations. Perception often matters more than intention in these circumstances. Individuals may not intend to attack others personally when discussing a contentious issue. However, a blunt and forceful critique of others' ideas can stir feelings of distress and anxiety, stimulate defensive behavior, and spark emotional counterattacks.

As noted in Chapter 1, "The Leadership Challenge," most managers have a difficult time engaging in task-oriented debate without sparking anger, personality clashes, and personal friction. That appears to be true whether we observe managers making decisions in real organizations, performing experimental studies, or asking students to evaluate their experiences after debating one another in a simple classroom exercise.[8] The latter results may be the most startling. Affective conflict does not emerge simply because the stakes are high, or because managers have a great deal of political capital tied up in a particular issue. It emerges even when individuals seemingly have little to gain or lose, at least of a material nature, by virtue of the outcome of a debate.[9]

How does a leader know whether he has managed conflict effectively during a decision process? A simple diagnostic exercise can be helpful. Think for a moment about a recent high-stakes decision that you have made. Now consider the questions shown in Table 5-2, and ask others involved in that decision to share their responses with you. Be sure to ask people to cite specific examples of affective conflict and to explain why they believe interpersonal disagreement emerged.

TABLE 5-2:   Evaluating the Two Dimensions of Conflict

Cognitive Conflict

1   How many disagreements were there over different ideas about this decision?

2.   How many differences about the content of this decision did the group have
       to work through?

Affective Conflict

1.   How much anger was there among the group members over this decision?

2.   How much personal friction was there in the group during the decision-
       making process?

Source: A. Amason. (1996). "Distinguishing the effects of functional and dysfunctional conflict
on strategic decision making," *Academy of Management Journal*. 39(1): 123–148.

You may find it helpful to present the group with the matrix
shown in Figure 5-1, and ask them to locate the decision-making
process in one of the four quadrants. Perhaps some of you will be fortunate enough to discover that the group believes the process fits in
Quadrant 4. Unfortunately, my research, teaching, and consulting
work indicates that most groups find themselves in one of the other
three quadrants. Each of those, of course, tends to lead to suboptimal
decision making, either because not enough dissent has surfaced
(Quadrant I) or too much interpersonal tension has emerged
(Quadrants II and III). If you find that many of your decision
processes fit in one of these three quadrants, do not be disheartened.
Getting to Quadrant IV might not be easy, but leaders can take action
to move their teams in that direction. Diagnosing the problem—and
developing a shared understanding of it within your organization—
represents an important first step in the improvement process.
Having done that, let's turn now to the strategies that leaders may
employ to manage conflict effectively.

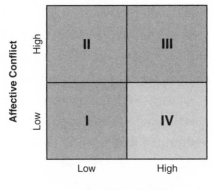

FIGURE 5-1: Cognitive versus affective conflict

Curbing Affective Conflict

Sometimes, people believe that regulating affective conflict entails a dispassionate, unbiased approach to decision making. Yet, eliminating the passion and emotion from the decision-making process may not only be nearly impossible, but also counterproductive. In the Writer's Room, Caesar's team achieved success in part because everyone came to the table with great zeal and excitement for their ideas. The same can be said for the process of creating new video games at Electronic Arts. Bruce McMillan, a senior executive at the firm, explains that passion and emotion play a critical role in business decisions. He wants proponents of an idea to display ardor and enthusiasm, because he knows that those feelings will fuel a powerful drive to execute the product development project successfully. One cannot—and should not—simply ask people to put their passion aside. McMillan likens the situation to a disagreement with your wife. As he says, "Imagine saying to your wife, 'Honey, let's the take the emotion out of this issue for a moment.' What do you think her reaction would be?"[10] Effective leaders channel others' emotions; they do not eliminate them.

How then does one regulate affective conflict without squelching people's passion for their ideas? A successful approach involves a concrete set of actions undertaken before, during, and after the decision-making process (see Table 5-3). Before a group begins to debate an issue, effective leaders establish ground rules, clarify roles and responsibilities, and build mutual respect among team members. These preliminary steps create the context in which people will behave. During the deliberations, as affective conflict begins to bubble up, leaders can reframe the debate, redescribe important ideas in novel ways, and revisit underlying facts and assumptions to help the group resolve disputes and break stalemates. After the decision process, effective leaders take the time to reflect and learn, repair damaged relationships or hurt feelings, and ensure that people remember the ways in which they worked through disputes constructively. Each of these steps requires careful forethought on the part of leaders; they must prepare themselves, and their teams in some instances, to employ these strategies. Once again, we find that making upfront process choices enhances a leader's effectiveness.

TABLE 5-3:   Leadership Strategies for Managing Conflict

Before	During	After
Rules: Establish ground rules for how people should interact during the deliberations.	**Reframe:** Redirect people's attention and recast the situation in a different light.	**Reflect:** Evaluate the process and develop lessons learned for application in the future.
Roles: Clarify the role that each individual will play in the discussion.	**Redescribe:** Present ideas and data in novel ways to enhance understanding and spark new branches of discussion.	**Repair:** Attend to damaged relationships and hurt feelings that may not have been apparent to all during the process.
Respect: Build mutual respect, particularly with regard to differences in the cognitive styles of each team member.	**Revisit:** Revisit basic facts and assumptions when the group appears to reach an impasse.	**Remember:** Ensure that people remember, and even celebrate, the effective ways in which they handled difficult disputes.

Before the Debate

What can leaders do before people even commence deliberations on an issue? The steps outlined in this section often serve to raise shared awareness about several dimensions of interpersonal and group behavior. That awareness tends to facilitate conflict management.

Ground Rules

When a group becomes engaged in a difficult dispute, individuals often revert to certain well-established routines—habitual patterns of behavior that have become deeply ingrained in the organizational culture over time. For instance, when Paul Levy took over as CEO at the Beth Israel Deaconess Medical Center in January 2002, he found that the department heads—highly accomplished doctors who were world leaders in their respective fields—often behaved very consistently, yet unproductively, when contentious issues arose. They remained silent during the CEO's staff meeting when, in fact, they objected to a course of action under consideration. Then, they tried to undercut that plan outside of the meeting, often lashing out at administrators who did not agree with their concerns. Affective conflict tended to swamp task-oriented disagreement.

Levy needed to disrupt this ineffective routine. He needed to override the "unwritten rules" that typically guided behavior. To accomplish that, he took a number of steps, beginning with the distribution of a set of "meeting rules" that described how he expected people to behave within his senior team.[11] Note the similarity to the approach employed by Steven Caufield, as described in the example at the start of Chapter 4, " Stimulating the Clash of Ideas." He used an explicit set of process guidelines to help govern behavior during his firm's debate about a critical strategic alliance decision. In that case, executives told me that Caufield and the process facilitators invoked the ground rules repeatedly when the debate seemed to veer off track or turn too personal.

At the Beth Israel Deaconess, Levy's ground rules were by no means revolutionary; they included simple axioms such as "state your objections" and "disagree without being disagreeable." Of course, Levy knew that simply offering these tenets to the group would not improve its ability to handle conflict. What purpose then did the explicit establishment of these ground rules serve? Social psychologists Connie Gersick and Richard Hackman argue that interventions such as this one can lead to learning and improvement by *heightening people's awareness of their habitual, yet problematic, patterns of action.*[12] Indeed, after distributing the list, Levy led a discussion about the new ground rules, during he which he modeled many of the prescribed behaviors. Over time, he referred to the list during contentious decision processes, and he "called people on bad behavior" when they violated the basic tenets that he had established. In short, the ground rules became a *benchmark or yardstick* by which the group could reflect upon its behavior, evaluate its decision processes in real time, and enact corrective action.

Roles

Chapter 4 discussed how role playing can help stimulate divergent thinking. It turns out that it also can be helpful as leaders try to minimize affective conflict and resolve intense disputes. By putting individuals in others' shoes, a leader can help them to understand better the motivations and interests of people with different views on a contentious issue. Moreover, it stimulates people to listen more closely to one another, because individuals are less likely to simply repeat tired old arguments, or apply their usual analytical frameworks, when they are asked to take on a different role. Renowned negotiation scholars Roger Fisher and William Ury argue that conflict often becomes highly dysfunctional if people focus on their respective positions, rather than trying to understand one another's interests. They explain:

Positional bargaining becomes a contest of will... Anger and resentment often results as one side sees itself bending to the rigid will of the other while its own legitimate concerns go unaddressed. Positional bargaining thus strains and sometimes shatters the relationship between the parties...Bitter feelings generated by one such encounter may last a lifetime.[13]

At Sun Life Financial, business unit leader Kevin Dougherty used assigned roles to both stimulate cognitive conflict and help executives understand the interests and goals of their peers in other units of the organization. As mentioned in Chapter 4, he broke his management staff into four-person teams during a two-day strategy formulation meeting in the fall of 2000, and structured the session as a competition among the teams, with each seeking to develop the best concept for a new venture at the firm. Within the groups, he assigned each member to play a specific role during these sessions. The four roles were the new venture's CEO, COO, CFO, and vice president of marketing. Each role came with a different mission. For instance, the vice president of marketing examined the value proposition for the customer, while the COO analyzed how the new venture leveraged existing resources and evaluated how the business should be structured and organized. Dougherty asked individuals to play a role different from the one to which they were accustomed. For instance, he asked individuals from the marketing staff to play the role of CFO in their groups.

The meetings produced a great deal of divergent thinking; the management team developed some innovative ideas regarding how to grow the firm's revenues and expand into new lines of business. Debates among team members became lively, as the competitive juices flowed and as some proposals challenged longstanding beliefs about how to compete in the marketplace. Nevertheless, interpersonal friction remained at a low level. When asked to explain why, managers pointed out that they had been forced to move beyond their "own little silos," and they began to understand why others often raised a particular type of objection or assessed alternatives differently during key decisions. They took greater care trying to support their arguments, because they were operating in an area in which they were less familiar. Finally, people found themselves becoming much more cognizant of their own biases and predispositions.[14]

Dougherty's approach may seem rather elaborate, and perhaps overly structured for some situations. In that case, leaders might adopt a simpler approach; they can ask individuals to evaluate and defend a position that they do not support. At New Leaders for New Schools, a nonprofit organization whose mission is to train exceptional new principals for urban schools, the management team needed to make a critical strategic choice during the firm's start-up phase. After much discussion, the group remained split on how the firm should proceed. Monique Burns, a co-founder and the company president, recalls that the debate seemed to go back and forth without any progress or resolution. The team decided to ask each side in the debate to write up a complete strategic plan—roughly 10 pages in length—that outlined and advocated for the strategy that they had *not* endorsed to that point. That experience sharpened people's understanding of the strengths and weaknesses of each option. It made them more tolerant of opposing views, largely because individuals gained a much better understanding of *why* others made particular arguments. Ultimately, the group selected a strategy with little rancor and solid buy-in from all members.[15]

Respect

Few people would disagree that a high degree of mutual respect among team members tends to enhance their ability to disagree with one another in a constructive manner. Individuals listen more carefully and give more weight to opposing views if they value the capabilities and expertise of their colleagues and if they have a high

regard for the manner in which fellow team members tend to conduct themselves. However, if leaders want to minimize affective conflict, they need to be attuned to yet another dimension of mutual
respect. They must cultivate a shared understanding and mutual
appreciation of the different cognitive styles that individuals possess.
One should not be surprised that Caesar's writers had immense
respect for one another, and perhaps more importantly, they recognized and appreciated the different ways that individuals approached
the creative writing process.

Psychologist Mark Tennant defines cognitive style as "an individual's characteristic and consistent approach to organizing and processing information."[16] Many different measures and typologies of
cognitive style have been developed. Most people are familiar with
the Myers-Briggs personality type indicator—a simple instrument
that has been used for decades to help people think about how they
process information and solve problems. For instance, Myers-Briggs
distinguishes between those individuals who tend to make decisions
based on logic and objective analysis and those who prefer to employ
subjective value systems.[17] Teams need not employ a formal survey
instrument such as Myers-Briggs to assess each member's cognitive
style, although many groups find it beneficial to do so. Frequent
interaction and thoughtful reflection about these issues often proves
to be nearly as enlightening.[18]

Monique Burns' experience demonstrates that teams can benefit
from having a candid discussion of how different members prefer to
process information and make decisions. She points out that the core
management team at her organization initially consisted of six individuals: two business people, one political policy expert, and three
teachers. As you can imagine, these individuals had what Burns
described as "very different approaches to problem solving." At first,
the diversity of cognitive styles proved to be a formidable challenge
for the team. Individuals seemed to have difficulty understanding
how people came to a particular view on an issue. At times, they

appeared to be talking past one another; finding common ground proved rather challenging. People definitely brought a great deal of passion and emotion to the debates. Burns and her colleagues did not initially recognize the problem. The potential for affective conflict rises substantially in these types of situations. Fortunately, her two co-founders, Jon Schnur and Ben Fenton, began to realize that the wide diversity of cognitive styles had become a barrier to effective communication within the team. They initiated an open discussion of this challenge facing the group, and they helped everyone understand and appreciate these important differences within the team. With heightened awareness and mutual respect for their differences, the team members found it easier to engage in productive debate on new issues going forward.[19]

During the Deliberations

So you have prepared thoroughly before a debate begins—thinking carefully about roles, rules, and respect for diverse cognitive styles. Nevertheless, a moment arrives when managers find themselves locked in rigid camps with seemingly little inclination to compromise with others. Arguments perhaps begin to cross the line from the substantive to the personal. What do you do now?

Reframe

When individuals seem to be locked into their positions, leaders need to find a way to alter the way that people perceive the situation. Too often, when debates get heated, individuals begin viewing the situation as a contest to be won or a test of wills. They believe that they are playing a zero-sum game, when, in fact, win-win solutions still may be achievable. Individuals stop thinking about new sources of information that might be examined or the possibility of new alternatives that might prove superior to any of the options currently being debated. They begin to worry more about losing face if the decision does not go their way rather being concerned about the impact on the organization. In these circumstances, leaders need to shift the focus back to the problem that needs to be solved. Negotiation expert William Ury calls this "changing the frame." He explains the dynamic:

> **Reframing means redirecting the other side's attention away from positions and toward the task of identifying interests, inventing creative options, and discussing fair standards for selecting an option...Instead of rejecting their hard-line position, you treat it as an informative contribution to the discussion. Reframe it by saying, "That's interesting. Why do you want that? Help me understand the problem you are trying to solve." The moment they answer, the focus of the conversation shifts from positions to interests. You have just changed the game.**[20]

The infamous teleconference that occurred on the eve of the ill-fated Challenger space shuttle launch in 1986 represents a powerful example of the lost opportunity to reframe a debate.[21] During that meeting, Roger Boisjoly, an engineer at NASA contractor Morton Thiokol, tried to express his concerns about the potential for O-ring failure in the shuttle's solid rocket booster at the cold temperatures expected on launch day. The mood became confrontational, as Boisjoly stuck to his position that the shuttle should not be launched, while NASA managers remained firmly opposed to a delay. They demanded scientific proof to support Boisjoly's concerns. Unable to provide such evidence, Boisjoly resorted to repeating his basic argument with growing exasperation. The two sides became locked into their positions, and people became frustrated. Affective conflict began to surface. At one point, George Hardy, deputy director of science and engineering at Marshall Space Center, commented forcefully that he was "appalled" at the recommendations for a delay by the Thiokol engineers. Imagine how people perceived that reaction to a well-intentioned, logical argument against launching the shuttle. Showing his frustration at one point, Marshall's Larry Mulloy asked, "When do you want me to launch, Thiokol, next April?"[22] Clearly, the debate had become unproductive.

My colleague Amy Edmondson has pointed out that the meeting participants could have avoided dysfunctional debate—and perhaps prevented the disaster—by reframing the discussion as a collective-learning and problem-solving process. She points out that people did not ask inquisitive questions during the debate, but repeatedly defended their own positions. Individuals did not try to understand each other's thinking. The lack of inquiry meant that people did not learn from one another and leverage the collective expertise in the room. They simply became frustrated and emotional. If participants had refocused on the problem—trying to understand whether there was a correlation between O-ring failure and temperature—they might have recognized that they did have access to data that may have convinced everyone to delay the launch. During the meeting, Boisjoly presented data on the temperatures at launch for those past flights with O-ring incidents. The evidence showed no apparent correlation between temperature and O-ring failure; thus, managers remained unconvinced of the threat. However, if the group had added all flights to the graph, including those without O-ring incidents, the partici-pants would have recognized very quickly that a correlation did exist. No one asked for more data of this kind during the debate.[23]

Edmondson stresses the power of asking curious, nonthreatening questions to help reframe a contentious debate and break a stale-mate. For instance, she points out that someone could have asked Mulloy, "What kind of data would you need to change your mind and postpone the launch?" Edmondson argues that the likely response to that question ("I would need data that suggests a correlation between temperature and O-ring erosion on past shuttle launches") would have spurred a great deal of further investigation and learning within the group. Specifically, group members together may have uncovered the correlation data that would have convinced senior NASA executives to delay the launch.[24]

Ury concurs with this prescription for reframing a contentious deliberation: "The most obvious way to direct the other side's attention toward the problem is to tell them about it. But making assertions can easily arouse their resistance. The better approach is to ask questions."[25] Unfortunately, people locked in a heated argument often stop asking questions and resort to pointed assertions. Worse yet, they stop listening altogether. For this reason, the leader of a decision-making process must take the initiative; he needs to spot the opportunity to shift the group into a collective inquiry mode by querying people about their goals, assumptions, rationale, and supporting evidence. Effective leaders take great care in formulating and articulating these questions. Language makes a difference when it comes to managing conflict. Leaders can model the way in which they want people to select words that are less likely to trigger defensive responses (see Table 5-4). They should not make questions sound confrontational ("Why do you keep saying that?"); instead, they ought to present inquiries as a personal desire to develop a better grasp of others' thinking ("Help me understand…"). The tragic Challenger story reminds us that leaders would be well-served to remember Peter Drucker's sage advice: "The most common source of mistakes in management decisions is the emphasis on finding the right answer rather than the right question."[26]

TABLE 5-4: Reframing the Debate: Asking the Right Questions

Type of Question	Examples
Why?	Help me understand why you believe….
Why not?	Why not pursue these other options?
What if?	What if we found this assumption to be false?
What would you do?	What would you do if you were in my shoes?
What makes that optimal?	You must have good reasons for thinking that's an optimal solution. I'd like to hear them.

Source: Adapted from W. Ury. (1993). *Getting Past No: Negotiating Your Way from Confrontation to Cooperation*. New York: Bantam Books.

Redescribe

Sometimes, conflict becomes dysfunctional because one set of individuals tries hard to convey an important idea, but they cannot present the supporting evidence in a persuasive manner. They become increasingly frustrated, because they do not understand why others do not find the data compelling. It seems so obvious to them! Soon they begin to attribute the others' inability to comprehend their argument to a personal deficiency on the part of those they have failed to persuade. They think, "How could an intelligent person not understand this point?"

Cognitive psychologist Howard Gardner, a pioneer in the study of the multiple dimensions of human intelligence, has argued that people can avoid these frustrating situations through a strategy that he calls redescription. As Gardner writes, "Essentially the same semantic meaning or content, then, can be conveyed by different forms: words, numbers, dramatic renditions, bulleted lists, Cartesian coordinates, or a bar graph...Multiple versions of the same point constitute an extremely powerful way in which to change minds."[27]

Gardner uses a simple example to illustrate his point. Many people initially approach a particular task by focusing roughly equal amounts of time and effort on each of its elements. Gardner calls this the "50/50 principle"—a notion that he believes we adopt in our early childhood. Contrast that with the Pareto principle—the so-called 80/20 rule. For instance, 20 percent of the components may be the cause of 80 percent of the defects in a particular product. The Pareto principle proves to be applicable to a wide range of tasks and situations, yet Gardner points out that people's behavior in life often remains steadfastly consistent with the 50/50 principle. How might people be convinced to change their behavior? Gardner argues that one might describe the 80/20 principle using a variety of data formats. Tables, Cartesian grids, bar graphs, and even cartoons might be used to describe the concept. As the number of formats increases, the concept becomes more compelling. See Figure 5-2 for an example of how to demonstrate the Pareto principle using two different presentations of the same set of data.[28]

Redescription works in practice as well as in theory. In one of my classes recently, two students locked horns about a set of issues in a case study that I had assigned. As the debate began to heat up, another student realized that one might look at the data in a different way. This redescription helped one combatant understand the point that his opponent had been trying to make. With that new insight, frustrations eased, even though the debate continued on many fronts. Fortunately for me, their fellow student's timely intervention had defused the potential for affective conflict.

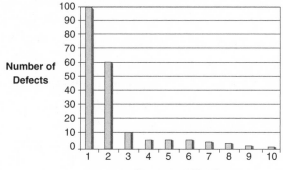

Component #	Percent of Defects
1	50.0%
2	30.0%
3	5.0%
4	2.5%
5	2.5%
6	2.5%
7	2.5%
8	2.0%
9	2.0%
10	1.0%

Source: Adapted from R. Koch. (1998). *The 80/20 Principle*. New York: Currency/Doubleday.

FIGURE 5-2: Illustrating the Pareto principle: same content, different format

Revisit

When stalemates emerge and heated debates appear ready to boil over, leaders also can ask participants to revisit key facts and assumptions. Here, leaders hope that they can get people to step back from the positions that they have taken, and help them discover precisely how and why they disagree about the appropriate course of action for the organization. Often, that process of reexamining underlying presumptions fuels new avenues for information gathering and analysis. Like the other techniques described here, circling back in this manner serves the purpose of trying to help people find some element of common ground. If individuals can surface and resolve a disagreement about a key assumption in an amicable manner, it may serve as a catalyst for more effective interpersonal communication later in the deliberations. In short, improved interpersonal relationships often begin to develop through the brokering of small agreements about a particular piece of analysis or a specific assumption.[29] Such "small wins" also help move groups to closure, as discussed in more detail in Chapter 8, "Reaching Closure."

One defense industry executive described how he handled difficult moments during a critical strategic choice:

> **Usually, people disagreed because they either thought something was different than perhaps somebody else did in terms of data, or they assumed that the customer wanted something different than what was being presented. And generally, we decided to check that out. Go see if the customer really wants that. Go see if that data is really different.**

This executive pointed out that this disciplined return to the data and the assumptions on numerous occasions enabled him to navigate a rather controversial issue without any major personal friction among his colleagues. In some sense, practice made perfect. As people focused on small areas of disagreement and managed to resolve those disputes, they developed a *capability* to deal with conflict in a constructive manner. The capability served them well as they approached the ultimate decision facing the organization. Instances of interpersonal tension seemed to diminish as the decision process unfolded.

After the Decision

Now the decision has been made. The debate has ended. If you are fortunate, the entire team has committed fully to the selected course of action. Even with such strong buy-in, your job remains incomplete. To manage debates effectively over time, leaders need to take certain steps at the end of a decision process to ensure that they will continue to develop and enhance their personal and organizational capabilities to deal with affective conflict successfully.

Reflect

Winston Churchill once said, "I am always ready to learn although I do not always like being taught." Learning from our failures indeed can be a painful experience.[30] If a group has struggled with affective conflict during a decision process, the members probably will not enjoy reviewing their missteps. However, as a leader, you need to make disciplined reflection an important part of the follow-up to each decision process. Looking back on a particular dispute, after tempers have cooled, often elicits some important lessons about how the conflict could have been managed more effectively.

Lessons-learned exercises often work best if they are conducted in a systematic manner and if groups make them a habit over time. Although many firms employ them to study large projects, one can and should adopt a similar approach to assessing decision-making processes. David Garvin's research shows that the U.S. Army has done a particularly good job of developing a routine mechanism for reflecting on past experience.[31] The army conducts after-action reviews after every mission. The discussion proceeds in four stages, each focused on a specific question:

1. What did we set out to do?

2. What actually happened?

3. Why did it happen?

4. What are we going to do next time?

In many organizations, people begin their reflection and review of past experience by jumping to questions 3 and 4. They want to discuss what went wrong and how to fix it. However, the army has found that it is critical to spend a substantial amount of time on the first two questions. People need to have a clear understanding of the goals and of the standards used to measure the achievement of those objectives. Here, you will want to have a candid discussion about your criteria for judging the quality of a decision process. You should share what you hoped to achieve during a particular debate. The army also has found that people need to develop a shared understanding of what happened in a particular situation before they can try to draw lessons from it. Think about a decision process in your organization. Do all the participants agree on how and why a particular dispute emerged during the deliberations? Did everyone perceive the interpersonal tension in a similar manner? Perhaps some people did not even attend the specific meeting in which tempers flared. Everyone needs a complete map of the territory if they are to contribute to the learning process.[32] Having accomplished this, you then can turn to analysis of why the conflict unfolded as it did, and how the group should change its approach in the future.

In many organizations, people only conduct post-mortems. That is, they only think about the need for reflection and review when they fail. The army takes a different approach; they examine all missions, regardless of the degree of success or failure. They recognize that, amid a largely successful mission, many mistakes occur. Likewise, even when the mission fails to achieve its primary goals, some things go right.[33] Leaders should adopt a similar approach when reflecting on past decision processes. Regardless of the overall outcome, instances of effective and ineffective conflict management may have occurred. Leaders need to capitalize on each of those moments as learning opportunities.

Repair

When decision-making processes end, it may not always be apparent to a leader, or even to some of the participants, that one or more individuals feel that they were criticized personally. Some people may believe that the conflict remained constructive, whereas others do not. People's feelings may be hurt, and bitterness may linger after a particularly ardent disagreement, yet they may keep those feelings largely to themselves. Leaders must take great care not to presume that everyone perceived the conflict as they did. Silence does not necessarily denote a uniformly positive affect about the decision process. Leaders should probe for negative emotions, damaged self-esteem, and frayed interpersonal relationships.

If leaders discover that some fallout has taken place after a difficult debate, they need to shift into repair mode. They need to address those issues head on before another contentious decision process takes place. If not, the personal friction among a few individuals may spill over and disrupt the entire team or even the organization as a whole. At Emerson Electric, Chuck Knight adopted a simple technique for keeping tabs on people's feelings and emotions after a tough debate. When one of his highly confrontational strategy reviews ended, he always tried to sit next to the business unit president at the dinner that immediately followed the conclusion of the meetings. Of course, that individual typically bore the brunt of the critical questioning from the corporate staff, including himself. He wanted to use the dinner conversation to assess whether the business unit president felt negatively about the discussions that had taken place earlier in the day. If Knight felt that he had damaged their working relationship in any way, he began to work on a plan to repair that connection.[34]

Adopting Knight's direct approach may not always unearth negative emotions. People may recoil further in some circumstances, seeking to suppress their feelings for fear that disclosure may harm their reputation in some way. They may not want to be perceived as "soft" or "thin-skinned." For that reason, leaders need to look for subtle signals of lingering interpersonal tensions. They might search for disruptions in the usual patterns of social interaction among their colleagues. Similarly, they might keep an eye out for sudden changes in the level of participation by a particular manager. If a typically talkative person suddenly becomes rather quiet during meetings, it may be a cause for concern. Similarly, if a rather reserved individual seems to be more argumentative than usual, one might pay a bit more attention to how past disputes may have affected him. In many instances, if leaders begin to look for these dangers signs, they will find that the signals are not all that subtle. They simply needed to become a bit more attuned to changes in people's usual patterns of behavior.

Remember

Finally, leaders want the organization to remember particularly striking examples of constructive conflict management. They want to celebrate those instances and build them in to the treasure chest of "classic stories" that people tell about the historical development of the organization. Leaders should do that as a reward for those who dealt with the disagreement in a positive manner. Moreover, they want to encourage others to emulate that behavior. Individuals may not always feel very positive about a contentious debate, even if they managed to keep affective conflict reasonably in check. The simple fact that they engaged in a rather confrontational discussion with a colleague—and perhaps danced close to the edge regarding personal criticism—may make them feel a bit uncomfortable. The leader ought to tell the story to others, showcasing it as an example of desirable behavior, to lessen people's anxiety about expressing dissent, particularly if the organization has had a "polite" culture in the past.

As noted earlier, Paul Levy took charge of an organization where people typically did not express dissent openly during meetings, and they did not effectively handle conflict when it did emerge. He desperately wanted to change that culture. During one committee meeting in his first few months on the job, it became apparent to him that two individuals disagreed strongly about a particular issue, yet the dispute bubbled beneath the surface. He intentionally sparked a fight between the two individuals. The rest of the group sat rather shocked and appalled that these people were shouting at one another. At the end of the meeting, Levy acknowledged their dismay, but he noted that he was glad that the disagreement had come to the surface and been discussed openly. The two sides worked through their disagreement very constructively, with his help, and they had arrived at a good solution for the organization by the next meeting. At that time, Levy again acknowledged the discomfort that many individuals felt about the contentious disagreement, but he asked the two "combatants" if they were glad to have addressed the dispute as they had. The two individuals responded that they were satisfied.

One of them actually concluded the meeting by singing a song that he had composed about the incident. He sang to the tune of "Down by the Levy"—a cute play on the CEO's name. Levy, of course, knew that the story of this wonderful resolution to the conflict would spread throughout the organization. He simply accelerated the dissemination of the story, and he made it clear that he was thrilled by how these individuals had handled the conflict. With that, he sent a strong signal to the organization about how he wanted them to deal with conflict in the future. He used this rather vivid memory as a powerful teaching moment.[35]

Building a Capability

This chapter has examined a number of mechanisms for alleviating or preventing affective conflict. We have learned that conflict management requires a substantial amount of skill and a great deal of forethought. Leaders must be adept at diagnosis, mediation, coaching, and facilitation. Often, they need to become personally involved to resolve heated disputes between managers in their organizations. We have argued that practice makes perfect; in other words, leaders become more adept at dispute resolution over time. Conflict management can become a personal capability that individuals feel quite comfortable drawing upon to ensure that decisions are made in a timely and efficient manner.

Consultants Charles Raben and Janet Spencer point out, however, that conflict management should not remain simply a personal competency of the leader. Leaders must coach their team members so that they become adept at managing disagreements constructively. Conflict management must become a shared responsibility, and ultimately, an organizational capability—not simply a personal one. Leaders cannot micromanage each disagreement. The authors write in reference to CEO behavior, but their argument applies to leaders at all levels:

> **The CEO must develop competency in the area of coaching and facilitation...In order to be a successful coach and facilitator, a CEO must be motivated by a genuine desire to help others become more adept at resolving conflicts. A CEO whose overarching concern is resolving the conflict at hand and getting everyone back to business as usual will lack the patience and commitment to see the process through to a successful conclusion. CEOs are, by nature, impatient and action-oriented; they see a problem, they want it solved. To**

develop competency as a coach/facilitator, then, often requires the CEO to develop new skills and adopt a new perspective.[36]

Freedom and Control

Leaders certainly cannot resolve every dispute that arises during a complex decision-making process. They need help. They must develop the skills of their subordinates. Moreover, after a leader unleashes the power of divergent thinking, they inherently give up some control over the ideas and options that are discussed. Yet, leadership always entails a broad responsibility for establishing the context in which people behave, as well as the processes that groups employ to initiate and resolve conflict. Leaders can and should shape and guide *how* people disagree, as well as the *atmosphere* in which that debate takes place. Along these lines, Larry Gelbart once reflected back on Sid Caesar's leadership of the wildly creative process in the Writers' Room. Gelbart remarked, "He had total control, but we had total freedom."[37]

PART III

BUILDING CONSENSUS

6

THE DYNAMICS OF
INDECISION

"Deliberate often. Decide once."

—Latin proverb

In 1996, a merger took place between the Beth Israel and the Deaconess hospitals, two large and well-respected health-care institutions in Boston, Massachusetts. The merged entity brought together more than 1,000 highly accomplished physicians and had revenues of nearly $1 billion. Senior executives at the newly formed Beth Israel Deaconess Medical Center (BIDMC) hailed the merger as a "good fit" and cited the potential for "tens of millions of dollars" in cost savings.[1] Not everyone remained convinced that the deal would pan out. The *Boston Globe* commented that "The concept is attractive; the reality may be a bit messy."[2]

The early years of the marriage did not go smoothly, to say the least. The financial losses escalated rapidly, topping $50 million per year in fiscal years 1998 through 2001. Several CEOs tried and failed to execute a turnaround. The Massachusetts attorney general began to pressure the board of directors to consider selling the institution to a for-profit health-care firm. Amid this turmoil, Paul Levy took over as chief executive in January 2002. As Levy assessed the situation, he noted that prior management *had* done a great deal of work analyzing the hospital's problems and discussing alternative proposals designed to restore the organization's financial health. Several consulting firms had performed extensive studies, and they had provided sound recommendations to the medical center's senior management team. Yet, substantive organizational changes never materialized. The organization seemed to be "all talk, no action." Levy explained:

> **This was not a question of not knowing what to do. Everyone knew what had to be done. This was an absolute failure to execute, which, ultimately, is a failure of leadership...BIDMC leadership was simply unable to reach an agreement on a programmatic plan for the hospital...I define the problem of the BIDMC as a curious inability to decide.[3]**

The BIDMC may sound like a particularly dysfunctional organization, but in fact, many organizations are plagued by the "curious inability to decide." In some cases, managers engage in plenty of debate, and they simply can never come to a consensus. The leader fails to bring deliberations to a close, make a decision, and move forward with a plan of action. The organization remains frozen in its tracks, while competitors gain the upper hand. The management team becomes a "debating society," or they find themselves embroiled in "analysis paralysis."[4] In other instances, a sense of false consensus emerges during decision processes. That is, people tend not to surface objections during meetings. Instead, they work around the decision process, laboring behind the scenes to kill projects or derail decisions in the early stages of implementation. The leader thinks a decision was made and is being implemented, but soon thereafter, he discovers that the course of action has not been enacted. In these organizations, decisions are apparently made, but they never survive long enough to be executed.

Napoleon Bonaparte once said that "Nothing is more difficult, and therefore more precious than to be able to decide." He recognized that many leaders find themselves unable to take decisive action when confronted with ambiguous information, dynamic environmental conditions, and conflicting advice from others. They cannot bring debates to a close, choose a course of action in a timely manner, and build the commitment and shared understanding required to implement their plans effectively. In this chapter, we examine why organizations experience the "curious inability to decide." Specifically, we examine the patterns of behavior, often deeply embedded in the organization's culture and processes, which create a systematic inability to reach closure in the decision-making process. In the two chapters that follow, we examine how leaders can overcome these barriers, build commitment and shared understanding, and reach closure in a timely manner.

A Culture of Indecision

People often conclude that organizational indecisiveness and inaction simply reflects the problematic leadership style or personality of a particular executive. They point to managers who are irresolute, undisciplined, and/or overly cautious. Those descriptors may very well apply to some executives who find it difficult to reach closure on critical decisions. However, the phenomenon of a "curious inability to decide" often stretches far beyond the leadership capabilities of a particular individual. In many cases, it tends to be a pattern of behavior that permeates the entire organization. Groups cannot arrive at a consensus because dysfunctional habits of dialogue and decision making have become second nature to many members of the organization.

Those habits manifest themselves through the manner in which dialogues and deliberations take place at all levels of the firm, in many different types of formal and informal teams and committees.

Ram Charan, a renowned adviser to the CEOs of many Fortune 500 firms, describes the problem as a "culture of indecision."[5] By culture, I mean the often taken-for-granted assumptions of how things work in an organization, of how members approach and think about problems.[6] In other words, certain patterns of behavior gradually become embedded in the way that work gets done on a daily basis, and sometimes those patterns lead to a chronic inability to reach closure on critical decisions. Over time, those patterns of behavior become taken for granted, and people engage in them without much forethought. In my research, I have found that such dysfunctional decision-making cultures come in three forms: a culture of no, a culture of yes, and a culture of maybe. Each comes with its own predictable and easily identifiable patterns of interaction and dialogue, and each has its own underlying causes. Yet, they all lead to a similar outcome—a chronic inability to move from conflict to consensus, from deliberation to action.

The Culture of No

When Louis Gerstner became IBM's CEO in 1993, he faced an enormous challenge. The company's performance had declined dramatically, after decades as the dominant behemoth in the computer industry. The company's share price had declined by 70 percent over the past 6 years. Mainframe revenues—once the company's mainstay—had dropped by nearly 50 percent since 1990. The firm lost $8.1 billion in 1993 alone. Prior to his arrival, the board of directors had even discussed the possibility of breaking up the company into several smaller independent firms.[7]

Gerstner set out to diagnose the problems at IBM, and he soon discovered that many problems were rooted in the firm's culture.

Once a competitive strength, the IBM culture had become insular and rigid. The firm had not kept pace with the dynamic changes taking place in the computing industry. It did not have deep insights regarding its customers' needs, nor a solid grasp of how rivals had a competitive edge in many areas.

Gerstner described one of IBM's problems in the early 1990s as "the culture of no." A cross-functional group could spend months working on a solution to a problem, but if a manager objected because of the deleterious impact on his business unit, he could obstruct or prevent implementation. In the IBM vernacular, a lone dissenter could issue a "nonconcur" in this type of situation and stop a proposal dead in its tracks. Gerstner discovered that IBM managers had actually designed a formal nonconcur system into the company's strategic planning process. In a rather incredible memo that Gerstner uncovered, an executive went so far as to ask each business unit to appoint a "nonconcur coordinator" who would be responsible for blocking projects and proposals that would conflict with the division's goals and interests. Gerstner described the "culture of no" as follows:

> **One of the most extraordinary manifestations of this "no" culture was IBM's infamous nonconcur system... The net effect was unconscionable delay in reaching key decisions; duplicate effort, as units continued to focus on their pet approaches; and bitter personal contention, as hours and hours of good work would be jeopardized or scuttled by lone dissenters. Years later, I heard it described as a culture in which no one *would* say yes, but everyone *could* say no.[8]**

A culture of no goes far beyond the notion of cultivating dissent or encouraging people to play the role of devil's advocate (see Table 6-1). In fact, it undermines many of the principles of open dialogue and constructive debate that we have espoused. It means that dissenters have veto power in the decision-making process, particularly if those individuals have more power and/or status than their peers.[9] The organization does not employ dissenting voices as a means of encouraging divergent thinking, but rather it enables those who disagree with a proposal to stifle dialogue and close off interesting avenues of inquiry. Such a culture does not force dissenters to defend their views with data and logic, or to explain how their objections are consistent with organization-wide goals as opposed to the parochial interests of a particular division or subunit. A culture of no enables those with the most power or the loudest voice to impose their will.

TABLE 6-1: Two Types of Dissent: Devil's Advocacy Versus Culture of No

Devil's Advocacy	Culture of No
Objective is to encourage divergent thinking and open new lines of inquiry.	Objective is to block proposals that conflict with one's own interests and objectives.
Dissenters have the ability to affect the decision process, but not dictate the outcome.	Lone dissenters have virtual veto power.
Dissenters have more impact if they present unbiased perspectives and if they provide equal levels of critical examination for all options under consideration.	Dissenters with more power and status, or who "pound the table harder than others," have more clout.
Dissenters share information freely with others so that others may form their own conclusions.	Dissenters horde information that might enable others to engage them in a productive debate.
Dissenters seek to generate many new options.	Dissenters tear down existing proposals without offering alternatives.
Dissenters focus on the extent to which assumptions underlying each option may be overly pessimistic as well as overly optimistic.	Dissenters focus only on downside risks associated with the specific proposals that they oppose.

A culture of no need not manifest itself in a formal system by which people issue objections, such as the bureaucratic procedures at IBM in the early 1990s. It can simply permeate the informal incentive structures and patterns of communication within an organization. Some cultures, for instance, reward people as much for what they say as for what they do. People garner attention and acclaim when they sound intelligent and insightful during meetings. Delivering a "gotcha" during a presentation becomes a badge of honor in such organizations. Group discussions become forums for impressing others, rather than a means of accelerating action on a key issue.

Scholars Jeffrey Pfeffer and Robert Sutton describe this phenomenon as the "smart-talk trap." Their research shows that "People who talk frequently are more likely to be judged by others as influential and important—they're considered leaders."[10] At first glance, that finding may not alarm you. Leaders do need the ability to articulate their ideas in a concise and persuasive way in public settings. However, Pfeffer and Sutton also have discovered that "smart-talk" tends to be overly negative and complex. When people strive to impress others in meetings, they tend to explain how and why a proposal will not work, rather than describing why it might succeed. Why the persistent emphasis on negativity? Based on the findings from field and experimental research, Pfeffer and Sutton argue that an individual is more likely to bolster others' perceptions of his intelligence by offering critiques rather than positive pronouncements about proposals and ideas under consideration. They find that many organizations encourage "the tendency to tear an idea down without offering anything positive in its place."[11] Smart talk becomes an impediment to open, constructive dialogue and an obstacle that prevents firms from moving from analysis to action. The behavior persists and even spreads throughout firms because individuals believe, often rightfully, that smart talk helps them get ahead. Unfortunately, many organizations do not understand how their reward structure—particularly the institution's informal reward and punishment system—promotes the development of a dysfunctional "culture of no."[12]

The Culture of Yes

Paul Levy faced a problem a bit different than the one encountered by Gerstner at IBM. Dissenters did not openly express their objections at the hospital. Nothing similar to the nonconcur system existed, and smart talk did not characterize the dialogue within the organization. Doctors gained prestige and power based upon the groundbreaking research that they published, not the clever pronouncements that they offered during meetings. The physicians often sat quietly during discussions of administrative issues; nevertheless, the organization found it difficult to reach closure on critical decisions. Levy traced the problem to a dysfunctional pattern of behavior that had become routine at the hospital:

> **People will not tell the truth during meetings about how their department would react to a given proposal... They will sit there quietly and you won't find out until a week later that they object to something... This behavior had become standard practice. If you object to a proposal, you get quiet during the meeting. Then later, when you leave the room, you undercut the consensus that appeared to have emerged.**[13]

A new manager in these circumstances might assume that silence means assent. However, Levy found that the hospital's culture discouraged those who said "no" during a meeting with their peers and superiors. Instead, people felt more comfortable conveying a sense of "yes" during group meetings, while working behind the scenes, often in one-on-one conversations, to convey their concerns and objections. Because of the lack of open and honest dialogue, the hospital executives found themselves constantly revisiting decisions that apparently had been made. Over time, new employees at the hospital learned how to behave in conformance with the cultural norms simply by observing others. A strong tacit understanding of accepted practice began to shape individual behavior.

Many firms find themselves in a similar predicament. (See Figure 6-1 for a depiction of the dynamics of indecision.) Reflecting on his experiences in executive suites around the world, Ram Charan points out that he has observed many instances in which "The true sentiment in the room was the opposite of the apparent consensus."[14] He argues that an overemphasis on hierarchy, excessive process formality, and a lack of interpersonal trust contribute to the problem. To be honest, I can recall a number of faculty meetings characterized by the very same dynamic; let's just say that management professors do not always practice what they preach!

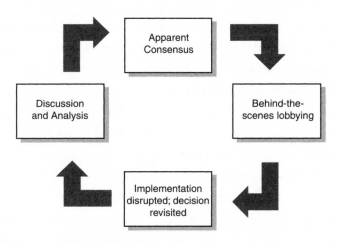

FIGURE 6-1: A cycle of inaction

Simply raising people's awareness of such dysfunctional behavior typically does not alter the "culture of yes." Recently, I conducted a full-day workshop on decision making with senior executives at a successful investment-banking firm. We spent much of the day talking about how to encourage more open dialogue and constructive dissent. The group performed a thoughtful diagnosis of the organization's approach to decision making, and it concluded that the "culture of yes" characterized some discussions within the firm. At the end of the day, the top executive at the session put forth a proposal for how to implement some changes based on what they had learned during the workshop. He asked the group whether they concurred with his recommendation, and no one raised any objections. Soon thereafter, he concluded the day's session. By the very next morning, he had

received a deluge of phone calls and e-mails from individuals expressing their concerns with the proposal!

Some leaders foster a "culture of yes" through the design of
their decision processes. That is, they develop routine procedures for
analyzing and reviewing alternative courses of action that actually
encourage managers to work behind the scenes to block decisions
with which they do not agree. Take the example of Don Barrett, a
division president at a discount sporting goods retailer. Barrett's
direct reports described him as someone who strove to build consensus on most important issues. However, even Barrett acknowledged
that his management team often found it difficult to reach closure:
"We tend to allow issues to resurface…If people don't agree with a
decision, then they tend to think they can keep bringing it up over
and over, and this will lead to a change in the decision." His direct
reports concurred. As one team member pointed out, "Something
prevents us from actually reaching a definitive conclusion on issues."[15]

What caused the problems at All-Star Sports? Barrett had a fairly
large senior team with 12 members besides himself. Decision making
could become rather cumbersome and slow in such a large group,
and the prospect of affective conflict concerned Barrett. Therefore,
the team developed a habit of asking a small subgroup to take contentious issues "off line" for further analysis. The subgroup worked
closely with Barrett to examine multiple alternatives. After complet-
ing extensive analyses, the subgroup presented Barrett with a tentative recommendation. He reviewed the analysis, discussed the
subgroup's assumptions, and often requested additional work.
Dissent and debate flowed freely during these sessions. Finally,
Barrett and the subgroup together selected a particular course of
action that they would recommend to the full management team,
which had responsibility for ratifying the decision.

Barrett expected the large team to raise questions about the
recommended course of action, yet such inquiries and objections
rarely surfaced. People felt that the subgroup's recommendations

represented a *fait accompli* because of the earlier communications with Barrett. Given the knowledge that he had endorsed the subgroup's conclusions, they withheld their concerns during the group meeting. However, conflict often emerged through informal channels after the meeting. People often found themselves asking, "Didn't we make this decision already?" Backroom lobbying became the norm at All-Star Sports. As one manager observed, "People don't invest heavily in what goes on in the room...The meeting is the wrong place to object, so people work around it." In sum, despite their good intentions, Barrett and his staff had designed a fairly rigid decision-making procedure that cultivated a "culture of yes."[16] Figure 6-2 summarizes how the "culture of yes" and the "culture of no" arrive at a similar undesirable outcome by taking different paths.

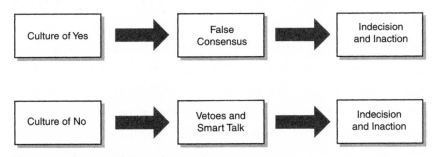

FIGURE 6-2:   Different pathologies, same results

The Culture of Maybe

Some organizations have highly analytical cultures. Managers in these firms strive to gather extensive amounts of objective data prior to making decisions. They try to apply quantitative analysis whenever possible, and they make exhaustive attempts to evaluate many different contingencies and scenarios. Scholars James Fredrickson and Terence Mitchell describe these decision-making processes as highly comprehensive. Naturally, this approach to decision making has its strengths. In their research, Fredrickson and Mitchell try to confirm that comprehensiveness leads to higher firm performance. They find that it does in organizations operating in relatively stable environments, but it has a negative relationship with performance for firms competing in relatively unstable environments. The scholars postulate that comprehensiveness slows down decision-making processes, and therefore, becomes a perilous handicap for firms competing in dynamic markets.[17]

Some organizations and their leaders find it difficult to cope with the uncertainty that characterizes turbulent environments. They go to great lengths to gather more information and perform additional formal analysis, in hopes of reducing the ambiguity associated with various options and contingencies. They strive for certainty in an inherently uncertain world—to turn every maybe into a simple yes or no. Indecision and a lack of closure result if managers cannot recognize the costs of trying to gather a more and more complete set of information.

Stanley Teele, a former dean of Harvard Business School, once said, "The art of management is the art of making meaningful generalizations out of inadequate facts." Yet, certain organizational cultures discourage managers from drawing conclusions based upon limited datasets. A "culture of maybe" prevails, in which people find themselves endlessly pursuing every unresolved question, rather than weighing the costs and benefits of gathering more information or performing more analysis. Many organizations do not recognize when the incremental, or marginal, value of additional information search has begun to decline. They continue to gather information even when the marginal costs of new data begin to rise dramatically, while the incremental benefits become very small.

Figure 6-3 shows a conceptual description of the information search problem that managers face. As the graph shows, when organizations gather the first bits of information associated with a decision, the incremental benefits are large, whereas the costs are low. As firms try to gather more information, the search becomes increasingly difficult and time-consuming. The incremental costs of an additional piece of information eventually begin to rise dramatically, while the marginal benefits of extra data diminish over time (i.e., the total cost curve in the chart begins to steepen, while the total benefit curve starts to flatten). An optimal level of information gathering occurs when the biggest gap exists between total costs and total benefits. When firms move beyond that point, the incremental costs of additional information exceed the marginal benefits.[18] Naturally, firms do not have a magic formula for calculating the value of information search, or for plotting it on a graph as in Figure 6-3. We have provided the chart for the purpose of making a critical conceptual point. However, managers can recognize the dynamic depicted in the chart and raise others' awareness of the value creation or destruction taking place as the organization searches for higher and higher levels of certainty and unassailable proof before taking action.

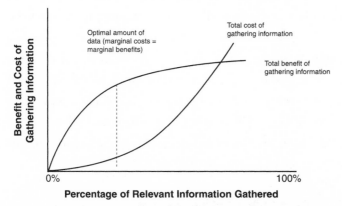

Source: Adapted from F. Harrison. (1996). *The Managerial Decision-Making Process,* 4th Edition. Boston: Houghton Mifflin. p. 49.

FIGURE 6-3: Optimal information search activity

Many factors explain why organizations become embroiled in a "culture of maybe" when faced with ambiguity and environmental dynamism. For starters, some firms have many members whose personality and cognitive style tend to favor rational and objective methods of problem-solving. Moreover, management education and training programs tend to preach the value of systematic analytical techniques. Employees often fall back on those methods when faced with complex problems.

Digging deeper, one finds that a natural human tendency also explains why many organizations place such emphasis on analysis and information gathering, even when the costs of doing so become prohibitive. Psychologists Irving Janis and Leon Mann argue that many individuals experience anticipatory regret when they make critical decisions. In other words, people become anxious, apprehensive, and risk averse as they imagine the negative emotions that they may experience if the decision does not transpire as expected. High levels of anticipatory regret can lead to indecision and costly delays.[19] Scholars have found that this anxiety and lack of confidence even affects very accomplished leaders, from U.S. presidents to top executives in Silicon Valley.[20] In some organizations, managers consistently fall back on formal analysis, planning systems, and intensive market-research studies as a means of overcoming anticipatory regret. They find cognitive and emotional comfort in the quantification and analytical rigor that characterizes such efforts. Unfortunately, managers often arrive at a false sense of precision in these circumstances, and these tactics exacerbate delays in the decision-making process, without truly resolving many outstanding questions.[21] For a brief summary of the three dysfunctional dynamics of indecision described in the preceding pages, see Table 6-2.

TABLE 6-2:   Three Cultures of Indecision

Culture of No	Culture of Yes	Culture of Maybe
Individuals tear down proposals without offering alternatives, exercise veto powers, and focus on obstacles rather than opportunities.	Individuals suppress objections during meetings, but then work behind the scenes to undermine the apparent consensus.	Individuals strive to resolve all uncertainty through formal analysis, and they engage in costly searches for new information.

Seeking Shortcuts

As executives become frustrated with the tendency for inaction within their organizations, they naturally search for strategies to accelerate decision making. Some managers conclude that decision complexity and ambiguity have paralyzed the organization, and therefore they adopt techniques for simplifying the situation so that they can make a judgment more quickly and easily. For instance, they reason by analogy, apply simple rules of thumb, and imitate other successful organizations. These strategies may help managers make accurate judgments amid a great deal of ambiguity, and they can provide a creative way to break stalemates or open up new ways of thinking about a problem. Moreover, these techniques do not require an overwhelming amount of formal analysis, yet even highly rational and analytical thinkers tend to find these decision-making strategies appealing.

Unfortunately, each of these strategies has serious drawbacks as well. When employing these techniques, many leaders draw the wrong conclusions, make biased estimates, pursue flawed policies, or impede the development of commitment within their management teams. Perhaps more importantly, these decision-making shortcuts do not tackle the fundamental cultural problems that consistently lead to indecision and inaction within the organization. They may enable an organization to arrive at one particular decision quite readily, but in the future, the same dysfunctional patterns of behavior tend to persist.[22]

Reasoning by Analogy

Business leaders often draw analogies to past experiences when faced with a complex problem for which the organization cannot seem to gain traction or arrive at a solution. They draw comparisons to similar situations or circumstances from their own past or from the history of other organizations, and they induce certain lessons from those experiences. John Rau, a former CEO and business school dean, argues that analogies provide a wealth of information: "The fundamental laws of economics, production, financial processes and human behavior and interaction do not change from company to company or industry to industry. Reading about other companies makes me a better decision maker because it provides a store of analogies."[23] Indeed, researchers have shown that people in a variety of fields, from foreign policy to firefighting, reason by analogy. Analogies prove especially useful when decision makers do not have access to complete information and do not have the time or ability to conduct a comprehensive analysis of alternatives. They enable people to diagnose a complex situation quickly and to identify a manageable set of options for serious consideration.

Unfortunately, most analogies are imperfect. No two situations are identical. Many decision makers quickly spot the similarities between situations, but they often ignore critical differences. In foreign policy, officials often refer to the "Munich analogy" when making decisions. When confronted with international aggression, many world leaders argue against appeasement by drawing comparisons to Hitler's belligerence during the 1930s. They argue that British Prime Minister Chamberlain's decision to appease Hitler in 1938 actually encouraged him to pursue further expansion. Political scientists Richard Neustadt and Ernest May point out, however, that not every situation parallels the circumstances in Europe in the late 1930s. For example, they argue that President Truman would have been well-served to identify the differences, as well as the similarities, between Korea in 1950 and Czechoslovakia in 1938. Ignoring these distinctions may have impaired the U.S. strategy during the Korean conflict.[24]

Business leaders often draw imperfect analogies as well. Take the dot-com boom of the late 1990s, for example. Several market-research firms projected the growth of online advertising by drawing analogies between the Internet and other forms of media. They examined the historical growth in advertising in these industries, and they projected Internet growth by selecting the analogy that they deemed most appropriate. In doing so, they failed to recognize critical differences between the Web and other forms of media, such as television and radio. Similarly, many research firms project the demand for new technologies by drawing analogies to the adoption rates for videocassette recorders, personal computers, and cell phones. Again, the differences between these technologies are often rather striking, yet they receive scant attention. In sum, reasoning by analogy can be a quite powerful tool. Managers encounter problems not because they choose to reason in this manner, but because they often do not select the appropriate analogies.[25]

Rules of Thumb

In many situations, managers seek to adopt a rule of thumb, or heuristic, to simplify a complicated decision. These shortcuts reduce the amount of information that decision makers need to process, and shorten the time required analyze a complex problem.[26] Often, an entire industry or profession adopts a common rule of thumb. For example, mortgage lenders assume that consumers should spend no more than 28 percent of their gross monthly income on mortgage payments and other home-related expenses. This provides a simple method for weeding out consumers with high default risk. Computer hardware engineers and software programmers have adopted many rules of thumb to simplify their work. Many of us are familiar with one such rule, Moore's law, which predicts that the processing power of computer chips will double approximately every 18 months.[27] Finally, the conventional wisdom in the venture capital industry used to suggest that firms should demonstrate four consecutive quarters of profits before an initial public offering. Alas, many venture capitalists regret abandoning this rule during the dot-com frenzy of the late 1990s.

In most cases, heuristics enable managers to make sound judgments in an efficient manner. Rules of thumb can be dangerous, however. They do not apply equally well to all situations—there are always exceptions to the rule. Whereas industries and firms employ many idiosyncratic rules of thumb, researchers also have identified several more general heuristics that can lead to systematic biases in judgment. Let's consider two prominent shortcuts: availability and anchoring. Individuals typically do not conduct a thorough statistical analysis to assess the likelihood that a particular event will take place in the future. Instead, they tend to rely on information that is readily available to them to estimate probabilities. Vivid experiences and recent events usually quickly come to mind and have undue influence on people's decision making. This availability heuristic usually serves people well. However, in some cases, easily recalled information does not always prove relevant to the current situation and may distort our predictions.

When making estimates, many people also begin with an initial number drawn from some information accessible to them at the time, and they adjust their estimate up or down from that starting point. Unfortunately, the initial number often serves as an overly powerful anchor and restrains individuals from making a sufficient adjustment. Researchers have shown that this "anchoring bias" affects decision making even if people know that the initial starting point is a random number drawn from the spin of a roulette wheel! In sum, many different rules of thumb provide a powerful means of making decisions rapidly, but they also impair managerial judgment when people do not recognize their drawbacks and limitations.[28]

Imitation

Some business leaders emulate the strategies and practices of other highly successful firms when faced with contentious and complex decisions. After all, why reinvent the wheel—one way to simplify a complex problem is to find someone else who has already solved it.

Learning from others can pay huge dividends. At General Electric, former CEO Jack Welch launched a major "best practices" initiative in 1988. He credits this initiative with fundamentally changing the way that GE does business and producing substantial productivity gains. Welch and his management team identified approximately 20 organizations that had long track records of more rapid productivity growth than GE. For more than a year, GE managers closely studied a few of these firms. They borrowed ideas liberally from these organizations and adapted others' strategies and processes to fit GE's businesses. For instance, they learned quick market intelligence from Wal-Mart and new product development methods from Hewlett-Packard and Chrysler. Over time, imitating others became a way of life at GE, and it produced amazing results.[29]

All this learning sounds wonderful, but imitation has its drawbacks. In many industries, firms engage in "herd behavior." They begin to adopt similar business strategies, rather than developing and preserving unique sources of competitive advantage. Take, for example, the credit-card industry. Many firms have tried to emulate the highly successful business model developed by Capital One. Over time, company marketing and distribution policies have begun to look alike, rivalry has intensified, and industry profitability has eroded. Consider too the many instances in which a leading firm decides to merge with a rival, touching off a wave of copycat acquisitions throughout an industry.[30]

At times, executives may feel safe imitating their rivals rather than going out on a limb with a novel business strategy. However, the essence of good strategy is to develop a unique system of activities that enables the organization to differentiate itself from the competition or to deliver products and services at a lower cost than its rivals. Simply copying the strategies and practices of rival firms will not produce a unique and defensible strategic position.[31] It takes great courage to stand alone when rivals engage in herd behavior, but it can pay huge dividends. Being different does not mean that a firm refuses to learn from others. For instance, General Dynamics studied its rivals very closely during the turmoil in the defense industry in the early 1990s, and observed that many firms had decided to pursue commercial diversification to compensate for diminishing military spending. The company's historical analysis indicated that aerospace firms had not fared well during past diversification efforts. Therefore, it chose to focus on defense despite the precipitous decline in industry demand. Many rivals ridiculed this strategy at the time, yet for the past decade, General Dynamics has generated shareholder returns well in excess of most large competitors.[32]

Failing to Solve the Underlying Problem

These decision-making shortcuts—reasoning by analogy, applying rules of thumb, and imitating others—clearly have their merits. Despite some limitations and pitfalls that we have identified, these strategies often serve a useful purpose for managers trying to make complicated decisions with incomplete information. However, these techniques do virtually nothing to alter the culture of indecision that often proves to be the true barrier to timely and effective execution within organizations. Tackling a culture of indecision requires leaders to focus not simply on the *cognitive* processes of judgment and problem-solving, but also the *interpersonal, emotional*, and *organizational* aspects of decision making. Leaders need to change the fundamental way that people interact with one another, both in and out of meetings, if they want to change a culture of indecision. They must teach others how to engage in more constructive and efficient dialogue and deliberation. They also must lead the decision process in a way that fosters commitment and shared understanding—a critical topic that the next chapter addresses.

The Origins of Indecisive Cultures

This chapter discussed the different patterns of behavior that constitute cultures of indecision. Leaders should keep in mind that those
behaviors may contribute to poor performance in the present, but the
roots of a culture of indecision often can be traced back to a time
when the organization performed remarkably well. Indeed, the very
same behaviors that contributed to the firm's past achievements may
have become problematic as internal and external conditions
changed.

How does this transformation from a decisive culture to an indecisive one take place? Where do dysfunctional behaviors emerge
from similar, yet constructive, patterns of interaction that took place
in the past? Take, for a moment, the example of Ken Olsen—the
founder and long-time CEO of Digital Equipment Corporation
(DEC). In his fascinating inside look at the company's history,
Massachusetts Institute of Technology Professor Edgar Schein
describes Olsen's decision-making philosophy:

> **I also observed over many meetings that Olsen had a**
> **genuine reluctance to say no. He preferred the group**
> **or the responsible manager to make the decision…It**
> **was pointed out over and over again in interviews that**
> **many of DEC's innovations were not Olsen's ideas but**
> **that Olsen created a climate of support for new ideas**
> **so that subordinates felt empowered to try new and**
> **different things.**[33]

Olsen liked to think of the company as a marketplace of ideas,
and he felt that the best strategies and decisions would emerge from
the conflict and competition in that marketplace. He enjoyed playing
the devil's advocate and probing people's thinking, but he did not
want to dictate choices to his people. Olsen let his people hash out
their own differences. The culture embodied Olsen's management

philosophy and style; in other words, his approach to decision making permeated all levels of the firm. The DEC style of decision making worked well during the early years when the company had little hierarchy, few lines of business, and everyone knew one another quite well. Over time, however, multiple organizational units emerged, and their interests diverged. People did not know others who worked in different functional areas. The marketplace of ideas began to break down; good concepts had trouble achieving priority and garnering resources, and bad ideas seemed to never die. Affective conflict, political stalemates, and endless recycling of ideas and proposals began to characterize the firm's decision-making processes. In short, the culture created by Olsen had become rigid, and it did not adapt as needs and pressures from the external environment and internal organization changed.[34]

Don Barrett experienced a similar problem at All-Star Sports. When Barrett launched the catalog division for the retailer, he had a small management team consisting of people with similar backgrounds and cognitive styles. He could tackle a complex issue one on one with an executive and then bring it back to the team for discussion and ratification, and the others had little reluctance expressing their concerns and objections candidly during staff meetings. However, as the catalog division grew rapidly, the organization became more complex. Through acquisition, the division now had multiple lines of business. The management team grew in size, and it now had members with different backgrounds, personalities, and leadership styles. When Barrett and others employed the decision-making approach that had worked so effectively in the past, it backfired. The newer members of the management team did not feel comfortable with the on line/off line approach, and the group found it difficult to reach closure in a timely manner. The context had changed, and the decision-making culture had not adapted.

This chapter argued that chronic indecisiveness does not simply reflect a problematic leadership style or personality deficiencies of an organization's leader. The problem tends to be deeply rooted in the tacit, often taken-for-granted, assumptions that people hold about how to work and interact with one another. Indecision often occurs at multiple levels of the firm and across many different functional units or lines of business. Habitual patterns of dialogue and interpersonal interaction are deeply rooted in an organization's history, perhaps stretching all the way back to the influence of its founders. Such patterns prove difficult to change, in part because a variant of that behavior contributed to the firm's prior success.

As a new leader takes charge and witnesses a tendency for indecision in an organization, he can take the first steps toward transforming the culture by examining how he interacts with his own senior management team. One can begin to alter the culture by modeling desired behaviors as he leads the top team's decision-making processes, fosters constructive conflict, and yet still achieves closure in a timely and efficient manner. Group members take their cues from those dialogues and deliberations. With some deft coaching and timely feedback, those managers can begin to change how they interact with their subordinates as well. As Ram Charan writes, "By using each encounter with his employees as an opportunity to model open, honest, and decisive dialogue, the leader sets the tone for the entire organization."[35] What, then, are these behaviors that leaders should model for others? How does one foster commitment and shared understanding and ultimately enhance the likelihood of achieving timely closure on contentious issues? For the answer to that critical question, one must turn the page.

7

FAIR AND LEGITIMATE PROCESS

"It is easier to make certain things legal than to make them legitimate."

—Sebastien-Roch Chamfort, French playwright

Mark Ager's firm had designed a software application that was earning rave reviews from its primary customer. The U.S. military employed the company's innovative expert diagnostic system for the control, maintenance, and repair of sophisticated weaponry. In the late 1990s, the company's engineers and programmers discovered, quite opportunistically, that a firm in the automobile industry had an interest in this software application. The company soon landed a lucrative contract with its first major nondefense customer. The technical staff worked feverishly to adapt the software to meet this client's needs, and they began to grow excited about the possibility of finding customers who could use the technology in a wide range of nonmilitary applications. As head of business development, Ager believed that the firm did not have the marketing and distribution capability required to commercialize the technology successfully. In his view, the company needed a strategic partner. He set out to find the perfect match. Moreover, he began to sell his colleagues on the concept of an alliance or joint venture.

Moving quickly, Ager identified several software firms offering similar types of products, and he initiated informal conversations with members of each organization. He consulted a few colleagues about the potential partners, but he chose to "play it close to the vest" until he learned more about each firm and come to some conclusions. Before long, he focused his attention on a rapidly growing company recognized for its strong national sales organization and a product line that appeared to complement his firm's new expert diagnostic system. At this point, he began to work closely with a fellow executive who maintained responsibility for the software product's development and financial performance. After more discussions with the potential alliance partner, Ager's intuition told him that he had found a good fit; his colleague agreed wholeheartedly. Now, they had to bring all their colleagues on board.

It took much longer than Ager expected to build consensus among senior managers, and he encountered substantial obstacles along the way. Why did he find it so time-consuming and challenging to achieve buy-in for his proposal? Interestingly, very few colleagues reported serious misgivings about his recommendation; they *did* have concerns about how he had managed the decision process. One executive said:

> **As champion, he sold it. He sold the concept that we had to have an alliance or a partnership. Once the process started, it was relatively secretive. I knew it was going on. If I asked some pointed questions, I'd get some answers, but there were no briefings, there was no discussion, there was no passing a document around for view, anything of that sort.**

This manager's feelings reflect the concerns expressed by many of Ager's colleagues. They thought that he had not managed an open and transparent process in which people with diverse perspectives, interests, and expertise had an opportunity to influence the final decision. Some managers indicated that they felt the choice was "preordained" by the time they had an opportunity to weigh in with their opinions. This dissatisfaction with the nature of the decision-making process impeded the development of commitment to the proposed course of action. Ager's troubles demonstrate an important lesson for all managers. Individuals do not care only about the *outcome* of a decision; they care about the nature of the *process* as well. Specifically, if members of an organization perceive a decision process as unfair and illegitimate, they are far less likely to commit to the chosen course of action, *even if* they agree with many aspects of the plan itself. This chapter explores the meaning of procedural fairness and legitimacy, and examines how these two process attributes form the building blocks of management consensus and pave the way for a smooth implementation effort.

Many leaders do not think in these terms when they try to build consensus and achieve closure in their firms. Naturally, they believe that consensus building on complex issues requires a healthy dose of persuasion coupled with the ability to negotiate compromises among senior executives whose interests sometimes clash.[1] Yet, building commitment and shared understanding begins with the construction of a solid foundation to the decision-making process; a leader tills the soil so that it is fertile for consensus building by creating processes that are fair and legitimate. Only then can leaders apply their persuasion and negotiation capabilities to craft decisions with strong buy-in from all key parties in the organization. Through it all, of course, leaders need to manage conflict effectively, so that interpersonal friction and personality clashes do not erode the development of commitment and impede the firm's ability to implement its plans.

Fair Process

During a decision-making process, some individuals will have their views accepted by the group, while other proposals garner little support. Advocates for each alternative hone their arguments, often believing that they must change others' minds to garner their commitment and cooperation during the implementation process. The presumption that one must alter the opinions of others to secure their buy-in to a plan proves to be false. Unanimity usually proves to be an elusive goal in a decision-making process. Not everyone will agree with the final choice, no matter how ardently advocates try to change the minds of their opponents. One may think that a lack of unanimity creates an obstacle to implementation. However, this absence of ultimate agreement may not be a problem, if everyone believes that the organization employed a fair and just process for arriving at a decision. People do not have to agree with a plan to support an organization's efforts to execute it. If individuals perceive the process of deliberation as fair, they are more likely to cooperate during implementation, even if they disagree with the chosen course of action. Naturally, leading a fair process does not guarantee commitment, but it raises the odds quite substantially.

Defining the Concept

What does it mean for a process to be fair? To answer this question, we begin by turning to an interesting stream of research in the field of law, which has subsequently had an enormous impact on those who study how decisions are made in business organizations. Scholars John Thibault and Laurens Walker first demonstrated that people engaged in a legal dispute do not care only about distributive justice (i.e., whether the outcome constituted a fair and equitable division of resources among the parties).[2] Their work challenged the fundamental notion that people only cared about the extent to which they receive a favorable verdict in a legal proceeding. Thibault and Walker illustrated that a disputant's satisfaction with a verdict was "affected substantially by factors other than whether the individual in question has won or lost the dispute."[3] In fact, the choice of procedure employed to resolve the legal dispute mattered a great deal. For instance, they showed that disputants cared a great deal about whether a particular procedure provided more or less opportunity for biases to affect the outcome.

Subsequent research by Tom Tyler and others showed that higher perceptions of procedural fairness tended to be associated with more favorable evaluations of the people and institutions involved in a legal proceeding as well as greater satisfaction with the entire court experience. Perhaps most interestingly, Tyler also demonstrated that the use of fair processes provides a "cushion of support" for authorities when they make a ruling that is objectively unfavorable for the individual involved.[4] When unfair procedures were employed, individuals receiving a favorable verdict expressed much higher levels of satisfaction with their legal experience. However, with fair procedures, people receiving an unfavorable verdict expressed a level of satisfaction much closer to the satisfaction levels of those who secured a favorable outcome! Other studies have confirmed this "cushion of support" effect provided by fair legal processes. Figure 7-1 shows the result from one such study by Adler, Hensler, and Nelson in 1983.

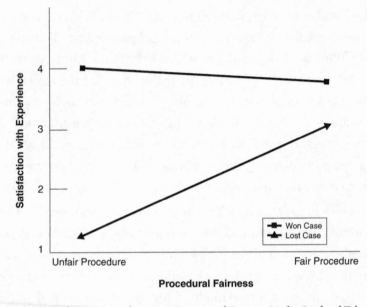

Reprinted with kind permission of Springer Science and Business Media. Lind and Tyler. (1988). *The Psychology of Procedural Justice*. Figure 4.3.

FIGURE 7-1:   Procedural fairness and the "cushion of support"

How do these findings in the field of law inform our understanding of how business leaders can build consensus when making critical choices in their firms? It turns out that individuals care a great deal about the perceived fairness of organizational decision-making processes, just as they care about the fairness of legal proceedings. Some managers equate fairness with "voice"—i.e., giving everyone a chance to air his views and ideas. Yet, procedural justice entails more than just allowing people to express their opinions openly and candidly. People want to feel that they have been heard when they have spoken, and they desire a real opportunity to affect the decisions made by their leaders.[5] They do not want to feel as though their leaders have engaged in what my colleague Michael Watkins refers to as a "charade of consultation"—a process steered by the leader to arrive at a preordained outcome (see Figure 7-2).

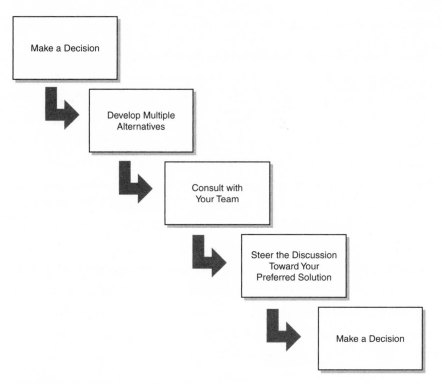

FIGURE 7-2: **The "charade of consultation"**

Specifically, individuals tend to perceive decision processes as fair if they

- Have ample opportunity to express their views, and to discuss how and why they disagree with other group members.

- Feel that that decision-making process has been transparent (i.e., the deliberations have been relatively free of secretive, behind-the-scenes maneuvering).

- Believe that the leader listened carefully to them and considered their views thoughtfully and seriously before making a decision.

- Perceive that they had a genuine opportunity to influence the leader's final decision.

- Have a clear understanding of the rationale for the final decision.[6]

Leading Fair Processes

What can leaders do to enhance the perceived fairness of a decision-making process? The answer is simple to articulate, yet frustratingly difficult to execute at times—they must demonstrate authentic consideration of others' views. That is, leaders have to show that they have paid close attention to the proposals put forth by their colleagues and advisers, and that they have contemplated and evaluated those views seriously and genuinely before choosing a course of action. In a fascinating experimental study, Audrey Korsgaard, David Schweiger, and Harry Sapienza showed that "the manner in which team leaders elicit, receive, and respond to team members' input affects their attitudes toward the decisions themselves and toward other members of teams, including the leaders."[7] In short, demonstrating consideration for others' views enhanced perceptions of fairness, commitment to the final decision, attachment to the group, and trust in the leader (see Figure 7-3).

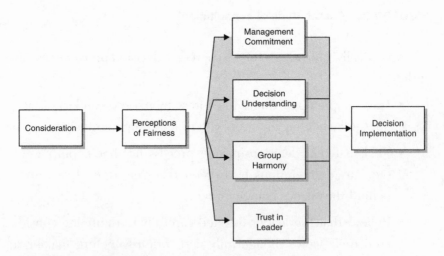

FIGURE 7-3:   The effects of consideration

Leaders can employ a number of techniques to ensure that others conclude that their views have been considered in a genuine manner (see Table 7-1). To begin with, a leader should make a concerted effort to provide a clear process roadmap, meaning that he describes how the decision process will unfold.[8] He explains the key steps in the process, the role that he will play in the discussion, and the manner in which he expects team members to contribute to the dialogue. The leader also makes it very clear how the final decision will be made (i.e., at what point and in what manner he will bring the discussion to a close and select a course of action). The theory is simple—no surprises!

TABLE 7-1: Demonstrating Consideration

Leader Techniques	Illustrative Statements
Provide a process roadmap	Here are the key steps in the decision process, and here is how I plan to make the final decision.
Reinforce an open mindset	I have some thoughts about how we should proceed, but my position is tentative. I am open to changing my mind. Let me remind you how I have amended my initial views in the past.
Listen actively	I think you are suggesting that none of the existing options enables us to meet our objectives. Have I understood you correctly?
Explain the decision rationale	I selected this course of action based upon the following criteria....
Explain how input has been used	Your views and advice regarding this decision influenced my thinking in the following way....
Express appreciation	I am very grateful for all of the input and advice that I have received. Everyone's comments have been valuable.

For instance, if one wanted to employ a Dialectical Inquiry approach to decision making, he should explain that the team will split into subgroups, generate alternatives, and then critique each other's proposals. He might even provide a bit of guidance as to how the subgroups should present their proposals to one another (i.e., written versus oral form, explicit statement of assumptions, clear documentation of supporting evidence, etc.) The leader would then go on to explain how he intended to interact with the subgroups, and perhaps state that he planned to make the decision after hearing a final debate between the subgroups. Naturally, a leader must remain flexible, and be willing to alter this process roadmap as deliberations unfold and unexpected twists and turns arise. Clearly, however, one must remember to communicate clearly how and why the original roadmap will be revised due to changing conditions.

Having established a vision of how the process will unfold, a leader must be proactive about countering the impression that the decision has already been made. He must ensure that others do not conclude that he simply wants to create the *appearance* of a consultative decision process. In many organizations, individuals have grown accustomed to "sham" decision processes. In those cases especially, leaders need to combat that deep-seated cynicism before moving forward. Some leaders accomplish that by choosing not to state their views at the start of the decision process, and by declaring that they need to hear everyone's thoughts and ideas before formulating an opinion on the matter at hand. Others may express an initial position on the issues, but make it very clear that they are open to changing their minds. A leader might even cite an instance in the recent past, when consultation with others had led to a complete reversal or significant adjustment in his views.[9]

After deliberations begin, leaders can demonstrate consideration by engaging in active listening, rather than sitting rather passively as people present ideas and proposals. Active listening shows that the leader is paying close attention to each speaker, and is trying hard to develop a thorough and accurate understanding of each person's views. When leaders engage in active listening, they ask questions for clarification or further explanation, test for understanding, and avoid interrupting people as they express their ideas. They take detailed notes as each person speaks, and they "playback" what they hear— that is, the leader summarizes each person's comments and asks the individual if that re-statement represents an accurate description of his proposal. Finally, leaders need to provide individuals with an opportunity to restate their recommendations if they believe that they have been misunderstood.[10] To evaluate your own listening skills, consider the questions shown in Table 7-2. If you answer "yes" to most of those questions, make a commitment to improving your capability to listen actively and effectively.[11]

TABLE 7-2:   Do You Listen Effectively?

1.	Do you avoid eye contact when others are speaking to you?
2.	Do you multitask during meetings?
3.	Do you interrupt often when others are talking?
4.	Do you rarely pause to solicit feedback or questions while you are speaking?
5.	Do you become easily distracted when others are presenting their ideas?
6.	Do you engage in side conversations on a regular basis during meetings?
7.	Do you provide many more answers than questions during group discussions?
8.	Do you rarely rephrase people's statements and confirm your interpretation?

Some leaders may believe that demonstrations of consideration end when deliberations are complete and they have chosen a course of action. That presumption proves to be false. Specifically, leaders tend to enhance perceptions of procedural fairness if they explain the rationale for their decision after it has been made. An effective explanation typically outlines the criteria employed to evaluate various alternatives and select a course of action. The leader also should explain how he incorporated each person's input into the final decision, as well as why he may have chosen not to take someone's advice. Individuals want to know how they contributed to the final outcome, and often, they even desire an explanation for why the leader has chosen not to heed key aspects of their advice.[12]

Finally, leaders enhance perceptions of fairness if they express appreciation for the input that they have received before announcing their choice. As they speak to their teams, leaders should note that, although they value all ideas, they may choose not to adopt the recommendations presented to them during the decision-making process. For instance, Andrew Grove, former CEO of Intel, made it clear to his managers that he valued their input, and would try to listen and understand, although he might not heed their advice in all cases. Grove recalled telling his troops: "Give your considered opinion and give it clearly and forcefully. Your criterion for involvement should be that you're heard and understood. Clearly, all sides cannot prevail in the debate, but all opinions have value in shaping the right answer."

As Mark Ager tried to persuade his colleagues that his firm should pursue an alliance with a software provider that he considered a perfect fit, he did not consider others' perceptions of procedural fairness. Having made up his mind by the time he consulted with many key parties, he had a difficult time overcoming the belief that he was driving the process to the conclusion that he desired. Although he asked for people's thoughts and opinions and may very well have wanted to hear their input, most individuals wondered whether they could affect the outcome of the decision process. Don Barrett faced a similar problem at All-Star Sports. When he asked his entire senior management team to ratify decisions he had arrived at with a small subgroup of advisors, many executives felt that it was too late to have a genuine opportunity to influence the final decision. Dismayed by the lack of transparency and the feeling that they could not reverse the decision at that point, they often did not speak their minds and raise objections during the staff meetings.

Fair Process in Action

When Paul Levy arrived at the Beth Israel Deaconess Medical Center, prior management often had presented plans to the staff without building a sense of collective ownership. People often felt that plans came down from on high as *fait accompli*. The chiefs (the physicians who led each department in the hospital) often became frustrated because they did not believe that management listened and *considered* their views. Levy went to great lengths to change the atmosphere and ensure that people had an opportunity to voice their opinions on major policy issues, and then he demonstrated consideration for their views while always making it very clear that he would make the final call. Before he took the job, a consulting firm had conducted an extensive study of the problems at the hospital, but they had not yet released their findings. In his very first week at the hospital, he posted the consulting firm's recommendations on the organization's intranet and asked for feedback. He responded *personally* to more than 300 e-mails from staff members. One month later, as Levy announced his plan for turning around the hospital, he explained why he had accepted some of the recommendations made by the consultants, but not others, and he explicated precisely how he had utilized the feedback that he had received from people throughout the hospital. People knew the rationale for his decisions, and they could see how their ideas had shaped and influenced his thinking. Because of higher perceptions of procedural fairness, most individuals respected the fact that he had rejected some of their advice. Once again, he posted his turnaround plan on the intranet. This time, he asked everyone to "sign" the plan, solidifying the sense of collective ownership and commitment to the new strategy.

After putting forth his strategic plan, Levy established a series of task forces to develop specific plans for how to achieve the goals that he had outlined. As he created the task forces, Levy made it clear how he expected the decision-making process to unfold. In short, he laid out a process roadmap and secured everyone's commitment to the *process*, long before anyone knew what recommendations the committees would develop. Specifically, Levy provided a broad outline of how the task forces would do their work—how they were to analyze how to improve certain areas of the hospital, as well as the role that he and the department chiefs would play in the final decision-making process. Levy did not want the chiefs to meddle in the work of each committee, leading once again to a pattern of indecision and action. He gave the task forces the freedom to collect data, evaluate options, and develop recommendations. Then, he expected the chiefs to assess the proposals put forth by each task force, and to offer him input and advice. Levy promised not to execute any major recommendations without consulting the chiefs. However, he retained the right to make the final decision if the chiefs could not come to an agreement. Levy made it clear that people had to voice their objections openly when he asked for advice, rather than staying silent and working behind the scenes to undermine key decisions as they had in the past. Because he created stronger perceptions of procedural fairness, individuals started to become much more comfortable expressing their views openly during staff meetings. The "culture of yes" began to change.

Note that Levy did not institute a democracy at the BIDMC. Far from it, indeed! He made tough decisions to cut costs, reduce headcount, and restructure operations—often making choices that went counter to the wishes of his staff. Despite his tough measures and decisive actions, he built commitment and shared understanding for his turnaround plan because people believed that he had operated in a just and transparent manner.

Some leaders may believe that fair process works fine without time constraints, but that the need for speed and efficiency precludes demonstrating consideration in times of crisis. This line of reasoning proves incorrect. Consider NASA's Apollo 13 mission to the moon in April 1970, in which an oxygen tank explosion aboard the spacecraft nearly led to catastrophe. Flight Director Gene Kranz led a remarkable creative effort to engineer a solution that would enable the astronauts to return to Earth safely.[13] He asked his team for unvarnished advice, and he listened carefully as technical experts debated multiple options for bringing the crew home. People trusted Kranz because he asked lots of questions, pushed for clarification when people made their arguments, tested for understanding, and demonstrated repeatedly that he could acknowledge when his initial thinking was incorrect. Kranz described the decision-making process:

I used the same brainstorming techniques used in mission rules or training debriefings, thinking out loud so that everyone understood the options, alternatives, risks, and uncertainties of every path. The controllers, engineers, and support team chipped in, correcting me, bringing up new alternatives, and challenging my intended direction. This approach had been perfected over years, but it had to be disciplined, not a free-for-all. The lead controllers and I acted as moderators, sometimes brusquely terminating discussions...With a team working in this fashion, not concerned with voicing their opinions freely and without worrying about hurting anyone's feelings, we *saved* time *[emphasis added]*. Everyone became part of the solution.[14]

Note that Kranz remained firmly in control, and he made tough, rapid decisions that often required him to reject the advice and input of very capable subordinates. Yet, people trusted him completely and dedicated themselves completely to the execution of his decisions. Their trust came, in part, from their admiration of his technical expertise; but, his leadership of the brainstorming process and his strong listening skills affirmed and enhanced that trust. Moreover, he found that leading a fair process "saved time" rather than causing costly delays, because he could quickly gather information and advice from a wide variety of sources.

Legitimate Process

When Jurgen Schrempp took over as CEO of Daimler Benz, he discovered that the company had become incredibly bureaucratic; division heads ran their units as independent fiefdoms, and many businesses did not earn an adequate return on capital employed. He sought to restructure the organization and streamline its complicated governance structure. He also wanted to assert control over the "feudal lords" that led key units. In particular, Schrempp decided to assert control over the highly independent Mercedes subsidiary. He wanted to fold Mercedes into Daimler, thereby eliminating the subsidiary's fiercely independent CEO and management board and reducing extensive duplication of functions between the corporate office and headquarters of the business unit. Yet, Schrempp did not just make the decision to restructure the organization. Instead, he asked a key lieutenant to develop eight alternatives for reorganizing the corporate governance structure, and all the while steering the discussion toward his preferred solution. Bill Vlasic and Bradley Stertz, authors of an insightful book that chronicled the events leading up to the Daimler-Chrysler merger, explained how the decision-making process unfolded:

> **Schrempp, the canny chess player, didn't want to bring his chosen solution to Daimler's management and supervisory boards as the only alternative. No, there must be a variety of choices to stimulate discussion, allow the board members to be part of the process, and dispel any notion that Schrempp was forcing it down their throats...[The management team] debated the various options. Schrempp always came back to Model Number Six, which merged Mercedes into Daimler and abolished the position of the Mercedes CEO.[15]**

Why did Schrempp present so many alternatives if he had already made up his mind? Why did he believe that he had something to gain by outlining eight alternatives? Schrempp clearly had a method to his madness; he had carefully thought through his strategy for leading the decision-making process. He believed that presenting multiple options provided a key benefit to him. However, in cases such as this one, managers often recognize how a leader has manipulated the decision process. That recognition shapes their perceptions moving forward, and it may imperil the implementation of future choices. In fact, Schrempp used this style of decision making again during the Chrysler merger deliberations, and in part, that may explain why the organization encountered such difficulties during the integration process.[16]

What Is Procedural Legitimacy?

The Daimler example highlights how efforts to enhance procedural legitimacy affect the development of consensus in organizations. What do we mean by *procedural legitimacy*? Organizational sociologists define the concept as the perception that organizational processes and techniques are "desirable, proper, or appropriate within some socially constructed system of norms, values, beliefs, and definitions."[17] That may seem like a mouthful, but the concept is rather simple. People come to believe that there is a "right way" to do certain things in organizations, and they are more accepting of outcomes if the process that they observe conforms to that "right way."

How do concerns about procedural legitimacy affect decision making in firms? Scholars Martha Feldman and James March once observed that "organizations systematically gather more information than they use, yet continue to ask for more."[18] They argued that firms employ information for its symbolic value, as well as for its effect on the quality of a decision. Gathering extensive amounts of information symbolizes that managers are engaging in a comprehensive and analytical decision-making process. Feldman and March suggest that social norms and values emphasize the merits of rational, or comprehensive, decision making. Thus, gathering extensive amounts of data *legitimizes* a decision process. Put another way, people feel more confident in the decision itself, because they recognize that the process was conducted in the "right way"—i.e., in a highly analytical, data-driven manner. Individuals will not commit to a decision if they believe the process was irrational, incomplete, or just plain sloppy.

As Feldman and March argued, "Using information, asking for information, and justifying decisions in terms of information have all come to be significant ways in which we symbolize that the process is legitimate."[19]

Other actions may symbolize rational choice, and thereby bolster procedural legitimacy. In particular, the generation of multiple alternatives and the utilization of formal analytical techniques (such as a discounted cash flow model or psychometric market research study) also signify that managers are employing a thorough and logical decision-making process.[20] Thus, Schrempp may have put forth eight options, because he knew that others expected to see an extensive analysis of alternatives for any major strategic choice. He recognized that board members would not accept and support a recommendation that lacked a comparative analysis of multiple options, even if the content of the recommended plan of action seemed sensible and feasible.

Managers hire external consultants to convey a sense of process legitimacy as well. To be sure, many readers have experienced this phenomenon. A firm's executives know what course of action they would like to take, but the use of well-known consultancies with highly respected reputations provides a "stamp of approval" for their plans. The consultants apply a series of analytical frameworks to justify the course of action that executives would like to undertake. The confirmation from a credible outside source, backed by formal analysis, helps to solidify internal support for a decision, and it protects managers from the potential charge that they did not think through the issue thoroughly before taking action.

Destroying Legitimacy

Unfortunately, efforts to enhance process legitimacy may not always produce the desired effect. Scholars Blake Ashforth and Barrie Gibbs point out that, in some cases, constituents may perceive attempts to legitimate processes as "manipulative and illegitimate."[21] Indeed, the findings of my research suggest that symbolic activity undertaken during the decision-making process may backfire, decreasing legitimacy and diminishing the formation of consensus.[22] For example, individuals may present a list of alternatives for purely symbolic reasons, rather than because they want to generate an authentic debate and consideration of those options. Others may perceive these proposals as "token alternatives"—think of seven of the eight possible restructuring plans outlined by Schrempp and his lieutenant—and conclude that individuals are attempting to manipulate the decision-making process. Similarly, someone may present a discounted cash flow model because executives within that firm typically value such structured techniques for evaluating capital investments, but the results may be skewed to justify a particular proposal rather than to evaluate multiple options equitably. If so, these attempts to enhance procedural legitimacy and persuade others to support a particular proposal actually will de-legitimize the process and reduce management buy-in.

Leaders must remember that individuals make critical attributions during decision-making processes. They attribute motives to others' actions.[23] They may perceive extensive information gathering, alternative generation, and the use of formal analytical techniques as authentic efforts intended to enhance the quality of the decision. On the other hand, they may believe that others are trying to manipulate, "rig," or preordain the process. If individuals perceive self-serving motives on the part of others, they become disenchanted with the decision process, and that disillusionment hinders the leader's ability to build consensus and achieve closure.

Just as leaders need to evaluate how their own actions affect perceptions of legitimacy, they also must monitor the legitimacy of others' actions. Ardent advocates of a proposal, such as Mark Ager, will strive for process legitimacy as they try to sell their ideas to superiors, peers, and subordinates. However, they can do more harm than good if the leader does not recognize and address the problem quickly.

Consider again Mark Ager's efforts to persuade others to support his alliance proposal. He offered a number of "token alternatives" during the decision process. A token alternative is a proposal that draws a significant amount of discussion and analysis, but is not ever considered seriously. A token alternative differs in an important way from a "straw man"—which has a great deal of value in a decision process. With a straw man, people understand that it will never be implemented, but they recognize the value of discussing it as a means of testing assumptions and stimulating critical thinking about a complex issue. In the case of token alternatives, people present options purely for symbolic reasons, rather than for their substantive value. Upon reflection, Ager recognized that he had offered token alternatives to the management team:

> **We did some internal analysis about who were the software tool providers that we should team with. We had a chart that said that what we ought to do is team with a tool provider. And we had a bunch of alternatives listed. And to be honest with you, between Bill and I— it was kind of a half-assed attempt, because we knew we wanted to go with ZTech. But, we were filling in the required work that said: Would you go with Jet Corp.? No, why not? Would you go with Keystone? No, why not? So, we had that list.**

The quote implies that Ager felt compelled to offer multiple options to make the process appear thorough and analytical, and to conform to the "standard way" in which people expected such decisions to be made at the firm. However, others understood the game being played. They perceived these efforts as manipulative. One executive noted, "I don't think we looked at anybody seriously except for ZTech." Another explained, "This was pretty ordained from the first day. They knew they were going to do this, and this six months of...this has just been goofing around."

Token alternatives appear to be a rather common feature of many firm's decision processes, and they typically do not fly under the radar—people recognize the self-serving behavior in most cases, and the leader often finds that the decision process grinds to a halt as procedural legitimacy collapses.

A similar phenomenon takes place with regard to information gathering in many organizations. Individuals naturally want to use data to support their arguments, justify assumptions, and persuade others to endorse their proposals. Often, they present extensive amounts of data to convince others that they have done a thorough investigation of the issues at hand. However, my research suggests that individuals employ two different approaches to disseminating that information prior to critical meetings. In some cases, managers provide each attendee with all available information prior to key deliberations. In other instances, managers provide some colleagues with more information than others. In many cases, this phenomenon occurs because individuals try to "pre-sell" a few key executives on the merits of their proposals prior to meetings, and to build a coalition that will support them during the group deliberations. To persuade these influential executives, individuals provide them with preferential access to key data prior to group discussions.

The failure to disseminate information to all participants prior to key meetings typically harms process legitimacy, rather than enhancing it. People feel disadvantaged if they are examining data for the first time, while others have reviewed it earlier. Individuals question whether their views and opinions are truly valued, if others have failed to share information with them. In addition, participants wonder whether they can influence the opinions of those with privileged access to data, or whether these individuals have established strong, unalterable preconceived notions.

An organizational restructuring decision at Ager's firm illustrates the problem caused by unequal dissemination of information. One executive shared data about various alternatives with only a few other staff members prior to a major offsite meeting. When he did provide extensive data to the entire group, individuals were not impressed by the thoroughness of the intelligence gathering effort, but instead, felt as though he was presenting them with a *fait accompli*. The vice president of engineering explained what happened at the start of the offsite meeting:

> **We had an offsite meeting, and Dave tried to show the team that he had investigated all the options carefully. Ron and I were the only people besides Dave who had examined the data at that point. It became apparent very quickly to the rest of the staff, after they didn't see me shrink like a violet in my chair, that I had seen the data already. So I'm a bad guy right away...I don't think that this decision was preordained, but that's what many people believed during and after that discussion, even to this day.**

Preserving Process Legitimacy

How, then, do leaders preserve the legitimacy of a decision-making process? They cannot eliminate symbolic behavior—at times, it has great value in organizations. People always will evaluate decision processes against a set of societal and organizational values and norms regarding what constitute the "right ways" to make complex choices.[24] Thus, individuals have an inherent incentive to signal that they have gathered extensive data, examined an exhaustive list of options, and employed favorite analytical methods.

Recognizing that fact, leaders still can take steps to ensure that symbolic behavior does not become a road block to consensus (see Figure 7-4). First, leaders must ensure that all participants in a decision process have equal access to information, to the greatest extent possible. If they want to build commitment, leaders need to create a level playing field before initiating a debate among their advisers and subordinates.

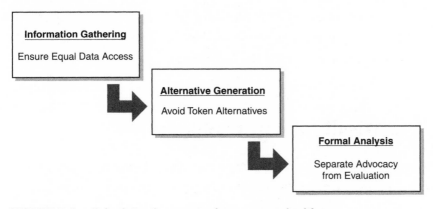

FIGURE 7-4:   Principles for preserving process legitimacy

Second, leaders can test for the presence of token alternatives, and then either take them off the table or force serious consideration of those proposals. They might have to push their teams to invent new options that do warrant genuine consideration. Moreover, leaders ought to distinguish clearly between a "straw man" being used to push critical divergent thinking and a token alternative being used in a manipulative manner.

Finally, leaders should strive to separate advocacy from evaluation. Recall the Kennedy handling of the Bay of Pigs decision. Presidential adviser Arthur Schlesinger states that the CIA presented "a proposal on which they had personally worked for a long time and in which their organization had a heavy vested interest. This cast them in the role less of analysts, than of advocates."[25] As political scientist Alexander George points out, flawed reasoning can go untested "when the key assumptions and premises of a plan have been evaluated only by the advocates of that option."[26] Interestingly, my research suggests that separating advocacy from evaluation does not only enhance the quality of decisions, but it also tends to enhance process legitimacy and management consensus. To separate advocacy from evaluation, leaders can ask multiple units of the organization to conduct independent evaluations of the proposals under consideration, as Kennedy did during the Cuban missile crisis. In some situations, leaders might even invite third parties—unbiased experts of some kind—to provide objective analysis of the alternatives put forth by various advocates within the organization.

The Misalignment Problem

Leaders face one additional challenge when trying to foster procedural fairness and legitimacy. Simply put, many leaders have a hard time detecting whether a group perceives a decision process in the same way that they do. For example, when I surveyed Don Barrett and his management team at All-Star Sports, the results proved quite enlightening. On a series of questions that asked individuals to rate the management team's effectiveness, Barrett consistently reported much higher scores than the average of all other team members.[27] Barrett's case is not unique. Similar misalignment often occurs with regard to perceptions of procedural fairness and legitimacy. On many occasions, a leader believes that he has managed a decision process in a just and legitimate manner, but his advisers and subordinates find that he has not demonstrated sufficient consideration, or they detect the presence of token alternatives. If a leader proceeds under a false impression of the team's satisfaction with the decision process, he may find himself surprised when implementation goes astray amidst a lack of management buy-in.[28]

How then can leaders test to make sure that their team's perceptions of the process match their own? One can begin by making it a habit to conduct "process checks" from time to time as a decision unfolds. Management teams should practice auditing their decision-making processes, with particular attention paid to their ability to generate dissent, manage conflict constructively, and maintain fairness and legitimacy. These audits need not wait until a process has ended and a decision has been made; teams can perform quick assessments in real-time to ensure that a process is on track.

Second, leaders can take individuals aside and hold one-on-one meetings to test for alignment. Some individuals may be more comfortable expressing their concerns about a decision process in a private setting, rather than doing so amidst a group discussion.

Third, the leader can absent himself from a group meeting and ask members to discuss their concerns about the team's approach to decision making among themselves. In the leader's absence, people will feel more open to divulge their reservations about, for example, the extent to which a leader listens attentively and demonstrates genuine consideration for others' views.

Finally, a leader must pay close attention to body language and other nonverbal cues during meetings and other interactions with advisers and subordinates. People often express dissatisfaction or reservations about a decision process through facial expressions, gestures, or changes in their posture. If leaders observe troublesome cues such as these, they need to find time, perhaps outside of a group meeting, to question the individual about their perceptions of the decision process. They may have concerns about the content of that particular decision. In that case, by pulling them aside, the leader can uncover critical dissenting views that had not emerged. At times, though, the leader may discover that the nonverbal cues point to process concerns rather than disagreement pertaining to the subject matter being examined and discussed.

Teaching Good Process

Leadership requires more than just the personal practice of good process to build consensus and achieve closure. Leaders must teach effective process to the members of their team as well. After all, the entire team benefits when all members, not just the leader, learn active listening techniques and begin to demonstrate greater authentic consideration of others' views. Preserving the legitimacy of a decision process requires teamwork, too. The leader may present preordained decisions from time to time, compromising process legitimacy and management consensus. However, team members often damage process legitimacy through their vigorous advocacy of pet projects and proposals. Sound process leadership requires more than a policing or monitoring capability; it means educating all team members regarding how to elevate the fairness and legitimacy of the group decision process. By teaching good process, leaders also enhance the likelihood that decision making will improve at all levels of an organization. Of course, teaching is not always easy—sometimes, it requires the delivery of negative feedback and the willingness to instill discipline.[29]

At the Beth Israel Deaconess, Paul Levy set out to tackle the curious inability to decide, and to build more collective ownership around key decisions. He knew that decision making needed to change at all levels, not just within the executive suite. By practicing some of the principles of fair process, he began to encourage people to stop remaining silent during group discussions, and then undermining, objecting, and obstructing plans later after an apparent consensus had been reached (classic indications of the culture of yes that had developed over the years). He tried to teach good process to people at all levels by establishing new norms, modeling desired behaviors, and giving people an opportunity to practice approaches to decision making that were both fairer and more disciplined.

Not everyone got the message. In Levy's second month on the job, he discussed an important issue with his staff, and by the end of the meeting, he thought that the group had reached consensus on how to proceed. He reminded everyone of his efforts to combat the "culture of yes" and asked whether everyone truly supported the decision. No one expressed objections or concerns. Just a few days later, one chief complained publicly about the decision, despite having remained silent in the staff meeting. Levy chose to reprimand the individual publicly, pointing out that he had been given numerous opportunities to voice his ideas and concerns in a constructive manner. Of course, public criticism can be dangerous, but in this case, Levy employed it judiciously to reinforce the new behavioral norms. It became a teaching moment, not just for that individual but for the entire management team.

Levy also delegated many tactical decisions and responsibilities, providing managers at all levels the opportunity to practice new approaches to problem solving and decision making. He took on the job of monitoring the way that people went about making those decisions to ensure that people embraced the new norms and employed them effectively to achieve consensus and reach closure in a timely manner. However, he did not micromanage. As groups went about their work, Levy chose to think of himself as the organization's version of an appeals court judge. He did not want to review all cases *de novo* (starting all over) and simply overrule decisions made by the lower court; instead, he strove to "review the decision process used by the lower court to determine if it followed the rules."[30] If so, its decision often stood. If not, he intervened to teach his managers how to lead more effective decision-making processes. He did *not* simply correct their choice.[31]

What About Conflict?

This chapter focused on building consensus. Some might wonder what happened to all the talk about conflict, dissent, and divergent thinking. How does one reconcile this discussion of fairness and legitimacy with earlier descriptions of how leaders can stimulate the clash of ideas? The answer is actually rather simple. Let's go back to our definition of consensus. It does *not* equal unanimity or even majority rule. It does *not* mean that teams, rather than leaders, make decisions. It does *not* mean that one must find a compromise solution that marries elements of multiple options. Consensus means that people comprehend the final decision, have committed themselves to executing the chosen course of action, feel a sense of collective ownership about the plan, and are willing to cooperate with others during the implementation effort.

Leaders can and should build consensus even when team members cannot reach unanimous agreement on a complicated issue. In fact, too much unanimity ought to be a warning sign that people might feel unsafe expressing their views. Striving for consensus certainly does not mean minimizing conflict among the members of your management team. In fact, to build a strong and enduring consensus, leaders need to stimulate conflict, not avoid it.

Although that last statement may sound counterintuitive, think about the concepts of procedural fairness and legitimacy again. The opportunity to engage in vigorous debate plays a critical role in shaping perceptions of fairness and legitimacy. Individuals will not perceive a decision process to be fair if they have not had an opportunity to air their diverse points of view, and to disagree with one another—and the leader—openly and candidly. People do not consider a process to be legitimate if they are steered toward a preferred solution or presented with token alternatives; they want the opportunity to debate a genuine set of options on an equal playing field with their colleagues. Scholars W. Chan Kim and Renee Mauborgne try to dispel the notion that one must avoid conflict to build commitment and foster active cooperation:

> **Fair process does not set out to achieve harmony or to win people's support through compromises that accommodate every individual's opinions, needs, or interests… Nor is fair process the same as democracy in the workplace. Achieving fair process does not mean that managers forfeit their prerogative to make decisions.**[32]

Those final words remind us that, when all is said and done, people need to be led if an organization is to move forward. Not everyone will agree with the decisions that a leader makes. Yet, we have learned that people care about process, not simply the outcome or verdict. By creating fair and legitimate processes, leaders can create the "cushion of support" that enables them to make tough decisions, about which reasonable people will disagree. As leaders make difficult calls, they will have to step in to bring lively and argumentative decision processes to a close. In those instances, they need only remember the words an observant manager once shared with me: "People just want their positions heard. Then, they really want a choice to be made."

8

REACHING CLOSURE

**"Nothing is particularly hard if you divide
it into small jobs."**
—Henry Ford

During World War II, General Dwight Eisenhower commanded one
of the most powerful military forces ever assembled in human history.
Under his skilled leadership, the Allied Forces stormed the beaches
of France, defeated Hitler's army, and liberated Europe. Several
years later, the American people elected the popular war hero as their
president. Naturally, not everyone believed that the retired general
would make a smooth transition to the Oval Office. During Harry
Truman's final months in the White House, he reflected on the challenges awaiting his successor: "He'll sit here, and he'll say, 'Do this!
Do that!' And nothing will happen. Poor Ike—it won't be a bit like the
army. He'll find it very frustrating."[1]

Truman spoke from experience. Getting his ideas and decisions implemented had been a formidable challenge at times. The obstacles did not always prove to be his opponents in Congress; at times, Truman encountered resistance from members of his own administration.[2] Political scientist Richard Neustadt, who worked for Truman and several other chief executives, once observed, "The president of the United States has an extraordinary range of formal powers... despite his 'powers,' he does not obtain results by giving orders—or not, at any rate, merely by giving orders."[3] Even the leader of the free world needs to build commitment and shared understanding if he wants his decisions to be executed in a timely and efficient manner.

As it turns out, Eisenhower could not simply issue dictums from on high, even as supreme commander of the Allied Expeditionary Force in World War II.[4] He needed to hold a complicated alliance together and balance the competing demands of many strong-willed individuals on both sides of the Atlantic, including the two heads of state, Churchill and Roosevelt; each nation's military chief of staff, Marshall and Brooke; and powerful field commanders such as Montgomery, Patton, Tedder, and Spaatz. Historian Stephen Ambrose has pointed out that Eisenhower's diplomatic skills often proved to be more important than his strategy-making prowess. He observed:

> **Although none of his immediate superiors or subordinates seemed to realize it, Eisenhower could not afford to be a table-thumper. With Montgomery's prestige, power, and personality, for example, had Eisenhower stormed into his headquarters, banged his fist on the table, and shouted out a series of demands, his actions could have been disastrous.[5]**

Eisenhower indeed proved adept at bringing people together and finding common ground. The enemy too recognized Eisenhower's strengths as a leader; the Germans once wrote that "his strongest point is said to be an ability for adjusting personalities to one another and smoothing over opposite viewpoints."[6]

Consider how Eisenhower chose the D-day invasion strategy amid much contentious debate among the heads of state and military commanders. He built commitment to the final plan by leading a fair and legitimate decision process. During often heated deliberations, Ambrose points out that Eisenhower "acted as chairman, listening judiciously to both sides, then making the final decision."[7] He ensured that everyone "received a fair hearing."[8] Moreover, "his basic method was to approach all problems objectively himself, and to convince others that he *was* objective."[9]

Eisenhower, however, did more than lead a fair process and make the final call when people could not reach agreement. He helped this group of incredibly powerful and strong-willed personalities reach closure on the D-day invasion strategy by breaking the complex issue down into manageable parts. Rather than settling on a strategy all at once, Eisenhower led a five-month process whereby the group gradually arrived at decisions regarding the date of the landings, the bombing strategy, the use of airborne troops, and whether to invade southern France at the same time as the cross-channel attack.

Eisenhower navigated contentious deliberations by seeking common ground whenever possible, often searching for agreement on key facts, assumptions, and decision criteria. According to Ambrose, when the commanders came together to debate whether to focus bombing on strategic targets within Germany or railway networks within France, Eisenhower ensured that the group "began by acknowledging those points on which everyone agreed."[10] When they could not agree on a possible invasion of southern France, he sought agreement first on the level of resources required to prosecute the cross-channel attack effectively. After the group came to a conclusion on that point, it became much clearer to everyone that an invasion of southern France must be delayed—a point of view that Eisenhower had not endorsed initially.

Throughout the D-day deliberations, Eisenhower adopted a disciplined, step-by-step approach to securing commitment and reaching closure. He brought the group along gradually, building upon points of common ground. Although "Eisenhower's practice was to seek agreement,"[11] he did make the tough call when all parties could not agree. Moreover, when he declared that matter closed and moved to the next area of debate, he did not allow people to revisit the matter and re-open it for further discussion.

Divergence and Convergence

Eisenhower's leadership in the months preceding the D-day invasion proves very instructive for those interested in understanding how to help a diverse group reach closure on a complex matter. In many ways, Eisenhower's approach challenges the conventional wisdom with regard to making complicated, high-stakes decisions.

Throughout this book, we have examined two pathologies that groups encounter as they try to make difficult decisions (see Figure 8-1). Some teams converge too quickly on a particular solution without sufficient levels of critical evaluation and debate. Others generate many alternatives, but cannot resolve conflict and achieve closure in a timely fashion.

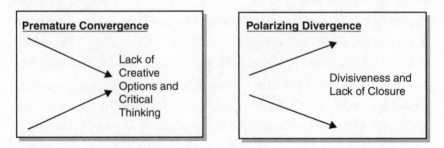

Source: Adapted from J. Russo and P. Schoemaker. (1989). *Decision Traps: The Ten Barriers to Brilliant Decision-Making and How to Overcome Them*. New York: Fireside. p. 153.

FIGURE 8-1:   Two pathologies

To avoid these problems, scholars and consultants often argue that groups should try to encourage divergent thinking in the early stages of the decision process, and then shift to convergent thinking to pare down the options and select a course of action. This sequential divergence-convergence model, depicted in Figure 8-2, represents the conventional wisdom often espoused by those who are advising managers on how to make decisions more effectively.[12] For instance, scholars J. Edward Russo and Paul Schoemaker make the following recommendation:

For the vast majority of decisions, especially those of any import, the best process is at first expansive, with sufficient time for different opinions, converging on a final decision only *after the* group has considered the problem from many diverse perspectives.[13]

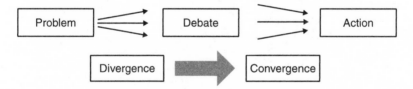

Source: Adapted from J. Russo and P. Schoemaker. (1989). *Decision Traps: The Ten Barriers to Brilliant Decision-Making and How to Overcome Them.* New York: Fireside. p. 153.

FIGURE 8-2: The divergence-convergence model

My research suggests that effective leaders direct an *iterative process* of divergence and convergence, much as Eisenhower did during the D-day deliberations (see Figure 8-3). Effective leaders do *not* encourage divergent thinking in the early stages of a decision process, and *then* turn their attention toward reaching closure and consensus in the latter stages of the deliberations. One does not achieve timely and sustainable closure by proceeding in this type of linear fashion Instead, leaders must actively seek common ground from time to time during the decision-making process. They cannot

completely defer judgment on all issues while engaging in brainstorming, alternative generation, and debate, nor can they restrict
convergent thinking to the latter stages of the decision process.[14]
They must reach intermediate agreements on particular elements of
the decision at various points in the deliberations, lest they find themselves trying to bridge huge chasms between opposing camps late in a
decision process.[15]

Like Eisenhower in the period before D-day, effective leaders
treat closure as a process nurtured over time rather than an event that
occurs at the culmination of an intense period of divergent thinking
and debate. They do not seek commitment and closure in a single act
of choice, but they strive for a series of "small wins"—concrete, intermediate points of agreement on elements of a problem—that bring
factions together and build momentum toward a final decision.

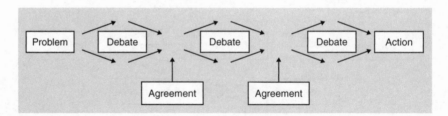

FIGURE 8-3:   An iterative process of divergence and convergence

To illustrate the power of an iterative process of divergence and
convergence, consider a critical decision made by CEO Andrew
Venton and his management team at a leading U.S. combat vehicle
and armament manufacturer. In the late 1990s, the firm sought to
compete for a joint British-American defense contract to design and
build an advanced armored combat vehicle. Venton knew that he
needed to put together an international joint venture, with several
other leading American and British aerospace firms, to win this
lucrative contract. It promised to be a complex decision with many
unknowns and multiple points of contention among his staff
members. For instance, much ambiguity existed about the precise

customer requirements for the program, and no one expected the two nations to clarify those specifications for some time. Venton recognized, too, that his managers would have disparate assessments of potential partners because of their vastly different experiences working with firms on past projects.

This decision provides examples of the types of debates and intermediate agreements that can occur as an iterative process unfolds. As Table 8-1 illustrates, Venton and his team did not move sequentially from a divergent thinking mode to a convergence mode during their deliberations. In particular, note that convergent thinking took place *at each major stage* of the decision-making process.

Managers conducted a broad information search, examining the needs of the customers, as well as the capabilities of potential partners, on both sides of the Atlantic. They eventually agreed on the problem's magnitude and urgency as well as on the firm's objectives (i.e., how fast the program would come to fruition, how large it would become, and what type of team would be needed to win the contract). The decision makers generated many different alternatives, but then agreed on a feasible set of options as well as the criteria to be utilized to evaluate them. They debated the different alternatives, but periodically agreed to eliminate some of those options. For instance, managers came to the conclusion that their firm must find a company with more advanced systems-integration capability to lead the joint venture; therefore, all options with their firm as prime contractor were taken off the table. Finally, they made a choice, contingent upon specific events. Specifically, managers reached a tentative agreement that the best course of action would be to serve as a subcontractor in a joint venture with three other British and American firms. However, several managers had concerns about this choice. They would only support this decision if the firm could negotiate an adequate joint venture agreement, particularly with regard to the division of work on future contracts. Managers agreed to commence negotiations with the potential partners, only after agreeing among themselves on the specific conditions under which the firm should proceed with the alliance.

In sum, the managers iterated between periods of debate and instances in which they found common ground. Gradually, they tackled a highly complicated issue and arrived at a decision that everyone understood and to which everyone was highly committed. Moreover, this iterative process did not take an inordinate amount of time. It turned out to be one of the most efficient decision-making processes that I examined at the firm, both in terms of managers' internal evaluations of the process as well as my assessment as an outside observer.

TABLE 8-1:   Profile of an Iterative Process[16]

	Problem Identification and Definition Stage	Alternative Generation and Development Stage	Evaluation and Selection Stage
Divergent Thinking	• Broad information search and inquiry process • Consideration of different situations analogous to current problem	• Generation of multiple alternatives • Consideration of multiple criteria	• Competitor role plays What-if scenarios
Convergent Thinking	• Agreement on goals and objectives • Agreement on magnitude and urgency of problem	• Agreement on set of plausible options • Agreement on decision criteria • Agreement on key facts and assumptions	• Agreement on elimination of alternatives • Agreement on choice contingent upon specific events • Agreement on contingency plans

The Psychology of Small Wins

Why is a "small wins" approach so effective when dealing with complex decisions? Modest agreements on a particular element of a problem bring new allies together, cause opponents to recognize their common interests, and consolidate and preserve progress that has been made during an intense set of deliberations. People begin to recognize that they can work constructively with one another despite their differences of opinion. One agreement serves as a catalyst for more productive debates and further agreements down the line. Psychologist Karl Weick explains:

> **By itself, one small win may seem unimportant. A series of small wins at small but significant tasks, however, reveals a pattern that may attract allies, deter opponents, and lower resistance to subsequent proposals. Small wins are controllable opportunities that produce visible results...Once a small win has been accomplished, forces are set in motion that favor another small win.**[17]

A "small wins" approach helps groups overcome two types of obstacles that impede decision making in complicated, high-stakes situations. One obstacle is cognitive in nature, and the other is socio-emotional. First, complex problems can overwhelm groups due to the cognitive limitations, or what is known as bounded rationality, of the decision makers. To put it simply, individuals do not have supercomputers in their brains. They cannot process reams of information effectively; they must be selective. They cannot examine every possible alternative in a given situation, or think through the consequences of each of those alternative courses of action. Individuals tend to think in terms of a limited set of data and a few plausible options at a time. In short, there are bounds, or cognitive limits, to their ability to examine a decision in a highly comprehensive manner.[18] Therefore, the cognitive challenge is to make the decision more manageable for the human mind. Small wins enable individuals and groups to do just that, by gradually structuring a highly unstructured and complex problem.[19]

Complicated issues also induce frustration, stress, and personal friction. Psychologists have shown that individuals become anxious and tense when they perceive a problem as beyond their capability to solve. People typically evaluate their skills, as well as the capabilities of the groups and organizations in which they work, and they assess whether those capabilities match the demands of a situation. If they perceive a mismatch—namely, that the demands of the situation exceed their skills and competences—they become flustered, worried, and stressed. Those emotions make it difficult to actually solve the problem and make an effective decision. Therefore, the socio-emotional challenge is to keep everyone engaged and committed to a decision process by coping effectively with these intra- and inter-personal tensions. A "small wins" approach proves effective when a problem appears overwhelming to people. As Weick writes, "A small win reduces importance ('this is no big deal'), reduces demands ('that's all that needs to be done'), and raises perceived skill levels ('I can do at least that')."[20]

The decision to reform Social Security in 1983 represents a vivid example of how groups can use a series of small wins to build toward closure on a complex, divisive issue. In January of that year, a small group of senior policy makers—known as the Gang of Nine—came together to tackle a crisis facing the nation's Social Security program. Without a decision to implement reforms immediately, the program would have become insolvent, and millions of senior citizens would not have received their monthly checks on time.[21]

The White House and Congress had tried to reach a compromise for more than one year, but had been unable to do so. President Reagan had appointed a bipartisan commission to address the issue, but it too had not been able to arrive at an acceptable solution. People on both sides of the political aisle had become exasperated by the enormity of the challenge and the intensity of disagreement on the issue. With time running out in early 1983, four White House staffers and five former commission members came together to tackle the problem once again. They came to an agreement acceptable to President Reagan and House Democratic leader Tip O'Neill. One Gang of Nine member described how they arrived at a decision: "It was an incremental process. There were no major breakthroughs, just a *bunch of small agreements* that added up to a major package" [*emphasis added*].[22]

The Gang of Nine arrived at a series of critical agreements before trying to negotiate a solution to the Social Security crisis itself. Those agreements laid the foundation for further constructive debate about various alternatives for reform. First, they argued about, and ultimately settled on, a set of economic and demographic assumptions regarding matters such as future economic growth, inflation, population growth, life expectancy, etc. Second, based on those assumptions, they reached agreement on the size of the overall problem ($168 billion in the short term) that they were trying to solve. Finally, the Gang of Nine agreed that any solution must be composed of 50 percent tax cuts and 50 percent benefit reductions. That principle, or criterion, would guide the evaluation of all options. Building on that common ground, the Gang of Nine debated various alternatives, and gradually began to concur, one by one, on a series of tax-increase and benefit-reduction proposals that comprised the final solution that they recommended to President Reagan and the congress. For instance, early on, the Gang of Nine agreed to delay cost-of-living increases. Later, they came to the conclusion that they should accelerate payroll tax increases, and in the final stages of their deliberations, the team agreed to impose a tax on Social Security benefits for senior citizens who chose to continue working past the official retirement age. As the group agreed on one proposal after another, they gradually pieced together a solution that would make up the $168 billion shortfall in the Social Security program. Through a "small wins" approach, the Gang of Nine had tackled the "third rail" of American politics, brought together political opponents, and solved a complicated and stressful problem.

Types of Intermediate Agreements

The Social Security reform decision illustrates two types of small wins that leaders can seek during a contentious decision-making process (see Table 8-2). One type does not involve the ultimate courses of action to be implemented, but focuses on the elements of the decision process itself. For instance, the group agreed on core economic and demographic assumptions, and individuals concurred on the 50/50 principle to which all solutions had to adhere. Those *process-oriented* small wins do not constitute courses of action that could be implemented to address the problem at hand, but they did lay the groundwork for productive discussions about a range of possible solutions. Another type of small win consists of a partial solution to the problem that could be executed in conjunction with a number of other proposals. For example, the agreement regarding the taxation of benefits represents a concrete course of action that could be implemented by the federal government. The taxation of benefits, by itself, could not solve the Social Security crisis, but it represented a small piece to the complex puzzle. It proved to be a critical *outcome-oriented* small win. As leaders strive for closure on complex issues, they need to search for opportunities to secure small wins of both the process and outcome variety.

TABLE 8-2: Examples of Small Wins

Process-Oriented Small Wins	Outcome-Oriented Small Wins
Goals and objectives	Taking alternatives off the table
Assumptions	Option-oriented agreements
Decision criteria	Contingency plans

Process-Oriented Small Wins

Although many types of process-oriented small wins exist (refer to Table 8-1), leaders would be hard-pressed to reach sustainable closure on a complex issue without agreement on three key elements:

goals, assumptions, and decision criteria. In nearly all decisions, management team members approach an issue with a mix of competing and shared goals. The functional areas, geographic units, and lines of business within a firm do compete with another to some extent, and their interests are not aligned perfectly. Moreover, individual executives have personal goals and ambitions that may conflict with the aspirations of their colleagues. To reach closure on a complex issue, leaders cannot eliminate clashing interests among their subordinates, but they can and must find common ground in terms of a superordinate goal about which managers can all agree.[23] As Stanford scholar Kathleen Eisenhardt and her colleagues discovered in their research on 12 senior management teams in high-technology firms, "When team members are working toward a common goal, they are less likely to see themselves as individual winners and losers and are far more likely to perceive the opinions of others correctly and to learn from them."[24]

In the Social Security decision, everyone recognized the common goal—restoring the solvency of the program—from the outset. However, some people held optimistic assumptions about economic growth, inflation, and the like, whereas others possessed a more pessimistic outlook. According to political scientist Paul Light, one participant felt that the early deliberations were "clouded by *massively incongruent* assumptions and datasets."[25] Dissimilar assumptions caused people to define the size of the problem quite differently. The Gang of Nine could not agree on a solution if they could not settle on the size of the deficit that needed to be closed. By reviewing historical data trends together, the group members came to an agreement on their economic and demographic presumptions. Senator Patrick Moynihan pointed out that focusing on hard facts helped immensely: "Everyone is entitled to their own opinions, but not to their own facts."[26]

Larry Bossidy, former CEO of Honeywell International, and consultant Ram Charan have pointed out that any effective strategic planning process must include a healthy discussion and debate about what managers assume will transpire in the external environment in the years ahead. They also have stressed that achieving a common view with regard to those presumptions is critical to achieving closure on contentious issues and moving forward smoothly and efficiently on the execution of a strategy. Reflecting on Bossidy's experience at Honeywell, they wrote:

> **Synchronization is essential for excellence in execution and for energizing the corporation. Synchronization means that all the moving parts of the organization have common assumptions about the external environment...Debating the assumptions and making trade-offs openly in a group is an important part of the social software...As they construct and share a comprehensive picture of what's happening on the outside and the inside, they hone their ability to synchronize efforts for execution. And they publicly make their commitments to execute.**[27]

Finally, an agreement on decision criteria can represent a critical small win that propels a group toward closure on a contentious issue. Leaders must consider a wide range of factors when comparing and contrasting alternative courses of action. In fact, many decision-making experts in academia and consulting have argued that managers make more effective choices when they consider a broader array of criteria, including both "hard" (quantitative) and "soft" (qualitative) factors.[28]

Of course, with such a wide range of factors to be considered, some managers may not recognize that they are evaluating a set of alternatives on dimensions that differ from those employed by their colleagues. It becomes difficult to make progress on a complex issue if people do not agree on the manner in which they will judge each option. When people discuss their evaluation criteria in an explicit fashion and settle on a set of factors to be used to examine each proposal, they often find that it helps them break deadlocks or impasses in the deliberations. Moreover, driving toward a common set of criteria can help dislodge some individuals from entrenched positions, encourage them to look at options in a whole new light and, ultimately, move a group toward closure. As one executive told me, "In order to get people to come together…we had to at least give them the opportunity to be comparing apples to apples."

Outcome-Oriented Small Wins

When it comes to selecting an actual course of action, leaders may piece together a series of partial solutions to address a large, complex problem, as the Gang of Nine did in the Social Security reform decision. Leaders also may emulate Eisenhower, who sought agreement on one element after another of a broad overall strategy. Each of these approaches takes advantage of the power of small wins. However, even when leaders are working toward one major final choice, as is sometimes necessary, they can seek a few types of outcome-oriented small wins along the way that can help them reach closure in a timely manner.

First, my research suggests that effective groups agree to eliminate options at critical junctures, rather than trying to simultaneously evaluate the entire set of feasible alternatives and select the single best course of action. For example, in one of the strategic alliance decisions described in an earlier chapter, the CEO explained how his team pared the list of options over time:

It was a winnowing process. What we were doing was taking things, gradually taking things off the table. In my mind, what you don't want to keep doing in a decision-making process is having to review all the alternatives over and over. You've got to start taking alternatives off the table.

Each time a group can agree to eliminate even one option, they secure a small win that may bring new allies together, shift the formation of coalitions within a management team, or break down some barriers among opponents. Taking one or more alternatives off the table also may cause some individuals to reexamine the remaining options from a new perspective, and perhaps to rank those proposals in a different order.

In contrast, some groups do not agree to eliminate options systematically, but instead, they try to revisit an entire array of alternatives repeatedly. Those teams tend to find their task cognitively overwhelming, particularly when a wide range of options exist. They find it harder to reach closure, or if they do reach an agreement, it represents a "mediocre compromise" that does not hold over time. For instance, reflecting on an important resource-allocation decision at his manufacturing firm, one executive explained how the management team's discussions seemed to wander aimlessly among five alternatives. Finally, the leader tried to build a patchwork solution that incorporated elements of each proposal. The staff member lamented, "We went through this whole harangue and analysis of all the options...and I think at the end of the day, it was sort of a decision. Maybe it's a compromise. We kind of did a little bit of everything."

Another type of small win, or intermediate agreement, occurs when managers make a tentative choice contingent upon *specific events* unfolding in the near future. In those instances, managers bridge their differences and move toward closure by agreeing to move forward definitively, but only if certain events transpire in the near future. For example, in the international joint venture decision described earlier, managers reached a tentative decision subject to certain conditions. This approach represented much more than a simplistic "keep your options open" mentality. The team agreed on a very specific set of parameters that needed to be negotiated with the alliance partners before moving forward with the joint venture. This

approach solicited the support of those who liked the choice of partners, but had grave concerns about becoming a minority member of
the joint venture with limited voice/influence on important matters.
In a capital investment decision at another manufacturing firm, an
executive explained that his management team came to a similar contingent agreement during a sometimes contentious decision process.[29]
In that case, the management team agreed to conduct a major facility
modernization project, but only if the firm could secure some tax
incentives from state and local governments. As one executive
explained, "We said we are going to do this, but we are going to do
this if we can get x, y, and z...It was always contingent on certain
events happening." This approach secured the support of those managers who recognized the many merits of the project, but did not
believe that the financial benefits justified the size of the capital
investment.

In some sense, this decision-making practice resembles a "real
options" approach to making progress on a complex and ambiguous
issue. A "real option" exists when firms have the ability to delay
investments and decisions until they acquire additional information.[30]
In these situations, managers must "purchase" this option by making
a small investment at the outset. That up-front spending may, for
instance, involve building a prototype of a new product and garnering
customer feedback. Managers may agree to launch a new product
line, but only provided that customers react favorably to a simple prototype, and/or that rivals do not beat the firm to market with a more
advanced product. This "option" approach to decision making may
help team members bridge their differences of opinion and move
beyond an impasse. It helps to alleviate people's concerns about a
decision prior to committing to full-scale implementation. Moreover,
this practice provides an opportunity for additional learning prior to a
final decision, and allows managers to resolve critical areas of uncertainty before moving forward in a definitive fashion.[31]

Finally, leaders may propel a group toward closure, and find an important patch of common ground, by seeking agreement on contingency plans that could be enacted during implementation if environmental conditions change. Many scholars and consultants have recommended a flexible approach to decision making when faced with high uncertainty.[32] A good backup or contingency plan provides managers with a thorough assessment of the risks associated with a decision, as well as a strategy for mitigating those risks. Contingency plans differ from the options approach described earlier, because managers do not wait to move forward with full-scale implementation, but they maintain a backup strategy for adapting their course of action if external conditions change substantially.

An agreement on a contingency plan may propel a group toward closure on a contentious issue, because it may help people with reservations about a decision to become more comfortable with the risks involved. Before settling on a contingency plan, some members of a management team may not feel comfortable supporting a particular proposal because they see a large potential downside under certain scenarios. They may present a worst-case scenario, and while acknowledging that it is improbable, still express their reservations about a decision that could produce that undesirable result. People may become more willing to endorse and commit to a decision if a group has developed and agreed on a plan for adapting the chosen course of action if a worst-case scenario begins to unfold during the implementation process.

Shifting into Decision Mode

Adopting a "small wins" approach may be effective, but leaders may still find it quite difficult to shift into decision mode. That is, they find it challenging to close down debate and act as the arbiter if team members have not been able to agree on a final decision. In these situations, leaders can become uncomfortable, or they can bring deliberations to a close in a way that diminishes satisfaction with the decision process and buy-in for the final choice. Some leaders may even experience anticipatory regret—i.e., strong nagging doubts that preclude them from making a tough call and result in delays that prove costly in the competitive marketplace.

Leaders may take three steps to make a smoother final transition from deliberation to decision. First, leaders can develop a clear set of expectations regarding how the final decision will be made, so that there are no misunderstandings within the management team. Second, they can develop a language system that helps them communicate how their role in a decision process will change at a critical juncture in order to achieve timely closure. Finally, leaders can build a relationship with a confidant who can not only offer sound advice, but also bolster the leader's confidence when they become tepid and overly risk averse in the face of high levels of environmental turbulence.

Leaders need to develop clear expectations about their role in the decision process if they hope to achieve sustainable closure. Suppose that team members believe that a leader will strive for unanimous agreement first, and then make the final call only if such congruence cannot be achieved. They will be surprised, and perhaps rather angry, if they find that the leader simply solicits advice in a series of one-on-one meetings and then announces a final decision, without ever convening a meeting at which all parties can exchange their views. That disappointment and anger may cause individuals to resist a speedy decision that the leader has made. In such circumstances, an apparent instance of timely closure can unravel rather quickly during the early stages of implementation. Leaders need to state clearly and plainly how they intend to garner input and then use that advice and data to make a decision. When they speak about "teamwork," they need to be clear that they do not mean democracy, nor do they mean autocratic rule. They also need to forewarn their staff members if, for good reason, they intend to make a particular decision largely without input from others.

Organizations often find it helpful if a leader has a language system for communicating how his role can and must change when the time comes for debates to end and final decisions to be made. Jamie Houghton, long-time CEO of Corning Incorporated, developed a simple way of talking openly about how he intended to participate in senior management team deliberations, and ultimately, bring them to a close. David Nadler, a consultant for many executive teams, explains Houghton's language system:

He talked about wearing "two hats." In his terms, there were times when he wanted to be a member of the team, to argue, to test ideas, to have people push him, to get into the rough and tumble of the team's work. In those cases, he saw himself as "one of the boys," and he talked about wearing a "cowboy hat." At other times, he was in the position of CEO, making a decision. In those cases, he was not looking for testing, push back, or argument. Instead, he would be wearing the "bowler."[33]

The metaphor may sound a bit odd, but it proved helpful because it made a clear distinction between his role and the team members' roles in the decision-making process. The two hats helped Houghton and his direct reports talk candidly about the stage of the decision process at which they stood. Nadler reports that team members often referred to the two types of hats during meetings, seeking to clarify whether the debate could continue or whether the time had come for Houghton to make the final decision. Houghton also could signal to the team that the "bowler" was coming soon if they could not reach agreement on a controversial issue. One could imagine that team members in a protracted disagreement might seek rapid opportunities to find common ground, if they knew that the "bowler" was coming in the near future.

On some occasions, leaders experience moments of indecision when faced with a complex issue, ambiguous data, and environmental instability. The team members know that the leader will make the call, and they clearly understand their roles, yet the leader himself cannot make the final leap. Stanford scholar Kathleen Eisenhardt argues that, in those instances, leaders may find it helpful to have a highly experienced confidant who can act as a sounding board. By walking through the analysis and conclusions one final time with that trusted adviser, the leader can become more comfortable with the decision that he is about to make. As Eisenhardt explains, a trusted counselor can "impart confidence and a sense of stability" in uncertain times, and enable leaders to overcome the anticipatory regret that often causes costly delay and indecision.[34]

Sustaining Closure

After a decision has been made, leaders need to make sure that they adopt a disciplined approach so as to sustain closure. Individuals who disagree with a decision often would like to re-open the deliberations. If leaders have directed a fair and legitimate process, they should not allow others to revisit a decision that has already been made. They need to affirm that the case is closed. Paul Levy adopted such a disciplined approach at the Beth Israel Deaconess Medical Center in Boston. Doctors and administrators at the hospital had become accustomed to revisiting decisions about which they disagreed whenever they felt it was to their benefit. Prior management had allowed such dysfunctional behavior to persist for years. Levy intervened when such detrimental conduct surfaced during his time as the chief executive, making sure that everyone understood that they could not revisit past decisions so long as they had been given a fair opportunity to voice their opinions earlier. In World War II, Eisenhower too needed to maintain discipline when powerful field commanders tried to continue debates that had long been brought to a close. At those times, Eisenhower often stressed the importance of "unity in command."

Leaders should not, however, remain stubbornly attached to a course of action, no matter what transpires after a decision has been made. Under certain circumstances, they should revisit past choices and re-open a matter for discussion and debate. In particular, decisions should be reexamined if extensive amounts of new information become available, or if several critical assumptions made during the decision process are proven to be false. A leader also might reconsider a past decision if it elicits unexpected and potentially deleterious responses from customers, rivals, and/or suppliers. Finally, issues may be re-opened for discussion if a subsequent initiative requires adjustments in past choices so as to ensure that the organization's entire set of activities and decisions remained aligned to achieve overall firm objectives.

The Importance of Trust

Fair and legitimate process helps build commitment, and small wins make it easier to navigate controversial deliberations and find solutions that people can endorse. In the end, however, leaders need to be trusted if they want to reach closure in a timely fashion and have people support and commit to that decision. Employing fair decision-making processes helps to build trust in a leader, as many studies have shown, but that is not enough.[35] Leaders need to work constantly, in all that they do, to maintain their credibility and sustain the confidence that others have in them. If people trust a leader wholeheartedly, they are more likely to put aside differences of opinion and commit to a chosen course of action.

Trust and credibility do not come overnight, and they do not derive simply from a past track record of making good decisions and accomplishing positive results. Take, for example, the tragic case of the 1949 forest fire in Mann Gulch, Montana, that killed 12 United States Forest Service smokejumpers. Wagner Dodge, an experienced and accomplished foreman, led the team of firefighters assigned to drop from an airplane and fight the fire in the gulch on August 5, 1949.[36]

Roughly one hour after the smokejumpers landed on the ground, the blaze accelerated dramatically. Dodge and his crew tried to sprint to safety at the top of a ridge. He soon came to the realization that the crew could not outrace the blaze. Dodge came to a rapid, intuitive decision without consulting with any of his crewmembers; in fact, he invented a tactic that no one had ever employed. He bent down and lit a small fire in the grassy area roughly 200 yards from the top of the ridge, placed a handkerchief over his mouth, and lay down in the smoldering ashes.

Dodge's crew did not understand what he was trying to accomplish. He pointed to his fire and yelled, "This way! This way!" Imagine what the smokejumpers thought as they watched Dodge pull out his tiny matchbook, a raging fire directly behind him. One firefighter described his impression at the time: "I thought, with the fire almost on our back, what the hell is the boss doing lighting another fire in front of us?"[37] As the crew raced by, one person reacted to Dodge by shouting, "To hell with that! I'm getting out of here!"[38] Everyone ran past Dodge, ignoring his frantic pleas. Sadly, all but two of the crewmembers perished in the race for the top of the ridge, whereas Dodge emerged completely unscathed after just a few moments. The fire blew right over him, because he had deprived it of grassy fuel in a small area.

Why did these men fail to commit to Dodge's decision to lie down in the smoldering ashes? He certainly had official authority as the foreman, and he had a solid track record. Furthermore, he had far more experience than the other smokejumpers. However, he had not developed a strong reservoir of credibility and trust. He had not participated in a three-week training session with the other crew-members during that summer. In fact, many of the men had never worked with Dodge prior to that day. As leadership expert Michael Useem has said, he had a "management style that fostered little two-way communication."[39] Many smokejumpers considered Dodge to be a man of few words. His wife concurred: "He said to me when we were first married, 'You do your job and I'll do mine, and we'll get along just fine'...I loved him very much, but I did not know him well."[40] Dodge, in fact, did not even know the names of many men on his crew. After the tragedy, one survivor told investigators, "Dodge had a characteristic in him...It is hard to tell what he is thinking."[41]

During the landing and initial attempts to fight the fire, Dodge had communicated very little with his crew. He did not ask for their assessments of the situation or for their advice regarding how to fight the fire. Dodge also never explained why he chose to attack the blaze as he did. Even later, as he became more alarmed, he offered terse statements about the increasing gravity of the situation, rather than explaining his situational diagnosis in depth. Dodge had not established a foundation of credibility and trust through his prior actions and management style. Therefore, as Useem argues, people would not commit to his decision at the critical moment of crisis:

Without revealing his thinking when it could be shared, Dodge denied his crew members, especially those not familiar with him, an opportunity to apprehend the quality of his mind. They had no other way of knowing, except by reputation, whether his decisions were rational or impulsive, calculated or impetuous... If you want trust and compliance when the need for them cannot be fully explained, explain yourself early.[42]

The Mann Gulch case provides an extreme example of a leadership failure in a time of grave crisis. Certainly, a business leader is unlikely to find himself in such a dangerous situation with many lives in the balance. However, the tragic story illustrates vividly that a leader's style of communication and approach to making decisions shapes the extent to which he garners the trust and respect of his subordinates. Despite respect for a leader's expertise and position of authority, individuals will not put their full and complete trust in someone who has not been open with them, built a relationship with them, and given them some input on past decisions. They also will not put their faith in someone who has not explained his rationale for past choices or illustrated how he approaches and solves tough problems.

On the matter of trust, we must return to General Eisenhower. According to Ambrose, who spent a lifetime trying to understand this extraordinary military leader, Ike's trustworthiness proved to be one of his greatest virtues, as well as his greatest asset when it came to dealing with powerful and opinionated men such as Churchill, Roosevelt, Montgomery, and Marshall. After reflecting on many of Eisenhower's fine attributes, Ambrose concluded, "Over and above these and the other factors that led to his success, however, one stood out. When associates described Eisenhower, be they superiors or subordinates, there was one word that almost all of them used. It was trust."[43]

PART IV

A NEW BREED OF
TAKE-CHARGE LEADER

9

LEADING WITH
RESTRAINT

"By failing to prepare, you are preparing to fail."
—Benjamin Franklin

In every direction that we turn these days, it seems that we hear people talking about the need for more leaders, as well as more effective leadership, in our private and public institutions. The strong desire for enhanced leadership in all aspects of society accelerated after the horrific tragedy of September 11, 2001. For good reason, people have become concerned about how institutions will cope with the extraordinary levels of ambiguity and turbulence in their external environments. Problems seem to be growing more complex, change seems to be happening more quickly than ever, and so many organizations seem ill-equipped to cope with these challenges.

Our institutions need leaders who can motivate people, manage organizational change, and align disparate groups behind a common goal. Decision making represents an important facet of leadership, as we have argued in this book. Now more than ever, leaders need to gather and assimilate divergent perspectives, choose based on incomplete information, test their assumptions carefully, reach closure quickly, and build strong buy-in so as to facilitate efficient execution. Perhaps most importantly, we hear many people argue that societal institutions need strong, decisive leaders—people who know how to make tough, and sometimes painful and unpopular, choices in a world of ambiguity and discontinuous change.

The recent emphasis on leadership—as well as the concerns about daunting social, political, and economic challenges—do not, of course, represent a completely new phenomenon. Nearly a decade ago, in a speech at the Minnesota Center for Corporate Responsibility, *Fortune* magazine editor-at-large Marshall Loeb offered this perspective based on his interaction with many prominent business executives:

> **As an editor travels across the country, listening to high executives he hears—over and over—one plaintive question: Where have all the leaders gone? Where are the patrician, eloquent, inspirational Churchills and Roosevelts, the rough-hewn, plain-spoken but ultimately charismatic Harry Trumans and Pope Johns, now that we need them so badly? We are *desperate* for leaders...Thomas Carlyle had it right I believe: All history is biography—as so all great companies are indeed the direct reflection of their *leaders*. The leader sets the tone, the mood, the style, the character of the whole enterprise.[1]**

Many people have echoed Loeb's comments in recent years. Business executives, politicians, and academics have all talked about a "crisis of leadership" in key business and government institutions. It's more than talk though; survey data suggests that employees feel a pressing need for more leadership in their organizations. In 2002, Watson Wyatt, a human resources consulting firm, conducted a survey of

12,750 U.S. workers across many industries, and they found that only 45% of respondents "have confidence in the job being done by senior management."[2] Moreover, Watson Wyatt reported in that same year that "less than half of employees (49%) understand the steps their companies are taking to reach new business goals—a 20% drop since 2000."[3] A comparable study conducted in Canada produced similar results.[4] Perhaps more disturbingly, a 2002 poll by *Workforce Management* magazine found that 83% of respondents perceived "a leadership vacuum in their organizations."[5]

What Type of Leaders?

If we need more effective leaders, the question becomes: What type of leaders should organizations seek? Naturally, the so-called management gurus disagree. Jim Collins, arguably the most widely read business writer in the world, conducted a study to determine how and why some companies move from a fairly long period of average financial performance to an era of sustained superior results. He found that only a small set of firms managed to make that leap, and their leaders possessed a distinct set of traits. According to Collins, the CEOs of those firms demonstrated great modesty and humility. They often proved quiet, reserved, and even shy. Collins extols those virtues, and he argues that organizations should seek leaders with these attributes, rather than simply chasing individuals who exhibit charisma.[6]

Tom Peters, another widely read business writer and consultant, disagrees vehemently. He thinks the current tumultuous business climate requires something quite different from the "stoic, quiet, calm leaders" that he hears Collins describe and extol. Peters exclaims, "Would you like to think that a quiet leader will lead you to the promised land? I think it's total utter bull, because I consider this to be a time of chaos."[7]

Peters does not believe that we can identify a single set of personality traits that are associated with superior leadership in all circumstances. He argues that different situations merit different types of leaders.[8] In fact, many scholars of leadership adopt this point of view. These academics endorse a theory of situational leadership—the notion that fit, or alignment, must exist between a leader's style and the contextual demands and pressures that he faces.[9] In short, institutions must seek a leader who is well-suited for the particular challenge that the organization faces at that moment. When making decisions, leaders need to adapt their approach based upon the nature of the problem they are trying to solve.

The Myth of the Lone Warrior

Some people bemoan the focus on leadership at the very top of the organization. They think that people place too much emphasis on the chief executive when it comes to explaining organizational performance. Surely, the business press enjoys crediting charismatic and forceful leaders such as Jack Welch and Lou Gerstner with the success that their firms achieved with them at the helm. Jim Collins criticizes the worship of charismatic and heroic CEOs; he prefers to heap praise on modest, relatively introverted leaders such as Darwin Smith at Kimberly-Clark or Colman Mockler at Gillette. Still, he places a great deal of emphasis on the person in the corner office.[10] Lest we forget, these organizations are large and complex, with hundreds of thousands of employees. Yet, so many people attribute much of their success to the leadership skills of one person—the heroic CEO.

Leadership scholar Ronald Heifetz wonders whether we expect too much of the person at the top, the individual who holds the most formal authority in our institutions. We believe that the individual at the top will have the answers to all the tough problems facing the organization. Is that really true? Can that possibly be true? Heifetz concludes, "The myth of leadership is the myth of the lone warrior: the solitary individual whose heroism and brilliance enable him to lead the way."[11] Warren Bennis points out that Michelangelo had plenty of help painting the Sistine Chapel; 16 others joined him in painting the ceiling that we all marvel at and praise him for today! Similarly, most firms do not accomplish great things without a team of people supporting and assisting the CEO. Bennis concludes that, in the business and government institutions of today, "The problems we face are too complex to be solved by any one person."[12]

Such talk elicits a visceral reaction from many top executives. They argue that firms cannot make critical strategic decisions by committee. Democracy, you will hear, has no place in the executive suite. These individuals believe that the chief executive needs to "take charge" when an organization faces tough problems that require speedy action. The person at the top simply has to make some tough calls on his own. To them, fostering dissent, striving for fair process, and building buy-in among multiple constituencies represent signs of weakness, rather than strength. Some worry that others will perceive a highly participatory approach as a sign of indecisiveness or loss of control. Others believe that such activities will waste precious time and provide competitors the upper hand in the marketplace.

Heifetz points out that many employees reinforce this viewpoint and help perpetuate the myth of the lone warrior. They adopt a very paternalistic view, in which they expect the top authority in the organization to look after them in troubling times and provide the right solutions to vexing problems. Heifetz explains:

> **In a crisis, we tend to look for the wrong kind of leadership. We call for someone with the answers, decision, strength, and a map of the future, someone who knows where we ought to be going—in short, someone who can make hard problems simple...Instead of looking for saviors, we should be calling for leadership that will**

challenge us to face problems for which there are no simple, painless solutions—problems that require us to learn in new ways.[13]

What would we make of a top executive who espoused this philosophy? Imagine if a CEO admitted that he did not know the answer to a pressing problem facing his organization. Imagine if he emphasized the need for a collaborative decision-making process and the requirement to build buy-in before taking action. Would we criticize that individual for not "taking charge" and demonstrating decisive leadership? It is not simply the people in positions of senior authority who perpetuate the myth of the lone warrior, sitting in the corner office making wise choices in a Solomon-like manner. Many of us who sit at a lower level in the organizational hierarchy expect that vision to become reality when our institutions face complex, pressing problems.

Must we espouse an either/or view of the world? Can top executives remain firmly in control of decision making when an organization encounters an exigent situation, yet still provide room for solutions to arise from below and for dissenting voices to be heard? In this book, we have argued that executives can be bold and decisive, while harnessing the collective intelligence of an organization and building buy-in from multiple constituencies.

Two Forms of Taking Charge

Effective leaders do take charge when confronted with difficult organizational decisions. However, there are two different approaches to taking charge. One kind of leader dives right into the problem, trying to find the best solution. This type of leader focuses on *what to do* to improve the organization's performance. A second type of leader takes a step back and focuses at first on *how* the organization ought to go about tackling the problem. This leader asks the question: What kind of decision process should we employ? This is not to say that the leader does not have an opinion about what to do, but he does not focus exclusively on finding the right *solution*. Instead, he focuses first on trying to find the right *process*.

Consultant and researcher David Nadler has argued that many top executives do not distinguish between these two approaches to taking charge. They believe that working with others in a collaborative problem-solving fashion signifies a shift toward "letting the team manage and decide for itself."[14] Nadler tries to clarify this misconception. He believes that leaders can be directive about a decision-making process, while providing subordinates plenty of room to offer divergent perspectives regarding the content of the issue at hand.

When I teach the Bay of Pigs and Cuban missile crisis case studies to executive audiences, I often ask: In which situation would you say that President Kennedy was a more "hands-on" leader? Invariably, nearly half of the class argues that he adopted a more "hands-on" approach in the Bay of Pigs; the others disagree. Who is correct? The answer is straightforward: Both sides are right! In the Bay of Pigs case, Kennedy became very involved in the details of how the invasion would be carried out. In that sense, he appears to have been a "hands-on" leader. However, Kennedy lost control of the decision-making process. He allowed the CIA officials to shape the decision process in a manner that would strongly enhance the probability of achieving the outcome that they desired. In short, Kennedy dove in to find the right solution, but he failed to take charge of the process. Ultimately, his failure to manage the process led to a flawed decision.

During the Cuban missile crisis, Kennedy became more directive about the decision process. He made careful choices about composition, context, communication, and control—the 4 Cs that together comprise how a leader decides how to decide. Kennedy considered how the deliberations should take place, what roles people should play in the process, and how divergent views should be welcomed and heard. Yet, he removed himself from several meetings. He resisted the temptation to micromanage all details of the situation. He offered his advisers some room to state their arguments, to debate one another, and to revise their proposals based upon the critique of others. Kennedy still retained the right to make the final call, and he clearly did not strive for unanimous agreement before moving forward. The president took charge of the decision process, knowing that he would not lose authority or control by offering others an opportunity to express their views. No one perceived Kennedy as weak or indecisive because he stepped back to give others room to state their case before he declared his own views on the matter.

Top executives will demonstrate true decisive leadership when they think carefully about how they want to make tough choices, rather than by simply trying to jump to the right answer. By deciding how to decide, they increase the probability that they will effectively capitalize on the wide variety of capabilities and expertise in their organization and make a sound decision. Moreover, they enhance the odds of being able to implement the chosen course of action effectively.

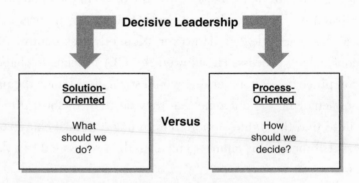

FIGURE 9-1:   Two forms of assertive leadership

Leading with Restraint

The brand of take-charge leadership called for in this book requires a great deal of restraint on the part of top executives. When faced with a complex problem, many executives will have a strong intuitive feeling about what to do based upon years of experience. That intuition will prove correct in many circumstances, but not all.

To make the most of the expertise and ideas that other members of their organizations possess, leaders need to refrain from pronouncing their solution to a problem, before others have had an opportunity to offer their perspectives. They must acknowledge that they do not have all answers, and that their initial intuition may not always be correct. They need to recognize that their behavior, particularly at the outset of a decision process, can encourage others to act in an overly deferential manner. Leaders must understand that the best choices mean very little if various, interdependent units of the organization are not willing to cooperate to execute the decision.

By leading with restraint, individuals in positions of authority recognize that their understanding and knowledge in a particular domain are often bounded, imprecise, and incomplete. They do not begin to tackle a problem by seeking confirmation of their preexisting hypotheses, but instead, recognize the existence of boundary conditions associated with each of their mental models (i.e. their theories may apply under certain conditions, but not in all circumstances).[15] Restrained leaders implicitly presume that their understanding of a specific domain consists of a set of nascent theories, which may be disproved over time and about which reasonable people may disagree. [16] Restrained leaders constantly search and explore for new knowledge, rather than seeking the data and opinions that confirm their preexisting understanding of the world around them.

Let's return to the 1996 Mount Everest tragedy for a moment. Just before Rob Hall and Scott Fisher made their final push for the summit, accomplished mountaineer David Breashears, the leader of the IMAX film expedition also on the mountain that year, faced a momentous decision. He felt uncomfortable with certain signs that suggested to him a possible deterioration in the weather during his team's ascent to the top.[17] Breashears turned to his team and sought their advice and input. After a dialogue with other expedition members, he chose to turn the team around and head back down to base camp. He recalled how difficult it was to encounter Hall and Fischer heading toward the summit, while he and his colleagues retreated. One of the expedition members remembered feeling a bit self-conscious about the decision to turn back: "We felt a bit sheepish coming down. Everybody is going up and we thought, 'God, are we making the right decision?'"[18] When Breashears came to my class at Harvard Business School a few years ago, he compared his experience on Everest in 1996 to the other expeditions that encountered tragedy. He talked about the need for skilled leaders on mountaineering missions; in his view, the world's greatest climbers did not necessarily comprise the world's best expedition leaders. Toward the end of that discussion, a student asked him what constituted great leadership. He argued that experience, formal authority, and expertise in one's field did not make someone a great leader. Instead, Breashears spoke of the need to exercise restraint when making decisions:

> **Some people have tremendous charisma, and they can dominate a room full of people, but all of that does not equal competence. Sure, leaders need to have a vision. But by restraint, I mean the ability to accept others' ideas without feeling threatened. Those are the people I found to be my role models—not the person who ordered me to go up the mountain, but the person who talked to the team, asking for a dialogue, not feeling threatened by the dialogue, because they still had the ability to make the final decision. Some people can tolerate no dissent. But, if you assemble a great team, don't you want to hear their ideas?[19]**

Breashears, of course, made a good decision in 1996 in part because he had set the stage for a successful choice. He certainly prepared well for the expedition, in terms of assembling the right equipment and supplies, organizing the logistics of the expedition, planning his group's acclimatization routine, and thinking through various dangerous scenarios that might unfold on the mountain. Those preparations helped him when conditions became more dangerous on the mountain. However, Breashears prepared for the problems that his team ultimately encountered in another important way. Long before arriving in Nepal, he had put some thought in how he wanted to make critical decisions, about the process that he would employ when faced with a tough call that needed to be made. When the signs of deteriorating weather emerged, Breashears took charge by directing a decision-making process that provided him with unvarnished advice and input, and that harnessed the vast expertise and knowledge of the other members of his expedition. Breashears succeeded by heeding the advice of Benjamin Franklin: "By failing to prepare, you are preparing to fail."

Questions, Not Answers

At Harvard Business School, we teach by the case method. We do not lecture our students. We provide a description of a management situation, and we ask students to put themselves in the shoes of the case protagonist, who has an important decision that he needs to make. Students learn inductively in this method of instruction. The professor does not hand the students a set of theories and principles and ask them to apply those ideas to the case study. Instead, the students discuss the issues facing the organization in the case, and principles and hypotheses about how to manage that situation effectively emerge from the class deliberations.[20]

What do students learn through the case method of instruction? Do they come away with a set of answers as to how to act in a specific situation? No, that is not our primary goal. We hope to teach our students *how* to make decisions, rather than provide them a set of prepackaged solutions to various management problems that they may encounter during their careers.

When asked what students learn at Harvard Business School, former Dean John McArthur once said, "How we teach is what we teach." What did he mean by that? Consider how an instructor behaves in the classroom. He asks questions—lots of them. He does not provide any answers, much to the chagrin of many students. Often, they want to hear the faculty member's recommended solution to the management problem described in the case. When pressed, most of us simply ask more questions, rather than provide answers. The case method instructor leads with restraint. By doing this, we aim to harness the collective intellect in the classroom and to create new knowledge through a process of inquiry and debate. We facilitate and moderate the deliberations. We stimulate dissent and divergent thinking, often employing the techniques described in Chapter 4, "Stimulating the Clash of Ideas," such as role play and mental simulation exercises. We try to establish a climate in which conflict can remain constructive. At times, we seek to bring opposing sides together, helping them to find common ground. To gain traction on complex problems, we often break them down into manageable pieces and tackle one aspect of the issue at a time—striving for a series of small wins as we build toward the denouement of a particular class session.

There is an important lesson here for all leaders. Consider again what Peter Drucker once said: "The most common source of mistakes in management decisions is the emphasis on finding the right answer rather than the right question." Indeed, proposing a solution often does not promote novel lines of inquiry, thought, and debate. It can shut down creative thinking or close entire avenues of discussion. By posing incisive questions, leaders can open up whole new areas of dialogue, unearth new information, cause people to rethink their mental models, and expose previously unforeseen risks. Much like the case method instructor, the effective leader uses sharp, penetrating questions to generate new insights regarding complex problems.

Those insights become the ingredients necessary to invent new options, probe underlying assumptions, and make better decisions.

For the case method instructor, the questions form long before the classroom session commences. Faculty members think carefully about how they want to lead the discussion. We anticipate the key points of debate and conflict. We devise mechanisms to spark divergent thinking. Faculty members consider the personalities in the room. We anticipate points of personal friction. We think about our role in the deliberations, and how we will intervene to advance the discussion. In short, we have a plan—albeit a highly flexible one. Great leaders, of course, behave as great teachers. They prepare to decide just as teachers prepare to teach. They have a plan, but they adapt as the decision-making process unfolds. Great leaders do not have all the answers, but they remain firmly in control of the process through which their organizations discover the best answers to the toughest problems.

ENDNOTES

Chapter 1 Endnotes

1. Many scholars have drawn this distinction between decisions that are quite novel, ill-structured, ambiguous, and highly consequential and those that are more routine, well-defined, and tactical in nature. For instance, see H. Simon. (1960). *The New Science of Management Decision*. New York: Harper & Row; P. Drucker. (1967). *The Effective Executive*. New York: Harper & Row; F. Harrison. (1996). *The Managerial Decision-Making Process*, Fourth Edition. Boston: Houghton-Mifflin. For an example of researchers who define strategic decisions in a manner similar to the approach employed in this book, see K. Eisenhardt and L. J. Bourgeois. (1988). "The politics of strategic decision making in high-velocity environments: Toward a midrange theory," *Academy of Management Journal*. 31(4): p. 737–770.

2. Henry Mintzberg and his colleagues conducted a landmark study in 1976 that documented the dynamic, iterative, and discontinuous nature of many strategic decision-making processes. See H. Mintzberg, D. Raisinghani, and A. Theoret. (1976). "The structure of 'unstructured' decision processes," *Administrative Science Quarterly*. 21: p. 246–275.

3. N. Tichy and D. Ulrich. (1984). "The leadership challenge—A call for the transformational leader," *Sloan Management Review*. 26(1): p. 63.

4. J. Byrne, L. Lavelle, N. Byrnes, M. Vickers, and A. Borrus. "How to fix corporate governance," *Business Week*, (May 6, 2002), p. 68.

5. Bill Wooldridge and Steven Floyd have defined and operationalized the construct of consensus as the multiplicative function of commitment and shared understanding. Their definition, survey instruments, and measurement methodology have now been used by a number of other scholars. See B. Wooldridge and S. Floyd. (1990). "The strategy process, middle management involvement, and organizational performance," *Strategic Management Journal*. 11: 231–241. To see how I have measured consensus following a similar methodological approach, see M. Roberto. (2004). "Strategic decision-making processes: Moving beyond the efficiency-consensus tradeoff," *Group and Organization Management*. 29(6): p. 625–658.

6. A. Amason. (1996). "Distinguishing the effects of functional and dysfunctional conflict on strategic decision making," *Academy of Management Journal*. 39(1): p. 125.

7. For more on what can happen when organizations achieve understanding without commitment, or vice versa, see S. Floyd and B. Wooldridge. (1996). *The Strategic Middle Manager: How to Create and Sustain Competitive Advantage*. San Francisco: Jossey-Bass.

8. J. Krakauer. (1997). *Into Thin Air: A Personal Account of the Mount Everest Disaster*. New York: Anchor Books. p. 356–357.

9. Many empirical studies have shown that organizational decision-making processes can be quite diffuse at times, and that they involve simultaneous activity at multiple levels of the firm. In Joseph Bower's seminal work on how resource-allocation decisions are made in organizations, he concluded that "Individual planning and investment decisions are made by managers at many levels of the firm...an idea is shaped as it proceeds up managerial levels until it emerges fully packaged as a request for capital or a business plan for consideration by corporate management. At the same time, each level of management influences the ones above and below it." See J. Bower. (1970). *Managing the Resource Allocation Process*. Boston: Harvard Business School Press. p. 19–20. For more empirical work consistent with Bower's findings, see R. Burgelman. (1983). "A process model of internal corporate venturing in the diversified major firm." *Administrative Science Quarterly*. 28: p. 223–244 as well as H. Mintzberg and A. McHugh. (1985). "Strategy formation in an adhocracy." *Administrative Science Quarterly*. 30(2): p. 160–197. An interesting reflection on the past few decades of research in this stream of literature can be found in R. Butler, H. Mintzberg, A. Pettigrew, and J. Waters. (1990). "Studying deciding: An exchange of views between Mintzberg and Waters, Pettigrew, and Butler." *Organization Studies*. 11(1): p. 1–16.

10. G. Allison and P. Zelikow. (1999). *Essence of Decision: Explaining the Cuban Missile Crisis*. Second edition. New York: Longman. p. 5. In Allison's book, he examines the Cuban Missile Crisis using three different conceptual lenses. The first—the rational actor model—presumes that one can explain an organization's behavior as the output of the thinking of a rational individual at the top of the institution. The other two conceptual lenses view organizational decisions and action as the result of a more complex set of routines and behaviors involving multiple actors, at different levels, who may have conflicting goals.

11. See M. Roberto. (2002). "The stable core and dynamic periphery in top manage-ment teams," *Management Decision*. 41(2): p. 120–131. In that paper, I provide results from a survey of 78 business-unit presidents at Fortune 500 firms, as well as from field research at several sites. The data show that a top management team performs a variety of monitoring and control functions within most firms, but that a single team with stable composition does not make strategic choices in most organizations. Instead, different groups, with members from multiple orga-nizational levels, form to make various strategic decisions. A stable subset of the top team forms the core of each of these multiple decision-making bodies.

12. D. Hambrick. (1994). "Top management groups: A conceptual integration and reconsideration of the team label," In B. M. Staw and L. L. Cummings (Eds.) *Research in Organizational Behavior*. Greenwich, CT: JAI Press. 172. Hambrick offered this acknowledgment one decade after launching the "upper echelons" literature, which focuses on the effect of top management team composition on strategic choices and organizational performance. See D. Hambrick and P. Mason. (1984). "Upper echelons: The organization as a reflection of its top man-agers," *Academy of Management Review*. 9: p. 193–206.

13. J.B. Quinn. (1980). *Strategies for Change*. Homewood, IL: Irwin. p. 13.

14. For interesting case studies that demonstrate the critical role of "offline" activity as it relates to senior management team decision making, see L. Hill. (1993). "Rudi Gassner and the Executive Committee of BMG International (A)," Harvard Business School Case No. 494-055, as well as D. Garvin and M. Roberto. (1997). "Decision-Making at the Top: The All-Star Sports Catalog Division," Harvard Business School Case No. 398-061.

15. For a comprehensive overview of cognitive bias research, see M. Bazerman. (1998). *Judgment in Managerial Decision Making*. New York: John Wiley & Sons. To access another useful guide for managers, see J. E. Russo and P. Schoemaker. (2002). *Winning Decisions: Getting It Right the First Time*. New York: Fireside.

16. For more on the sunk-cost trap, see B. Staw and J. Ross. (1989). "Understanding behavior in escalation situations." *Science*. 246: p. 216–220; H. Arkes and C. Blumer. (1985). "The psychology of sunk cost," *Organizational Behavior and Human Decision Processes*. 35: p. 124–140; J. Brockner. (1992). "The escalation of commitment to a failing course of action," *Academy of Management Review*. 17(1): p. 39–61.

17. Kathleen Eisenhardt and L. Jay Bourgeois found that political behavior—defined in terms of activities such as withholding of information and behind-the-scenes coalition formation—leads to less-effective decisions and poorer organizational performance. See K. Eisenhardt and L.J. Bourgeois. (1988). However, other studies show that certain forms of political behavior can enhance organizational performance. For instance, Kanter, Sapolsky, Pettigrew, and Pfeffer each have conducted studies that show that political activity such as coali-tion building can prove helpful in building commitment and securing support for organizational decisions. See R. Kanter. (1983). *Change Masters*. New York: Simon and Schuster; Sapolsky. (1972). The *Polaris System Development: Bureaucratic and Programmatic Success in Government*. Cambridge: Harvard University Press; A. Pettigrew. (1973). *The Politics of Organizational Decision*

Making. London: Tavistock; J. Pfeffer. (1992). *Managing with Power.* Boston: Harvard Business School Press. Why the discrepancy in these studies? It appears that the results will depend on precisely how scholars define politics, as well as precisely how managers employ political tactics in organizations.

18. In a classic study of more than 200 capital investment choices, Eberhard Witte found that the decision processes almost never followed a simple linear progression from problem identification to selection of a course of action. See E. Witte. (1972). "Field research on complex decision-making processes—The phase theorem." *International Studies of Management and Organization.* Fall: p. 156–182.

19. James March has described the "garbage-can model" of decision making in which solutions, problems, and decision makers often come together haphazardly, with the outcome sometimes being that solutions are in search of problems to solve. See J. March. (1994). *A Primer on Decision Making.* New York: Free Press.

20. See A. Langley. (1989). "In search of rationality: The purposes behind the use of formal analysis in organizations," *Administrative Science Quarterly.* 34: p. 598–631; M. Feldman and J. March. (1981). "Information in organizations as signal and symbol," *Administrative Science Quarterly.* 26: 171–186.

21. For more on Iacocca and the Ford Mustang story, see R. Lacey. (1986). *Ford: The Men and the Machine.* Boston: Little Brown; D. Halberstam. (1986). *The Reckoning.* New York: William Morrow; L. Iacocca. (1984). *Iacocca: An Autobiography.* Toronto: Bantam Books.

22. See K. Weick. (1995). *Sensemaking in Organizations.* Thousand Oaks, CA: Sage.

23. For more on the emergent nature of strategy formation, see H. Mintzberg and J. Waters. (1985). "Of strategies, deliberate and emergent," *Strategic Management Journal.* 6(3): p. 257–272.

24. Welch describes this concept of confronting reality in a video produced at the Harvard Business School that includes a compilation of Jack Welch speaking to students or being interviewed by HBS professors at a series of points during his 20-year tenure as CEO of General Electric. See J. Bower. (2002). *Jack Welch Compilation: 1981–2001.* Harvard Business School Video. Welch also describes what he means by dealing with reality in his book. See J. Welch. (2001). *Jack: Straight from the Gut.* New York: Warner Business Books.

25. Bower. (1970). p. 305.

26. In her book, *Men and Women of the Corporation*, Rosabeth Moss Kanter describes how managers have a tendency to search for subordinates who are similar to them in many ways, including people with similar outward appearances. She argued that homogeneity comforts people, in a sense, particularly during times of uncertainty. See R. Kanter. (1977). *Men and Women of the Corporation.* New York: Basic Books. Many scholars also have argued that demographic homogeneity may signify a lower level of cognitive diversity within a firm (i.e., a tendency for more like-minded people). For instance, see D. Hambrick and P. Mason. (1984).

27. For an example of the pressures to not disagree with a powerful chief executive, one might consider the case of Bill Agee, CEO at Morris Knudsen in the early 1990s. Brian O'Reilly describes his management style in great detail in an article

for *Fortune* magazine that appeared in May 1995, after a year in which Agee's firm lost more than $300 million, largely due to a flawed decision to move into locomotive and railcar manufacturing. In the article, O'Reilly quotes a rail company executive commenting on Morris Knudsen's attempt to move into this new business; that executive describes Agee's direct reports as "sycophants and yesmen." See B. O'Reilly. "Agee in exile," *Fortune.* (May 29, 1995): p. 50–61.

28. Ibid. (1997). p. 190.

29. Ibid. (1997). p. 260.

30. Ibid. (1997). p. 260.

31. Ibid. (1997). p. 245.

32. A. Boukreev and G. Weston DeWalt. (1998). *The Climb: Tragic Ambitions on Everest.* New York: St. Martin's. [p. 121].

33. Krakauer. (1997). p. 216.

34. Ibid. (1997). p. 219.

35. Ibid. (1997). p. 265.

36. For a complete conceptual analysis of the 1996 Mount Everest tragedy, see M. Roberto. (2002). "Lessons from Everest: The interaction of cognitive bias, psychological safety, and system complexity," *California Management Review.* 45(1): 136–158. For educators, the events also are detailed in a teaching case; see M. Roberto and G. Carioggia. (2002). "Mount Everest—1996," Harvard Business School Case No. 303-061.

37. A. Grove. (1996). *Only the Paranoid Survive: How to Exploit the Crisis Points That Challenge Every Company.* New York: Currency-Doubleday. p. 116.

38. See Amason (1996) for a detailed discussion of the relationship between cognitive and affective conflict, as well as the effect that these two forms of conflict have on outcomes such as commitment, understanding, and decision quality.

39. Many people have speculated about cross-cultural differences with respect to the role of conflict in organizational decision-making processes. I believe that many of the ideas presented in this book represent universal principles, but naturally, managers need to apply these core principles with sensitivity for the cultural settings in which they work. For instance, many people have wondered whether conflict must be handled differently in certain countries, such as Japan. I have chosen not to speculate in this book about cross-cultural differences, given that most of my research has taken place in the United States, Canada, and Great Britain. Moreover, other scholars have not yet arrived at definitive research conclusions with regard to cross-cultural differences in senior management decision-making. More work needs to be done in this area.

40. For more on the leadership style of Bill Parcells, see B. Parcells. (2000). "The tough work of turning around a team," *Harvard Business Review.* 78(6): p. 179–184.

41. H. Einhorn and R. Hogarth. (1978). "Confidence in judgment: Persistence in the illusion of validity," *Psychological Review.* 85: p. 395–416.

42. For more on overconfidence bias, see S. Lichtenstein, B. Fischhoff, and L. Phillips. (1982). "Calibration of probabilities: The state of the art to 1980," in D. Kahneman, P. Slovic, and A. Tversky, eds., *Judgment Under Uncertainty: Heuristics and Biases*. New York: Cambridge University Press.

43. B. Staw, L. Sandelands, and J. Dutton. (1981). "Threat-rigidity effects on organizational behavior," *Administrative Science Quarterly*. 26: p. 501–524.

44. For more on social identity theory and self-categorization theory, see H. Tajfel. (1978). "Social categorization, social identity, and social comparison." In H. Tajfel (ed.). *Differentiation Between Social Groups in the Social Psychology of Intergroup Relations*. p. 61–76. London: Academic Press; J. Turner. (1985). "Social categorization and the self-concept: A social cognitive theory of group behavior." In E. J. Lawler (ed.). *Advances in Group Processes: Theory and Research*. p. 77–122. Greenwich, CT: JAI Press. For a recent empirical study applying these theories to better understand the impact of diversity on work groups, see J. Polzer, L. Milton, and W. Swann, Jr. (2002). "Capitalizing on diversity: Interpersonal congruence in small work groups," *Administrative Science Quarterly*. 47(2): p. 296–324.

45. C. Argyris. (1990). *Overcoming Organizational Defenses*. Needham Heights, MA: Simon and Schuster.

46. A great deal of empirical research has shown that certain process attributes tend to enhance decision-making outcomes (i.e., a higher quality process leads to higher quality choices). For instance, see I. Janis. (1989). *Crucial Decisions*. New York: Free Press; J. Dean and M. Sharfman. (1996). "Does decision process matter?," *Academy of Management Journal*. 39: 368–396. For a review of studies in this area, see N. Rajagopalan, A. Rasheed, and D. Datta. (1993). "Strategic decision processes: Critical review and future directions," *Journal of Management*. 19: p. 349–364.

Chapter 2 Endnotes

1. T. Sorensen. (1966). *Kennedy*. New York: Bantam. p. 346.

2. D. Halberstam. (1972). *The Best and the Brightest*. New York: Random House. As an example of the caliber of the intellects gathered in the White House at that time, consider McGeorge Bundy—Kennedy's national security adviser. He received tenure at Harvard after only two years on the faculty, and he was appointed dean of the Faculty of Arts and Sciences in 1953 at the remarkably young age of 34.

3. This account of the Bay of Pigs decision draws upon two critical sources: A. Schlesinger, Jr. (1965). *A Thousand Days*. Boston: Houghton Mifflin; I. Janis. (1982). *Groupthink*. Second edition. Boston: Houghton Mifflin.

4. Schlesinger. (1965). p. 250.

5. The Bay of Pigs decision represents one of the classic cases of "groupthink" described by Irving Janis. According to Janis, groupthink is "a mode of thinking

that people engage in when they are deeply involved in a cohesive in-group, when the members' striving for unanimity override their motivation to realistically appraise alternative courses of action." Janis. (1982). p. 9.

6. For a discussion of the changes Kennedy made after the Bay of Pigs failure, see Janis. (1982). In addition, see Schlesinger. (1965); R. Johnson. (1974). *Managing the White House: An Intimate Study of the Presidency*. New York: Harper Row; A. George. (1974). "Adaptation to stress in political decision making: The individual, small group, and organizational context." In G. Coelho, D. Hamburg, and J. Adams (eds). *Coping and Adaptation*. New York: Basic Books.

7. For a detailed, first-hand account of the decision making that took place during the Cuban missile crisis, see R. Kennedy. (1969). *Thirteen Days: A Memoir of the Cuban Missile Crisis*. New York: W.W. Norton.

8. Janis. (1982). p. 141.

9. This analysis of the two decisions draws heavily upon a discussion in D. Garvin and M. Roberto. (2001). "What you don't know about making decisions," *Harvard Business Review*. 79(8): p. 108–116.

10. Schlesinger. (1965). p. 248.

11. The material that follows draws heavily upon empirical research reported in M. Roberto. (2002). "The stable core and dynamic periphery in top management teams," *Management Decision*. 41(2): p. 120–131.

12. For more on the filtering of information and its potentially detrimental effect on organizational decision making, see A. George. (1980). *Presidential Decision Making in Foreign Policy*. Boulder, Colorado: Westview Press. The book is an excellent analysis of the dynamics of decision making at the most senior levels of government, but the conceptual ideas also apply to many other types of complex organizations.

13. For a conceptual analysis of why NASA downplayed the risks associated with the foam strike that took place during the Columbia's launch in January 2003, see A. Edmondson, M. Roberto, R. Bohmer, E. Ferlins, and L. Feldman. (2005). "The recovery window: Organizational learning following ambiguous threats." In M. Farjoun and W. Starbuck (eds). *Organization at the Limit: NASA and the Columbia Disaster*. London: Blackwell. In that chapter, we define the concept of a recovery window as the finite time period between a threat and a major accident (or prevented accident) in which constructive collective action is feasible. We argue that executives do not downplay threats such as the foam strike simply because of negligence or incompetence; instead, we propose that organizations are naturally predisposed to downplay threats when they are ambiguous. That predisposition to under-respond derives from certain factors related to human cognition, team design and dynamics, and organizational structure and culture. The paper also outlines an alternative, learning-oriented approach to addressing ambiguous threats that leaders can employ to reduce the risk of catastrophic failures.

14. For more about involving people responsible for implementation in the strategic decision-making process, see L. Jay Bourgeois and K. Eisenhardt. (1988). "Strategic decision processes in high velocity environments: Four cases in the microcomputer industry," *Management Science*. 34(7): p. 816–835. The authors

explain how the CEOs of successful firms in their study tended to consult people responsible for implementation during the decision process, and in particular, involved them deeply in the development of execution triggers, defined as the stream of "subsequent decisions to be triggered by a schedule, milestone, or event" in the initially chosen course of action (p. 829–830).

15. K. Eisenhardt. (1989). "Making fast strategic decisions in high-velocity environments," *Academy of Management Journal.* 12: p. 543–576.

16. Eisenhardt. (1989). p. 559.

17. M. Roberto. (2002). "The stable core and dynamic periphery in top management teams," *Management Decision.* 41(2): p. 120–131.

18. Irving Janis and Leon Mann describe the apprehension and anxiety that individuals sometimes experience before making a consequential decision as "anticipatory regret." For a detailed discussion of the concept and its impact on decision makers, see I. Janis and L. Mann. (1977). *Decision Making: A Psychological Analysis of Conflict, Choice, and Commitment.* New York: Free Press.

19. Eisenhardt. (1989).

20. For a thoughtful summary and analysis of the research on demographic heterogeneity, see K. Williams and C. O'Reilly. (1998). "Demography and diversity in organizations: A review of 40 years of research." In B. Staw and R. Sutton (eds). *Research in Organizational Behavior:* p. 77–140. Greenwich, CT: JAI Press. It should be noted that many scholars have criticized the literature on top management team demographics for reasons beyond the fact that it has produced a series of conflicting findings. For instance, my 2002 article in *Management Decision* shows that strategic choices are not made by a stable top team within a firm, but by a dynamic blend of participants depending on the situation at hand. Therefore, it becomes hard to argue that the demographic attributes of the top team can accurately predict organizational outcomes. Other scholars have pointed out that most demographic studies cannot determine the direction of causality, pay insufficient attention to intervening team processes which some data suggest matter more than structural attributes, and fail to account for situation-specific factors that affect team process and performance. For an insightful critique of the research on top management team demographics, see A. Pettigrew. (1992). "On studying managerial elites," *Strategic Management Journal.* 13: p. 163–182.

21. Leaders also should consider the power structure within a top management team and its effects on the decision-making process. Recent studies suggest that scholars who have focused on demographic heterogeneity may not have accounted sufficiently for power imbalances within top management teams. For an insightful study that looks at both power structure and demographics within senior teams over time, see P. Pitcher and A. Smith. (2001). "Top management team heterogeneity: Personality, power, and proxies," *Organization Science.* 12(1): p. 1–18.

22. Joseph Bower introduced the concept of structural context in his study of resource allocation processes within multidivisional firms. See J. Bower. (1970). Subsequent studies by many of Bower's doctoral students have further explored how structural context shapes strategic decision making within firms. For

example, see C. Christensen and J. Bower. (1996). "Customer power, strategic investment, and the failure of leading firms," *Strategic Management Journal.* 17: p. 197–218.

23. J. Kotter and D. Cohen. (2002). *The Heart of Change.* Boston, MA: Harvard Business School Press.

24. Janis and Mann. (1977).

25. F. Fiedler. (1992). "Time-based measures of leadership experience and organizational performance: A review of research and a preliminary model," *Leadership Quarterly.* 3(1): p. 4–23.

26. J. R. Hackman. (2002). *Leading Teams: Setting the Stage for Great Performances.* Boston: Harvard Business School Press.

27. A. Edmondson. (1999). "Psychological safety and learning behavior in work teams." *Administrative Science Quarterly.* p. 44: 354.

28. For more details regarding the impact of psychological safety on team learning and performance, see A. Edmondson, R. Bohmer, and G. Pisano. (2001). "Disrupted routines team learning and new technology implementation in hospitals," *Administrative Science Quarterly.* 46: p. 685–716; A. Edmondson. (2003). "Speaking up in the operating room: How team leaders promote learning in interdisciplinary action teams," *Journal of Management Studies* 40(6): p. 1419–1452.

29. R. Farson and R. Keyes. (2002). "The failure-tolerant leader," *Harvard Business Review.* 80(8): p. 67.

30. A. Edmondson, M. Roberto, and A. Tucker. (2002). "Children's Hospital and Clinics," Harvard Business School Case No. 302-050.

31. Experimental studies have been conducted that compare the different group decision-making procedures discussed in this section (Consensus vs. Dialectical Inquiry vs. Devil's Advocacy). The analysis in these pages draws upon the results of that research. For instance, see D. Schweiger, W. Sandberg, J. Ragan. (1986). "Group approaches for improving strategic decision making," *Academy of Management Journal.* 29: p. 51–71. My colleague David Garvin and I have developed a set of group exercises, based on these experimental studies, that enable students to experience these different approaches to decision making, and to compare and contrast their evaluations of the three methods. See D. Garvin and M. Roberto (1996). Decision-Making Exercises (A), (B), and (C). Harvard Business School Cases No. 397-031, 397-032, 397-033. The teaching note accompanying those exercises examines these three methods in depth. Moreover, we discuss these approaches in D. Garvin and M. Roberto. (2001). "What you don't know about making decisions," *Harvard Business Review.* 79(8): p. 108–116.

32. E. De Bono. (1985). *Six Thinking Hats.* Boston: Little, Brown.

33. For a more in-depth discussion of the strengths and weaknesses of each method, see the following articles: D. Schweiger, W. Sandberg, J. Ragan. (1986); R. Priem, D. Harrison, and N. Muir. (1995). "Structured conflict and consensus outcomes in group decision making," *Journal of Management,* 21(4): p. 691–710; A. Murrell, A. Stewart, and B. Engel. (1993). "Consensus vs. devil's advocacy," *Journal of Business Communication.* 30(4): p. 399–414.

34. Recall, for instance, the finding of Solomon Asch in his famous experiments conducted in the early 1950s. He exposed an individual to a group that was instructed to unanimously articulate a position in clear violation of the facts. The individual often experienced enormous pressures for conformity. However, when the experimenter introduced a second person unaware of the experimenter's instructions for the majority, Asch found that the two individuals tended to be less likely to succumb to conformity pressures. See S. Asch. (1951). "Effects of group pressure upon the modification and distortion of judgments." In H. Guetzkow (ed). *Groups, Leadership, and Men*: p. 177–190. New York: Russell and Russell.

35. Priem, Harrison, and Muir. (1995); Murrell, Stewart, and Engel. (1993).

36. I have created a set of group exercises that explore the impact of a leader announcing an initial position at the outset of a meeting. See M. Roberto. (2001). "Participant and Leader Behavior: Group Decision Simulation (A)-(F)," Harvard Business School Case Nos. 301-026, 301-027, 301-028, 301-029, 301-030, 301-049. The teaching note accompanying those exercises describes the legitimacy, conformity, and framing effects, and it provides sample data pertaining to the impact that taking an initial position has on perceptions of fairness, levels of commitment, etc.

37. J. Russo and P. Schoemaker. (1989). *Decision Traps: The Ten Barriers to Brilliant Decision-Making and How to Overcome Them*. New York: Fireside. p. 15.

38. My colleague, Michael Watkins, has coined the phrase "charade of consultation."

39. D. Balz and B. Woodward. "America's chaotic road to war: Bush's global strategy began to take shape in first frantic hours after attack," *The Washington Post*. January 27, 2002: p. A01.

40. I have written a case study documenting the way in which President Bush and his advisers decided to go to war in Afghanistan in the days after the September 11 tragedy. See M. Roberto and G. Carioggia. (2002). "Launching the War on Terrorism," Harvard Business School Case No. 303-027.

41. A. Edmondson, M. Roberto, and M. Watkins. (2003). "A dynamic model of top management team effectiveness: Managing unstructured task streams," *Leadership Quarterly*. 14(3): p. 297–325.

42. G. Stasser and J. Davis. (1981). "Group decision making and social influence: A social interaction model," *Psychological Review* (88): p. 523–551; G. Stasser and W. Titus. (1985). "Pooling of unshared information in group decision making: Biased information sampling during discussion," *Journal of Personality and Social Psychology*. (48): p. 1467–1478; G. Stasser. (1999). "The uncertain role of unshared information in collective choice." In L. Thompson, J. Levine, and D. Messick (eds). *Shared Cognition in Organizations*. p. 49–69. Mahwah, NJ: Lawrence Erlbaum Associates.

43. An experimental study by University of Illinois-Chicago Professor Jim Larson and his colleagues supports the proposition that a more activist leadership style may induce people to share more private information. See J. Larson, P. Foster-Fishman, and T. Franz. (1998). "Leadership style and the discussion of shared and unshared information in decision-making groups," *Personality and Social Psychology Bulletin*. 24(5): p. 482–495.

44. K. Eisenhardt, J. Kahwajy, and L.J. Bourgeois. (1998). "Conflict and strategic choice: How top management teams disagree." In D. Hambrick, D. Nadler, and M. Tushman (eds). *Navigating Change: How CEOs, Top Teams, and Boards Steer Transformation.* p. 141–169. Boston: Harvard Business School Press.

45. Edmondson, Roberto, and Watkins. (2003). p. 312. We draw our definitions of mediation and arbitration from D. Lax and J. Sebenius. (1986). *The Manager as Negotiator: Bargaining for Cooperation and Competitive Gain.* New York: Free Press.

46. Edmondson, Roberto, and Watkins. (2003). p. 312.

47. Eisenhardt. (1989). Note that authors, researchers, and managers have used the term *consensus* in many different ways. It might be useful at this point to recall that we have defined consensus in this book as the combination of commitment and shared understanding. That definition differs from the use of the term employed by Eisenhardt, in which it refers to agreement among group members. It is important to point out that one could employ the approach to reaching closure described by Eisenhardt, which many leaders do, but not achieve high levels of commitment and common understanding.

48. D. Garvin. (2000). *Learning in Action: A Guide to Putting the Learning Organization to Work.* Boston: Harvard Business School Press.

49. It should be noted that former President Dwight Eisenhower may have encouraged President Kennedy to engage in process-centric learning after the Bay of Pigs failure. In late April 1961, Eisenhower traveled to Camp David at Kennedy's request. Kennedy explained his views regarding the causes of the failure: faulty intelligence, tactical mistakes, poor timing, etc. According to historian Stephen Ambrose, Eisenhower offered the following inquiry: "Mr. President, before you approved this plan did you have everybody in front of you debating the thing so you got pros and cons yourself and then made your decision, or did you see these people one at a time?" Apparently, Kennedy acknowledged that he and his advisers had not debated the plan openly in a full team meeting. See S. Ambrose. (1984). *Eisenhower: The President, Volume 2.* New York: Touchstone. p. 638.

Chapter 3 Endnotes

1. Welch. (2001). p. 96. In Chapter 7 of Welch's book, he provides a vivid description of General Electric's culture when he began as CEO. For a case study of Welch's leadership of the transformation at GE during the 1980s, see J. Bower and J. Dial. (1994). "Jack Welch: General Electric's Revolutionary," Harvard Business School Case No. 394-065.

2. In Bower and Dial's case about Jack Welch, they include a quote from one of Welch's colleagues, who comments that the CEO's decision-making style reflected his early years playing ice hockey as a child in Salem, Massachusetts: "Hockey is the kind of game where people bang you up against the boards and then go out and have a drink with you after...Jack will chase you around the

room, throwing arguments and objections at you. Then you fight back." Bower and Dial. (1994). p. 3–4.

3. Russo and Schomaker have described this situation as a "debating society." See Russo and Schoemaker. (1989). Note that several studies show a positive correlation between cognitive conflict and team performance, with no evidence of a curvilinear relationship. See Amason. (1996) and L. Pelled, K. Eisenhardt, and K. Xin. (1999). "Exploring the black box: Group diversity, conflict, and performance," *Administrative Science Quarterly*. 44: p. 1–28. On the other hand, Karen Jehn performed a study in 1995 that did show a curvilinear relationship between cognitive conflict and team performance. See K. Jehn. (1995). "A multimethod examination of the benefits and detriments of intragroup conflict." *Administrative Science Quarterly*. 40: p. 256–282.

4. I am not suggesting that personality plays no role whatsoever. Some people clearly are more comfortable with conflict than others. Some individuals find it easier to express dissenting views than others, independent of the context in which they are operating.

5. ABC News. (2003). "Final mission," *Primetime Live*.

6. This material on the Columbia accident is drawn from a year of intensive research that I conducted along with my colleagues Amy Edmondson and Richard Bohmer and our research associates, Erika Ferlins and Laura Feldman. I am deeply indebted to them for enabling me to join them in such a fruitful and intellectually stimulating research program. Along with reviewing all the publicly available materials about the accident, we conducted our own interviews with key experts. For educators wanting to teach about the Columbia accident, we have developed a traditional case study (Harvard Business School Case No. 304-090). In addition, we have created an innovative multimedia case study (Harvard Business School Case No. 305-032) that puts students in the shoes of six key managers and engineers at NASA, and enables them to experience the first eight days of Columbia's final mission as those individuals did. In our classes, we then role play a critical management meeting that took place on Flight Day 8. The case discussion is unlike any other we have experienced, because students come to class with asymmetric information, reflecting the reality at NASA during the mission itself. In the multimedia case, students receive a wealth of information, all based on actual communications that took place within NASA. Students hear audio reenactments of meetings that took place (based on actual transcripts), read internal NASA reports, see e-mails sent and received (and can even open attachments), obtain "while you were out" notes denoting phone calls that took place, view Microsoft PowerPoint slides shown at key meetings within NASA, etc. We also have conducted interviews with experts such as members of the Columbia Accident Investigation Board and a former shuttle astronaut. Those video clips are interspersed throughout the simulation. The teaching note accompanying the multimedia case explains how to lead the class discussion of this material.

7. This account of the events that took place during Columbia's final mission draws heavily upon the detailed account in the Columbia Accident Investigation Board's official report on the accident. For those unfamiliar with this report, it is one of the most remarkable accident investigation reports that I have ever read.

In large part, that is because the report goes "beyond the widget" as board member Duane Deal (a retired brigadier general) has said. That is, they did not stop with a finding of the technical cause of the tragedy. They examined the underlying organizational causes in great depth, and in so doing, they drew heavily upon social science research and organization theory to help explain why NASA behaved as it did before and during the mission. See "Columbia's Final Flight," Columbia Accident Investigation Board (CAIB) report. August 26, 2003. Washington, D.C. For Brigadier General Duane Deal's perspective, see D. Deal. (2004). "Beyond the widget: Columbia accident lessons affirmed," *Air and Space Power Journal*. Summer issue.

8. NASA Web site, http://www.nasa.gov/pdf/47227main_mmt_030121.pdf, accessed February 25, 2004.

9. Columbia Accident Investigation Board report. Vol. 1: p. 157.

10. James Glanz and John Schwartz. "Dogged engineer's effort to assess shuttle damage," *The New York Times*. September 26, 2003.

11. ABC News. (2003). "Final mission." *Primetime Live*.

12. Ibid.

13. T.Halvorson. "Judgment errors similar to Challenger, Ride says," *Florida Today*. April 8, 2003.

14. Interview with D. Vaughan conducted June 24, 2004. Professor Vaughan wrote an extraordinary book on the Challenger accident. In that analysis, she argued that NASA's behavior leading up to the Challenger disaster represented a "normalization of deviance." In other words, as time passed, small deviations from the official specifications became acceptable within NASA, because the shuttle continued to return safely despite O-ring problems. Over time, as Vaughan told us, "The unexpected becomes the expected becomes the accepted." In other words, what to outsiders may seem like serious signals of impending danger do not appear to be risky or dangerous to those within the organization who have gradually become accustomed to a deviation from the original standards. One could argue that a similar normalization of deviance occurred with regard to foam strikes in the years leading up to the Columbia accident. See D. Vaughan. (1996). *The Challenger launch decision: Risky technology, culture, and deviance at NASA*. Chicago: The University of Chicago Press.

15. Vaughan argues eloquently that the problems at NASA are systemic, and she certainly puts a great deal of weight on that level of explanation rather than the issue of individual behavior. On the other hand, I do not think she means to absolve individuals of accountability by looking to the organizational and cultural determinants of behavior.

16. I recognize that this distinction between "hard" and "soft" becomes blurry at times. Naturally, organizational structure and culture are intricately intertwined. Structure and culture shape and influence one another over time.

17. Welch. (2001). p. 96.

18. See J. Bower. (2002). "Jack Welch Compilation: 1981–2001," Harvard Business School Video.

19. Interview with Dr. Widnall conducted May 21, 2004.

20. This description and analysis of the incident draws heavily from the insightful examination found in S. Snook. (2000). *Friendly Fire: The Accidental Shootdown of U.S. Black Hawks over Northern Iraq.* Princeton, NJ: Princeton University Press.

21. Snook. (2000). p. 90–91.

22. For a discussion of the pros and cons of a CEO-COO structure at the top of a firm, see D. Hambrick and A. Cannella, Jr. (2004). "CEOs who have COOs: Contingency analysis of an unexplored structural form," *Strategic Management Journal.* 25(10): p. 959–979. This paper provides an empirical investigation of the CEO-COO structure. The authors find that firms with a COO perform worse than those without a COO. They argue that the negative performance may be due to problems such as the filtering of information and the partial separation of responsibility for strategy formulation from implementation. However, they also suggest that CEOs who select COOs may be less comfortable and/or competent in their roles than those who choose not to hire a COO.

23. See A. George. (1980). p. 153.

24. Rumsfeld, Donald. "Rumsfeld's Rules," Revised September 10, 2001.

25. Karl Weick and Kathleen Sutcliffe offer an example of an industry and a firm in which senior teams tend to consist of members who have been together for a lengthy period of time. In particular, they point out that Union Pacific had a strong inclination for appointing people with long tenures in the railroad industry to the top management team, particularly after a time when an outsider had brought changes that were not readily accepted by experienced railroad industry veterans. Moreover, Weick and Sutcliffe suggest that this preference for long-tenured industry executives has its risks: "It makes for a cohesive top management team. But that team is of one mind simply because the minds that compose it are redundant. Everyone sees the same warning signals and is blind to the same unexpected warnings." K. Weick and K. Sutcliffe. (2001). *Managing the Unexpected: Assuring High Performance in an Age of Complexity.* San Francisco: Jossey-Bass.

26. R. Foster and S. Kaplan. (2001). *Creative Destruction: Why Companies That Are Built to Last Underperform the Market—And How to Successfully Transform Them.* New York: Currency.

27. For a discussion of how senior management team dynamics may change over time as CEO tenure and overall team tenure grows, see D. Hambrick and G. Fukutomi. (1991). "The seasons of a CEO's tenure," *Academy of Management Review.* 16(4): p. 719–742. Also see D. Hambrick. (1995). "Fragmentation and the other problems CEOs have with their top management teams," *California Management Review.* 37(3): p. 110–127.

28. A. Edmondson, R. Bohmer, and G. Pisano. (2001). "Speeding up team learning." *Harvard Business Review.* 79(9): p. 125–134; A. Edmondson, R. Bohmer, and G. Pisano. (2001). "Disrupted routines team learning and new technology implementation in hospitals," *Administrative Science Quarterly.* 46: p. 685–716; A. Edmondson. (2003). "Speaking up in the operating room: How team leaders promote learning in interdisciplinary action teams," *Journal of Management Studies.* 40(6): p. 1419–1452.

29. ABC News. (1995). "Friendly fire: death over Iraq." *Primetime Live*.

30. I am deeply indebted to Leslie Freeman, a leader in learning and leadership development activities at Morgan Stanley Dean Witter, who has helped me identify the parallels between this friendly fire incident and problems that occur in business settings of various kinds. Freeman has co-authored a teaching case about this incident. See S. Snook, L. Freeman, and J. Norwalk. (2004). "Friendly Fire," Harvard Business School Case No. 404-083.

31. J. Andrus. (1994). *AFR 110-14 Aircraft Accident Investigation Board Report of Investigation: U.S. Army Black Hawk Helicopters 87-36000 and 88-26060*. U.S. Air Force. TAB V-026: p. 18.

32. M. Salter. (2003). "Innovation Corrupted: The Rise and Fall of Enron," Harvard Business School Case No. 904-036.

33. Widnall interview. (2004).

34. I have written a teaching case about the Storm King Mountain fire. See M. Roberto and E. Ferlins. (2003). "Storm King Mountain." Harvard Business School Case No. 304-046. For a more detailed analysis of the fire, see J. Maclean. (1999). *Fire on the Mountain: The True Story of the South Canyon Fire*. New York: William Morrow and Company. For academic perspectives on decision making during this incident, see the following articles: M. Useem, J. Cook, and L. Sutton. (forthcoming). "Developing leaders for decision making under duress: Wildland firefighters on Storm King Mountain and its aftermath," *Academy of Management Learning and Education*; K. Weick. (1995). "Findings from the wildland firefighters human factors workshop." Paper presented at the Decision Workshop on Improving Wildland Firefighter Performance Under Stressful, Risky Conditions: Toward Better Decisions on the Fireline and More Resilient Organizations. Missoula, Montana. June 12–16, 1995.

35. Edmondson, Roberto, and Tucker. (2002).

36. The concepts in this section are described in depth in Edmondson, Roberto, Bohmer, Ferlins, and Feldman. (2005).

37. Columbia Accident Investigation Board Report. (2003). p. 22.

38. For more on framing for execution vs. learning, see A. Edmondson. (2003). "Framing for learning: Lessons in successful technology implementation." *California Management Review*. 45(2): p. 34–54.

39. Vaughan interview. (2004).

40. Interview with R. Tetrault conducted May 24, 2004.

41. M. Roberto and E. Ferlins. (2004). "Massport (A)-(D)," Harvard Business School Case Nos. 304-081, 304-097, 304-098, 304-099.

42. E. Schein. (1992). *Organizational Culture and Leadership*. Second edition. San Francisco: Jossey-Bass.

43. Interview with T. Durden conducted May 26, 2004.

44. D. Garvin and M. Roberto. (1997). "Decision-making at the top: The All-Star Sports Catalog Division," Harvard Business School Case No. 398-061.

45. Columbia Accident Investigation Board Report. (2003). p. 170.

46. W. Langewiesche. (2003). "Columbia's last flight," *The Atlantic Monthly*. 292(4): p. 58–87.

Chapter 4 Endnotes

1. The term *confrontational by design* has been used by Charles Knight, former chairman and CEO of Emerson Electric, to describe the strategic planning process that he created and led for many years at his firm. See C. Knight. (1992). "Emerson Electric: Consistent profits consistently," *Harvard Business Review*. 70(1): p. 57–70.

2. As noted in an earlier chapter, building a more diverse team—one with more demographic heterogeneity—may increase cognitive conflict, though it could spark affective conflict as well. For an example of the empirical research on the link between demographics and cognitive conflict, see D. C. Pearce, K. G. Smith, J. Olian, H. Sims, K. A. Smith, and P. Flood. (1999). "Top management team diversity, group process, and strategic consensus," *Strategic Management Journal*. 20: 445–465. One should note, however, that demographic heterogeneity certainly may be helpful, but naturally, it does not guarantee a higher level of cognitive diversity or divergent thinking. In fact, one study showed that group process was a stronger predictor of top management team performance than demographic composition. See K. G. Smith, K. A. Smith, J. Olian, H. Sims, D. O'Bannon, and J. Scully. (1994). "Top management demography and process: The role of social integration and communication," *Administrative Science Quarterly*. 39(3):p. 412–438.

3. Naturally, as mentioned in the preface, leaders also need to take into account the national culture in which they are working. Some would argue that certain principles regarding conflict are not universal; that is, certain national cultures tend to deal with conflict differently, people in some countries tend to be more averse to conflict in group settings, etc. Because I have not conducted a great deal of research in non-Anglo Saxon cultures, I have chosen not to speculate in this book regarding cultural differences. In my view, some cultural differences do exist, although it is not clear to me that the typical stereotypes about certain countries are always accurate. There is certainly a need for more academic research on cultural differences in this area.

4. D. Scott. "Hot off his Manning impersonation, Huard now mimics Delhomme," *The Charlotte Observer*. January 24, 2004

5. Eisenhardt and her colleagues also have written about the importance of role-play exercises. See Eisenhardt, Kahwajy, and Bourgeois. (1998).

6. Grove. (1996). p. 89.

7. Grove. (1996). p. 92–93. For an insightful academic analysis of Intel's exit from the DRAM business, see R. Burgelman. (1994). "Fading memories: A process theory of strategic business exit in dynamic environments," *Administrative*

Science Quarterly. 39(1): p. 24–56. In this work, Burgelman describes how middle managers gradually shifted resources at Intel from the DRAM business to microprocessors, thereby altering the firm's competitive strategy. During this time, senior management continued to maintain that DRAMs represented a core element of Intel's corporate strategy; by the time Moore and Grove came to their epiphany, the organization's strategy had already been altered substantially. They were, in a sense, engaging in post-hoc rationalization of the new strategy that had taken hold at lower levels.

8. G. Klein. (1999). *Sources of Power: How People Make Decisions.* Cambridge, MA: MIT Press; G. Klein. (2003). *Intuition at Work: Why Developing Your Gut Instincts Will Make You Better at What You Do.* Boston: Harvard Business School Press.

9. P. Wack. (1985). "Scenarios: Uncharted waters ahead," *Harvard Business Review* 63(5): 72–79; P. Wack. (1985). "Scenarios: Shooting the Rapids," *Harvard Business Review.* 63(6): p. 139–150.

10. Eisenhardt, Kahwajy, and Bourgeois. (1998). p. 163.

11. J. Clawson and J. Grayson. (1996). "Scenario planning," Darden Business Publishing No. UVA-G-0260.

12. Klein. (2003).

13. M. Roberto. (2001). "Strategic Planning at Sun Life," Harvard Business School Case No. 301-084

14. The problem, of course, is that the selection of a particular conceptual lens entails the implicit selection of a frame for the problem at hand. How one frames a problem, of course, drives the type of solutions that are generated and considered. Therefore, scholars often advocate the explicit generation and consideration of multiple frames. See Schoemaker and Russo. (1989).

15. M. Roberto and G. Carioggia. (2003). "Polycom's Acquisition Process," Harvard Business School Case No. 304-040.

16. Schweiger, Sandberg, and Ragan. (1986). For more information, see also Garvin and Roberto (1996) and Garvin and Roberto (2001).

17. M. Roberto and G. Carioggia. "Electronic Arts: The Blockbuster Strategy," Harvard Business School Case No. 304-013.

18. A. George. (1980). George's comments build on the work of Richard Tanner Johnson, who wrote a book about different presidential decision-making styles. He described Franklin Roosevelt's style as a "competitive" model of decision making. Johnson contrasted Roosevelt's approach with the "formalistic" model adopted by presidents such as Eisenhower and Truman. That style emphasized the hierarchical flow of information by well-defined channels and procedures. Subordinates had clearly defined roles and areas of expertise, and the president synthesized the input received from various advisers. Kennedy, in contrast, employed a "collegial" model of decision making. According to Johnson, this approach emphasized a team-oriented approach to problem solving in which a great deal of informal communication occurred. Moreover, advisers behaved more as generalists than as specialists expected only to provide input on matters

related to a narrow domain of expertise. The president did not receive information filtered through and synthesized by one cabinet head or by the chief of staff, but rather worked closely with the whole group to hear the debate among his advisers. See Johnson. (1974).

19. J. Thompson, Jr. (1968). "How could Vietnam happen?—An autopsy," *The Atlantic Monthly*. 221(4): p. 47–53. Thompson provides an insightful analysis of the decision making about the conflict in Vietnam, writing with the perspective of having spent five years working in the White House and State Department for Presidents Kennedy and Johnson. For instructors wanting to teach about the Johnson administration's decision-making processes with regard to the war in Vietnam, I highly recommend asking students to view the movie *Path to War*, produced by HBO. The film provides an up-close look at how Johnson drew upon the input and counsel of his staff to make important decisions. I have written a brief orientation guide that I ask students to read before watching the movie. The guide provides a bit of background about the conflict, and it provides brief biographies of Johnson and each of his key advisers. See M. Roberto. (2004). "Orientation for Viewing 'Path to War," Harvard Business School Case No. 304-088.

20. Janis. (1982). p. 115.

21. Ibid.

22. Jeffrey Pfeffer has pointed that agenda control represents an important lever by which managers exert power. Moreover, he notes that some managers may purposefully crowd an agenda so as to avoid an intense focus on a subject about which they do not want lengthy debate. See Pfeffer (1992) and J. Pfeffer (1981). *Power in organizations*. Marshfield, MA: Pitman Publishing.

23. The adoption of a production, or routine operational, frame provides a powerful explanation of the organization's behavior during the Columbia recovery window (Deal, 2004). That framing partially explains why NASA emphasized schedules and deadlines as much as it did. Moreover, it contributes to our understanding of why Mission Management Team meetings were run in a very regimented, orderly, and efficient manner—after all, in a routine production environment, meetings are typically conducted in that manner. In short, Ham led the meeting in a manner consistent with the "operational frame" in which the shuttle program was organized. Her behavior is partially a product of the context in which she worked. That argument fits with Vaughan's analysis of the organization; as she said, "This was no personality problem. This was a structural and a cultural problem. And if you just change the cast of characters, the next person who comes in is going to be met with the same structure, the same culture, and they're going to be impelled to act in the same way." Vaughan interview (2004). For a lengthier discussion of the impact of the operational framing of the shuttle program, see Edmondson, Roberto, Bohmer, Ferlins, and Feldman, (2005).

24. Deal. (2004).

25. My colleague David Garvin often has pointed out that the subgroups in the Cuban missile crisis only spent a few days together, not many weeks or months. The limited timeframe may explain, in part, why people did not become so wedded to their subgroup positions as to induce a great deal of affective conflict and/or impede implementation of the final decision.

26. Lengthy time spent in subgroups may induce and accelerate social categorization processes, in which individuals may adopt highly positive perceptions about their in-group (their own subgroup) and negative perceptions about their out-group (the other subgroup). As Polzer and his colleagues have noted, such categorization activity can have a detrimental effect on team communication, conflict management, and performance. See Polzer, Milton, and Swann. (2002).

27. Langley. (1989).

28. M. Roberto and G. Carioggia. (2003). "Polycom's Acquisition Process," Harvard Business School Case No. 304-040.

29. A related problem in acquisition decision-making concerns the effects of momentum. Scholars Philippe Haspeslagh and David Jemison have described how many acquisition decision processes take on a "life of their own." In that atmosphere, it becomes difficult to question the strategic logic of a deal that appears destined to be completed, and for which all debates seem only about the fine points of the quantitative analysis. See P. Haspeslagh and D. Jemison. (1991). *Managing Acquisitions: Creating Value Through Corporate Renewal.* New York: Free Press.

30. D. Schweiger, W. Sandberg, and P. Rechner. (1989). "Experimental effects of dialectical inquiry, devil's advocacy, and consensus approaches to strategic decision making," *Academy of Management Journal.* 32: p. 745–772.

31. Bower and Dial. (1994). p. 4.

32. Welch. (2001).

33. Knight. (1992).

Chapter 5 Endnotes

1. This account of the Caesar comedy-writing team draws from an Institute for Management Development case study about the group, as well as Sid Caesar's autobiography. See B. Fischer and A. Boynton. (2002). "Caesar's Writers," IMD Case No. 3-1206, and S. Caesar. (1982). *Where Have I Been?* New York: Crown.

2. Fischer and Boynton, (2002). p. 7.

3. Caesar. (1982). p. 5.

4. Fischer and Boynton. (2002). p. 8.

5. My colleague David Garvin and I have described these two modes of decision making as advocacy and inquiry. See Garvin and Roberto. (2001). Chris Argyris and his colleagues have described advocacy vs. inquiry in a slightly different way in their work on group process and learning. See C. Argyris, R. Putnam, and D. Smith. (1985). *Action Science: Concepts, Methods, and Skills for Research and Intervention.* San Francisco: Jossey-Bass.

6. M. Roberto. (2004). "Strategic decision-making processes: Moving beyond the efficiency-consensus tradeoff," *Group and Organization Management*. 29(6): 625–658; K. Eisenhardt, J. Kahwajy, and L. Bourgeois. (1997). "How management teams can have a good fight," *Harvard Business Review*. 75(4): p. 77–85.

7. C. Lord, L. Ross, and M. Lepper. (1979). "Biased assimilation and attitude polarization: The effects of prior theories on subsequently considered evidence." *Journal of Personality and Social Psychology*. 37: p. 2098.

8. Many studies have reported a relationship between cognitive and affective conflict. For instance, see Amason. (1996) and Pelled, Eisenhardt, and Xin. (1999).

9. My colleague David Garvin and I created a set of group decision-making exercises modeled after the experiments found in Schweiger, Sandberg, and Ragan. (1986). See Garvin and Roberto. (1996). When we conduct these exercises with MBA students and executive education students at Harvard Business School, cognitive conflict often leads to affective conflict despite the fact that teams discuss simple, disguised case studies in their decision-making processes, and of course, the choices do not pertain to real issues in their own organizations.

10. Interview with B. McMillan conducted August 19, 2002. See also M. Roberto and G. Carioggia. "Electronic Arts: The Blockbuster Strategy," Harvard Business School Case No. 304-013.

11. David Garvin and I have developed an innovative multimedia case study about Levy's turnaround of the Beth Israel Deaconess Medical Center. The research's distinguishing feature is that we were able to track the turnaround in real time; in fact, we conducted lengthy (2+ hours) video interviews with Levy every two to four weeks during the first six months of the turnaround. The multimedia case study includes clips from those interviews, internal e-mails and documents, and articles that appeared in the press—all of which document the turnaround in great depth. The material has been organized in a calendar, where students can see the major activities that took place each month, and then drill down deeper to hear Levy's comments about the event, read e-mails and other internal documents that may pertain to it, and examine press accounts as well. The case also presents a representative week from Levy's actual calendar/schedule so that students can understand precisely what he does on a day-to-day basis as he launches the turnaround. See D. Garvin and M. Roberto. (2003). "Paul Levy: Taking Charge of the Beth Israel Deaconess Medical Center," Harvard Business School Multimedia No. 303-058. A detailed teaching note explains how to teach this multimedia case. In addition, we have written an article examining some of the leadership lessons from this story. See D. Garvin and M. Roberto. (February 2005). "Change through persuasion," *Harvard Business Review*. 83(2): p. 104-113.

12. C. Gersick and J.R. Hackman. (1990). "Habitual routines in task-performing groups," *Organizational Behavior and Human Decision Processes*. 47: 65-97.

13. R. Fisher and W. Ury. (1991). *Getting to Yes: Negotiating Agreement Without Giving In*. New York: Penguin Books. p. 6–7.

14. M. Roberto. (2001). "Strategic Planning at Sun Life," Harvard Business School Case No. 301-084

15. Interview with Monique Burns was conducted September 12, 2003.

16. M. Tennant. (1988). *Psychology and Adult Learning*. London: Routledge. p. 89.

17. For more information about the Myers-Briggs personality types, see I. Myers Briggs and P. Myers. (1995). *Gifts Differing: Understanding Personality Type*. Mountain View, CA: Davies-Black Publishing.

18. It is interesting to note, however, that students in the MBA and advanced management program (executive education) at Harvard Business School, and at similar programs at other institutions, often complete the Myers-Briggs test soon after arriving on campus. Perhaps discussion of the survey results enhances people's respect for others' cognitive styles, and thereby improves our ability to stimulate constructive debates in our classrooms. To my knowledge, we have not examined the impact of the Myers-Briggs evaluations on subsequent student interaction in our classrooms, but I believe that this question may warrant further investigation.

19. Interview with Burns. (2003).

20. W. Ury. (1993). *Getting Past No: Negotiating Your Way from Confrontation to Cooperation*. New York: Bantam Books. p. 78.

21. See Vaughan (1996) for a detailed description of the events that took place during the teleconference prior to the final launch of the Challenger space shuttle. See also Presidential Commission on the Space Shuttle Challenger Accident. (1986). *Report to the President by the Presidential Commission on the Space Shuttle Challenger Accident*. Washington, D.C.: Government Printing Office. Many different analyses of this teleconference have been done, from various conceptual angles. For instance, James Esser and Joanne Lindoerfer argued that the managers and engineers engaged in "groupthink" during the critical prelaunch meeting. See J. Esser and J. Lindoerfer. (1989). "Groupthink and the Space Shuttle Challenger accident: Toward a quantitative case analysis," *Journal of Behavioral Decision Making*. 2: 167–177. Vaughan, however, argues that many of these other analyses do not offer either accurate or complete explanations of the accident. For instance, she makes the case that the groupthink hypothesis does not fit the facts with regard to what took place at the teleconference. See Vaughan. (1996). p. 525.

22. Vaughan. (1996). p. 6.

23. A. Edmondson and L. Feldman. (2003). "Group Process in the Challenger Launch Decision (A), (B), (C), and (D) (TN)," Harvard Business School Teaching Note No. 604-032. For educators who are interested in teaching these concepts, Edmondson's teaching note explains how she uses an ABC film (*Challenger*—a 1990 movie directed by Glenn Jordan) to stimulate discussion about the Challenger launch decision. In class, she then conducts a role play of the deliberations that took place at the midnight teleconference on the eve of the launch. As students engage in the role play, she encourages them to think about how posing the right type of questions can foster an inquiry orientation and more effective collaborative learning process. She also describes how certain types of comments simply lead to a hardening of positions and more affective conflict.

24. Edmondson and Feldman. (2003). p. 14.

25. Ury. (1993). p. 80.

26. P. Drucker. (1954). *The Practice of Management*. New York: Harper Row. p. 351.

27. H. Gardner. (2004). Changing *Minds: The Art and Science of Changing Our Own and Other People's Minds.* Boston: Harvard Business School Press. p. 11, 14. Gardner's book provides a useful framework for thinking about how to engage in effective persuasion during a situation in which others disagree with you. Specifically, Gardner identifies seven levers that one can use to convince others to reconsider their position on a subject. The book builds upon Gardner's earlier work on the nature of human intelligence. See H. Gardner. (1983). *Frames of Mind: The Theory of Multiple Intelligences*. New York: Basic Books.

28. In *Changing Minds*, Gardner's description of the power of representational redescription uses the example of the Pareto principle, and it includes graphs such as those shown in Figure 5-2. Gardner draws his example from a book about the Pareto principle. See R. Koch. (1998). *The 80/20 Principle*. New York: Currency/Doubleday.

29. K. Weick. (1984). "Small wins: Redefining the scale of social problems," *American Psychologist*. 39(1): p. 40–49.

30. In some organizations, finger-pointing and the designation of blame crowd out learning opportunities when failures take place. Moreover, individuals often do not want to talk about their failures, because they are embarrassed, or because they do not want to admit their mistakes in a public forum. For more on how to enhance tolerance of failure in organizations, see Farson and Keyes (2002). For additional insight as to why organizations do not learn effectively from failure, see A. Tucker and A. Edmondson. (2003). "Why hospitals don't learn from failures: Organizational and psychological dynamics that inhibit system change," *California Management Review*. 45(2): p. 55–72.

31. Garvin. (2000). Garvin's book, *Learning in Action*, provides a detailed analysis of the U.S. Army's after-action reviews. For additional information about this learning process, see D. Garvin. (1996). "Putting the Learning Organization to Work," Harvard Business School Publishing Video.

32. At Children's Hospital and Clinics in Minnesota, the staff has come to a similar conclusion with regard to how they conduct "focused event studies"—lessons learned exercises that take place after a medical accident has taken place. The doctors, nurses, and administrators at Children's Hospital have discovered that a focused event study must begin with a detailed mapping of the events that took place leading up to the accident, before people turn to a discussion of the causes of the failure. In part, staff members have come to this conclusion because each individual often does not know the full chain of events that took place. A similar situation may exist with regard to a complex decision-making process. For more details on focused event studies at Children's Hospital, see Edmondson, Roberto, and Tucker (2002).

33. Garvin. (2000).

34. C. Knight. Discussion during Harvard Business School class, February 23, 2004.

35. D. Garvin and M. Roberto. (2003). "Paul Levy: Taking Charge of the Beth Israel Deaconess Medical Center." Harvard Business School Multimedia No. 303-058.

36. C. Raben and J. Spencer. (1998). "Confronting senior team conflict: CEO choices." In D. Hambrick, D. Nadler, and M. Tushman (eds). *Navigating Change: How CEOs, Top Teams, and Boards Steer Transformation.* Boston: Harvard Business School Press. p. 188.

37. Boynton and Fischer, (2002). p. 1.

Chapter 6 Endnotes

1. M. Gendron. "Beth Israel, Deaconess to merge," *Boston Herald.* February 24, 1996.

2. Editorial, *Boston Globe.* October 8, 1996.

3. Levy's description of the merger and the subsequent problems at the hospital leading up to his hiring are described, in his own words, in a brief paper case that accompanies the multimedia study that David Garvin and I have developed about the turnaround at the BIDMC. See D. Garvin and M. Roberto. (2003). "Paul Levy: Taking Charge of the Beth Israel Deaconess Medical Center (A)," Harvard Business School Case No. 303-008.

4. Russo and Schoemaker (1989) employ the term *debating society* in their book.

5. R. Charan. (2001). "Conquering a culture of indecision," Harvard Business Review. 79(4): p. 74–82.

6. This definition of culture has been developed by Ed Schein, an expert on the subject who teaches at MIT's Sloan School of Management. See E. Schein. (1992).

7. L. Gerstner, Jr. (2002). *Who Says Elephants Can't Dance? Inside IBM's Historic Turnaround.* New York: Harper Business.

8. Gerstner. (2002). p. 192–193.

9. The exercise of power plays a vital role in a culture of no. At IBM, the heads of the various business units had a great deal of power, and they could exercise it in the nonconcur process. In some organizations, of course, power is highly centralized, with a large gap between the CEO's power and that of others on the senior team. In others, the business unit chiefs operate independent fiefdoms, control a vast amount of resources, and they have a large degree of independence. The culture of no is more likely to exist in the latter case.

10. J. Pfeffer and R. Sutton. (1999). "The smart-talk trap," *Harvard Business Review.* 77(3): p. 134–142. p. 137. Interestingly, the authors argue that management education may encourage smart talk in organizations. They point out that students in MBA programs are rewarded for making clever comments, and they are especially lauded if they offer contrarian views and sharp critiques of ideas presented in the case or by others in the class. Furthermore, Pfeffer and Sutton highlight the fact that the students do not need to implement their ideas to be successful in MBA programs; they need only formulate ideas that sound smart and sophisticated.

11. J. Pfeffer and R. Sutton. (1999). p. 138. One interesting study that the authors cite in their article was conducted by Teresa Amabile. She found that book reviewers who offered negative critiques were viewed by others as more intelligent than those who issued positive evaluations. See T. Amabile. (1983). "Brilliant but cruel: Perceptions of negative evaluators," *Journal of Experimental Social Psychology* 19: p. 146–156.

12. An interesting example of "smart talk" may be the interaction that took place between the finance executives and the manufacturing and engineering managers at Ford in the 1950s. Ford President Robert McNamara had recruited a cadre of "whiz kids"—highly intelligent young people, with stellar academic credentials, who were adept at employing sophisticated quantitative techniques to analyze business issues. In David Halberstam's book about the auto industry, *The Reckoning*, he argues that the finance managers were adept at critiquing the plans and ideas of the "car guys," but their strictly analytical approach also may have stifled innovation and adaptation to the changing business environment in later years. See Halberstam. (1986).

13. Levy speaks about the decision-making problems at the hospital in great detail in a section of the multimedia case study that we have developed. He explains why decisions were not made effectively in the past, as well as how he overcame the "curious inability to decide." Later chapters of the book explain, in part, how he addressed the problem of indecisiveness at the hospital.

14. Charan. (2001). p. 76.

15. For more detail on this example, see D. Garvin and M. Roberto. (1997). "Decision-Making at the Top: The All-Star Sports Catalog Division," Harvard Business School Case No. 398-061. Please note that the names of the company and executives in this case study have been disguised.

16. Jon Katzenbach offers a similar example in his book on senior management teams. See the example about CEO Winston Newberry of Best Fuel Distribution Corporation (disguised case) in Chapter 3 of his book: J. Katzenbach. (1998). *Teams at the Top: Unleashing the Potential of Both Teams and Individual Leaders*. Boston: Harvard Business School Press.

17. A pair of articles describes these findings regarding the link between comprehensiveness and performance in stable vs. unstable environments. See J. Fredrickson. (1984). "The comprehensiveness of strategic decision processes: Extension, observations, and future directions," *Academy of Management Journal*. 27: p. 445–466; J. Fredrickson and T. Mitchell. (1984). "Strategic decision processes: Comprehensiveness and performance in an industry with an unstable environment," *Academy of Management Journal*. 27: p. 399–423. I should note that other scholars disagree with these findings. For instance, Bourgeois and Eisenhardt found that, "In high velocity environments, effective firms use rational decision-making processes." See Bourgeois and Eisenhardt. (1988): p. 827. However, in subsequent work, Eisenhardt argues that the high-performing microcomputer firms in her sample did not become handicapped by the comprehensiveness of their decision-making processes because they examined real-time information, rather than relying on elaborate planning systems. Moreover, the effective firms examined a wide range of options, but they worked through them simultaneously so as to conserve time. Less-effective firms moved

through different alternatives in a sequential fashion. In short, high-performing firms in a turbulent environment tended to act rationally or comprehensively, but they chose strategies that economized on time without compromising decision quality. See Eisenhardt. (1989).

18. Harrison. (1996). The type of marginal analysis described here is often used in economics. For instance, economic theory posits that competitive firms will maximize profits at the point at which marginal revenue equals marginal cost. In other words, if the incremental revenue of producing one more unit of good does not exceed the incremental cost required to produce it, then the firm will not manufacture that additional unit. For more on the cost of gathering additional information, as well as the optimal level of information search, see K. Brockhoff. (1986). "Decision quality and information." In E. Witte and H. Zimmerman (eds). *Empirical Research on Organizational Decision Making*. New York: Elsevier Science Publishers.

19. Janis and Mann. (1977).

20. See George. (1980) and Eisenhardt. (1989).

21. Henry Mintzberg has described the reliance on planning systems in many organizations, as well as the problems associated with an emphasis on formal planning as a means of making strategic decisions. See H. Mintzberg. (1994). *The Rise and Fall of Strategic Planning*. New York: Free Press.

22. This section draws heavily upon an article that I wrote several years ago about how managers cope with ambiguity in decision making. See M. Roberto. (2002). "Making difficult decisions in turbulent times," *Ivey Business Journal*. 66(3): p. 15–20.

23. J. Rau. (1999). "Two stages of decision making." *Management Review*. 88(11): p. 10.

24. Neustadt and May offer an extensive and insightful analysis of the promise and peril of reasoning by analogy, with many vivid historical examples. They also offer a useful framework to help decision makers scrutinize their analogies carefully, so as to avoid drawing inappropriate parallels to past situations. See R. Neustadt and E. May. (1986). *Thinking in Time: The Uses of History for Decision-Makers*. New York: Free Press.

25. My colleagues Jan Rivkin and Giovanni Gavetti have begun exploring the use of analogies in the formulation of competitive strategy within firms. See G. Gavetti and J. Rivkin. (2004). "Teaching students to reason well by analogy," *Journal of Strategic Management Education*. 1(2): p. 431-450.

26. Russo and Schoemaker. (1989); See also M. Bazerman. (1998). *Judgment in Managerial Decision Making*. Fourth Edition. New York: John Wiley and Sons.

27. G. Moore. (1965). "Cramming more components on to integrated circuits," *Electronics*. 38(8): p. 114–117.

28. Russo and Schoemaker. (1989); Bazerman. (1998).

29. Bower and Dial. (1994).

30. In relation to the pervasive tendency for firms to imitate one another, strategy expert Gary Hamel once offered this rather humorous observation: "In nearly every industry, strategies tend to cluster around some central tendency of industry orthodoxy. Strategies converge because success recipes get lavishly imitated... Aiding and abetting strategy convergence is an ever-growing army of eager young consultants transferring best practice from leaders to laggards... The challenge of maintaining any sort of competitive differentiation goes up proportionately with the number of consultants moving management wisdom around the world." See G. Hamel. (2000). *Leading the Revolution*. Boston: Harvard Business School Press. p. 49. Many firms do imitate others because they seek to find and emulate best practices. However, sociologists have offered alternative explanations for why imitation of strategies, structures, and processes occurs. They describe the phenomenon by which organizations begin to look more alike as isomorphism. See J. Meyer and B. Rowan. (1977). "Institutionalized organizations: Formal structure as myth and ceremony," *American Journal of Sociology*. 83: p. 340–363; P. DiMaggio and W. Powell. (1983). "The iron cage revisited: Institutional isomorphism and collective rationality in organizational fields," *American Journal of Sociology*. 48: p. 147–160.

31. M. Porter. (1996). "What is strategy?," *Harvard Business Review*. 74(6): p. 61–78.

32. I worked as a financial analyst at the nuclear submarine division (Electric Boat) of General Dynamics Corporation during this time. Many people expressed serious doubts about the strategy pursued by CEO William Anders at that time. They attributed his desire to focus on defense, while gradually selling off units of the aerospace conglomerate, as a strategy being pursued to maximize his compensation under a highly controversial pay-for-performance plan put in place when he was hired. Although Anders did make a great deal of money, the firm also performed remarkably well. Meanwhile, many competitors struggled mightily as they pursued commercial diversification strategies and mega-mergers. General Dynamics has continued to perform near the top of its industry since Anders's departure, and it is still focused almost entirely on defense. For more on Anders's controversial tenure at the firm, see K. Murphy and J. Dial. (1993). "General Dynamics: Compensation and Strategy (A) and (B)," Harvard Business School Case Nos. 494-048 and 494-049.

33. E. Schein. (2003). *DEC Is Dead, Long Live DEC: The Lasting Legacy of Digital Equipment Corporation*. San Francisco: Berrett-Koehler Publishers. p. 64, 69.

34. Schein (2003) provides a fascinating account of DEC's rise and fall, combining academic insights with first-hand observations based upon his time as a consultant to the organization over many years.

35. Charan. (2001). p. 76.

Chapter 7 Endnotes

1. The ability to persuade, of course, does matter a great deal. For more on persuasion, see R. Cialdini. (1993). *Influence: The Psychology of Persuasion*. Second Edition. New York: Quill; J. Conger. (1998). "The necessary art of persuasion,"

Harvard Business Review. 76(3): p. 84–95; D. Garvin and M. Roberto. (forthcoming February 2005).

2. J. Thibault and L. Walker. (1975). *Procedural Justice: A Psychological Analysis.*
   Hillsdale, NJ: L. Erlbaum Associates.

3. A. Lind and T. Tyler. (1988). *The Social Psychology of Procedural Justice.* New
   York: Plenum Press. p. 26. This book provides a comprehensive overview of the
   empirical research on procedural justice through the late 1980s.

4. Lind and Tyler. (1988). p. 72.

5. For a discussion of how the concept of fair process applies to decision making in
   the business context, see D. Garvin and M. Roberto. (2001). In addition, see W.
   Kim and R. Mauborgne. (1997). "Fair process: Managing in the knowledge
   economy," *Harvard Business Review.* 75(4): p. 65–75.

6. This definition of *fair process* draws upon my field research as well as numerous
   studies by other scholars. In particular, see M. Korsgaard, D. Schweiger, and
   H. Sapienza. (1995). "Building commitment, attachment, and trust in strategic
   decision-making teams: The role of procedural justice," *Academy of
   Management Journal.* 38(1): p. 60–84; D. Shapiro. (1993). "Reconciling theoret-
   ical differences among procedural justice research by re-evaluation of what it
   means to have one's views 'considered': Implications for third party managers,"
   R. Croponzano (ed). *Justice in the Workplace: Approaching Fairness in
   Human Resource Management.* Hillsdale, NJ: Erlbaum: p. 51–78; W. Kim and
   R. Mauborgne. (1991). "Effectively conceiving and executing multinationals'
   worldwide strategies," *Journal of International Business Studies.* p. 24: 419–448;
   Kim and Mauborgne, (1997); Lind and Tyler, (1988); Thibault and Walker,
   (1975).

7. Korsgaard, Schweiger, and Sapienza. (1995). 76. As mentioned in endnote 36 for
   Chapter 2, I have created a set of group decision-making exercises patterned
   after the experiments conducted by these scholars. They enable students to
   experience situations in which leaders employ more vs. less fair decision-making
   processes. At the conclusion of the exercise, students learn that giving people
   voice, by itself, does not engender commitment. Small changes in leader behavior matter a great deal with regard to others' perceptions of procedural fairness,
   and therefore, their level of commitment to a decision. See M. Roberto. (2001).
   "Participant and Leader Behavior: Group Decision Simulation (A)-(F)," Harvard
   Business School Case Nos. 301-026, 301-027, 301-028, 301-029, 301-030,
   301-049.

8. Anthony Iaquinto and James Fredrickson have conducted research demonstrating a correlation between top management team agreement about the comprehensiveness of decision processes and organizational performance. Their study
   suggests that senior teams with a clear, shared understanding about process comprehensiveness perform more effectively because of less role ambiguity and
   clearer norms of behavior, which in turn generate a greater focus on the problem
   that needs to be solved. Although their study focuses on comprehensiveness, it
   suggests that a clear up-front understanding about overall process design facilitates more effective decision making. See A. Iaquinto and J. Fredrickson. (1997).
   "Top management team agreement about the strategic decision process: A test
   of some of its determinants and consequences," *Strategic Management Journal.*
   18(1): p. 63–75.

9. For instance, the story of the development of Insulate at 3M has become legendary. Despite repeated rejections by top management, engineers continued to pursue development of the new product. Ultimately, they made substantial progress, and they convinced top management to allocate resources to enable the completion of the product development process. CEO Desi DeSimone used to tell the story of how he had been the executive who refused to allocate resources to the Thinsulate effort. Ultimately, he became convinced that the product had great potential, and he often reminded his managers that he had made a mistake and changed his mind when that became clear. See C. Bartlett and A. Mohammed. (1995). "3M: Profile of an Innovating Company," Harvard Business School Case No. 395-016. In addition, see Farson and Keyes. (2002).

10. Korsgaard, Schweiger, and Sapienza. (1995).

11. For a useful discussion regarding active listening skills, see T. Phelan. (1994). *1-2-3 Magic: Effective Discipline for Children 2-12*. Glen Ellyn, Illinois: Child Management Inc. Specifically, see Chapter 26. It may seem odd to cite a book about child development when talking about business leadership, but in fact, the ideas presented in Phelan's book apply equally well in a wide variety of settings. Charles Gragg also has written an interesting perspective on listening in an article about teaching and learning. He points out that listening can be a difficult task: "The imaginative reception of another's thoughts, often only partially created and certainly often poorly expressed, is a grueling task." Gragg makes a powerful case for why listening is essential for teachers to stimulate true learning. His ideas too apply equally well in a variety of settings. See C. Gragg. (1994). "Teachers also must learn." In L. Barnes, C. R. Christensen, and A. Hansen (eds). *Teaching and the Case Method*. Third Edition: p. 15–22. Boston: Harvard Business School Press.

12. M. Korsgaard, D. Schweiger, and H. Sapienza. (1995).

13. For more on the decision making that took place at NASA during the Apollo 13 mission, see G. Kranz. (2000). *Failure Is Not an Option: Mission Control from Mercury to Apollo 13 and Beyond*. New York: Berkley Books. In addition, see M. Useem. (2000). *The Leadership Moment*. New York: Times Books. Instructors who want to teach about the Apollo 13 crisis should consider asking students to view a documentary about the mission. See R. Whittlesey and N. Buckner. (1994). *Apollo 13: To the Edge and Back*. Universal Studios.

14. G. Kranz. (2000). p. 321.

15. B. Vlasic and B. Stertz. (2000). *Taken for a Ride: How Daimler-Benz Drove Off with Chrysler*. New York: William Morrow: p. 140–141. My understanding of the decision-making dynamics during the Daimler-Chrysler merger process was greatly enhanced by my opportunity to spend a half day with the authors of this book, Bill Vlasic and Brad Stertz, when they graciously accepted my invitation to come to the Harvard Business School to lead a seminar about that merger.

16. For a case study of the Daimler-Chrysler merger, see A. Cohen and D. St. Jean. (2004). "Daimler Chrysler Merger: The Quest to Create One Company," Babson College No. 404-084.

17. M. Suchman. (1995). "Managing legitimacy: Strategic and institutional approaches," *Academy of Management Review*. 20: p. 574.

18. M. Feldman and J. March. (1981). "Information in organizations as signal and symbol," *Administrative Science Quarterly*. 26: p. 171.

19. M. Feldman and J. March. (1981). p. 178.

20. See A. Langley. (1989); see also J. Bower. (1970). He focuses on the role of the "integrator" in his study of resource-allocation decisions. The integrator is a middle manager who provides impetus to some projects proposed by technical/market specialists, and he tries to convince upper management to approve those capital requests which he endorses. Bower explains the pressures that integrators feel to portray the decision in quantitative terms, even if they have not relied mainly on the financial data to select the projects to which they want to provide impetus: "Managers performing the integrating phase tasks must use strategic measures as well as financial ones…They must be intimately familiar with the strategic aspects of a variety of product-market units and measure of performance of those units in strategic terms. On the other hand, they must defend their judgments to top management in financial terms," Bower. (1970). 307, 309.

21. B. Ashforth and B. Gibbs. (1990). "The double-edge of organizational legitimation," *Organization Science*. 1: p. 177.

22. My research on procedural legitimacy has been published in M. Roberto. (2004). "Strategic decision-making processes: Moving beyond the efficiency-consensus tradeoff," *Group and Organization Management*. 29(6): p. 625–658.

23. For more on how individuals make attributions about others, see E. Jones and T. Pittman. (1982). "Toward a general theory of strategic self-presentation." In J. Suls. (ed). *Psychological Perspectives on the Self.* Hillsdale, NJ: Erlbaum. p. 231–262.

24. Feldman and March. (1981).

25. Schlesinger. (1965). p. 241.

26. George. (1980). p. 130. George points out that some presidents have attempted to create a "multiple advocacy" system—a systemized approach to ensure that issues are examined from diverse perspectives, and to prevent one bureaucratic agency or department from controlling all information and analysis pertaining to a particular decision. He describes how the national security adviser typically plays a special role as the "custodian-manager of the policy-making process" when presidents attempt to employ variants of a multiple advocacy model. That person becomes responsible for a number of key activities such as "strengthening weaker advocates" as well as "bringing in new advisers to argue for unpopular options." See George. (1980). p. 191–206.

27. D. Garvin and M. Roberto. (1997). p. 17.

28. When I conduct group decision-making exercises regarding procedural fairness in my classes at Harvard Business School, I plot charts that display the level of misalignment within teams. For instance, in one chart, I measure a team leader's perception of procedural fairness on the x-axis and the team members' perceptions of procedural fairness on the y-axis. We then discuss why some teams find themselves, for instance, in the lower-right portion of the chart (high leader perceptions, low member perceptions). For a detailed discussion of misalignment, including a discussion of how I employ survey data to address the topic in the

classroom, see M. Roberto. (2001). "Participant and Leader Behavior: Group Decision Simulation (Case Series) TN," Harvard Business School Teaching Note No. 301-120.

29. For a discussion of the role of the leader as a teacher, see N. Tichy. (2002). *The Leadership Engine: How Great Leaders Teach Their Companies to Win.* New York: Harper Business.

30. Quotation from Paul Levy. See D. Garvin and M. Roberto. (2005).

31. David Garvin and I discuss Levy's role as a teacher in great depth in the teaching note that accompanies our case study. Specifically, we discuss how he tackled the "curious inability to decide." See D. Garvin and M. Roberto. (2003). "Paul Levy: Taking Charge of the Beth Israel Deaconess Medical Center (A), (B), and (C) (TN)," Harvard Business School Teaching Note No. 303-126.

32. Kim and Mauborne. (1997). p. 69.

Chapter 8 Endnotes

1. R. Neustadt. (1980). *Presidential Power.* New York: John Wiley and Sons: p. 9.

2. Reflecting on the inefficiencies of decision making within the U.S. government, Truman once said, "When you have an efficient government, you have a dicta-torship."

3. Neustadt. (1980). p. 10.

4. This discussion of the decision-making process leading up to the D-day invasion draws from historian Stephen Ambrose's book on Eisenhower's war years. See S. Ambrose. (1970). *The Supreme Commander: The War Years of Dwight D. Eisenhower.* New York: Doubleday. For instructors wanting to teach about Eisenhower's approach to planning the D-day invasion, they might consider ask-ing students to view a film about the decision-making process that the general led during the first half of 1944. See R. Harmon. (2004). *Ike: Countdown to D Day.* Columbia Tristar.

5. Ambrose. (1970). p. 323.

6. Ibid. p. 323.

7. Ibid. p. 324.

8. Ibid. p. 371.

9. Ibid. p. 664.

10. Ibid. p. 366.

11. Ibid. p. 351.

12. For instance, see Russo and Schoemaker. (2002) as well as S. Kaner, L. Lind, C. Toldi, S. Fisk, and D. Berger. (1996). *Facilitator's Guide to Participatory Decision-Making.* Gabriola Island, Canada: New Society Publishers.

13. Russo and Schoemaker. (2002). p. 164.

14. Scholars often talk about how groups should defer judgment and focus on idea generation in the early stages of a creative brainstorming process. In other words, people should not critique other ideas at the outset, but instead focus on generating as many out-of-the-box ideas as possible. See S. Parnes. (1962). *A Sourcebook for Creative Thinking.* New York: Scribner.

15. Strategy process scholars have spoken about the iterative nature of strategy formulation processes in firms. They do not address the issue of closure, per se, but they do describe benefits from iterative behavior in the strategy process. See J.B. Quinn. (1978). "Strategic change: 'Logical incrementalism,'" *Sloan Management Review.* 20(1): p. 7–21; T. Noda and J. Bower. (1996). "Strategy making as iterated processes of resource allocation," *Strategic Management Journal.* 17: p. 159–192.

16. One should note that the types of divergent thinking described in this table emerge naturally in many firms—that is, leaders do not necessarily have to spark such divergence in a forceful fashion. Divergent thinking may arise because people in different units within an organization have disparate mental models regarding the firm's strategy, technological capabilities, customer needs, etc. Deborah Dougherty describes these sometimes conflicting mental models across various organizational units as the "thought worlds" within a firm. She also shows how the existence of multiple "thought worlds" can create obstacles in the product development process. See D. Dougherty. (1992). "A practice-centered model of organizational renewal through product innovation." *Strategic Management Journal.* 13: p. 77–92.

17. K. Weick. (1984). "Small wins: Redefining the scale of social problems," *American Psychologist.* 39(1): p. 43.

18. Herbert Simon outlined the theory of bounded rationality in response to the rational choice model put forth by economists. He wrote, "It is obviously impossible for the individual to know all his alternatives or all their consequences, and this impossibility is a very important departure of actual behavior from the model of objective rationality." See H. Simon. (1976). *Administrative Behavior: A Study of Decision-Making Processes in Administrative Organization.* Third edition. New York: Free Press. p. 67.

19. Maier and Maier conducted an experimental study in the 1950s that demonstrated that groups tend to be more effective when they employ a problem-solving process that is broken down into a few concrete stages, rather than trying to engage in a completely unstructured problem-solving approach. See N. Maier and R. Maier. (1957). "An experimental test of the effects of developmental vs. free discussions on the quality of group decisions," *Journal of Applied Social Psychology.* 41: p. 320–323.

20. Weick. (1984). p. 46.

21. This account of the 1983 Social Security reform is drawn from P. Light. (1985). *Artful Work: The Politics of Social Security Reform.* New York: Random House.

22. Light. (1985). p. 185.

23. For more on the concept of a superordinate goal, see M. Sherif. (1979). "Superordinate goals in the reduction of intergroup conflict." In W. Austin and S. Worchel (eds). *The Social Psychology of Intergroup Relations.* California:

Brooks/Cole. One way to focus attention on super-ordinate goals can be through the compensation system. For instance, Nucor—the mini-mill steel producer that enjoyed remarkable success for many years—employed group-level incentives. More specifically, people's bonus pay was linked to performance at one level higher in the organizational hierarchy. Front-line employees were compensated based upon the productivity of their production group. Similarly, the bonus pay of department heads depended on overall factory performance, and the compensation of plant managers hinged on the performance of the entire corporation. See P. Ghemawat. (1995). "Competitive advantage and internal organization: Nucor revisited," *Journal of Economics and Management Strategy*. 3(4): p. 685–717.

24. Eisenhardt, Kahwajy, and Bourgeois. (1997). p. 80.

25. Light. (1985). p. 184.

26. Ibid. p. 185.

27. L. Bossidy and R. Charan. (2002). *Execution: The Discipline of Getting Things Done*. New York: Crown Business. p. 234, 237.

28. J. Hammond, R. Keeney, and H. Raiffa. (1999). *Smart Choices: A Practical Guide to Making Better Decisions*. Boston: HBS Press.

29. Scholars may see a resemblance here to the concept of contingent contracting described by negotiation scholars. See M. Bazerman and J. Gillespie. (1999). "Betting on the future: The value of contingent contracts," *Harvard Business Review*. 77(5): p. 155–162.

30. For an overview of real options theory, see L. Trigeorgis. (1995). *Real Options in Capital Investment: Models, Strategies, and Applications*. Westport, CT: Praeger. For a discussion of how managers should apply the concept to capital investment decisions and strategy formulation, see W. C. Kester. (1984). "Today's options for tomorrow's growth," *Harvard Business Review*. 62(2): p. 153–160; T. Luehrman. (1998). "Strategy as a portfolio of real options," *Harvard Business Review*. 76(5): p. 89–99. One example of a largely effective "real options" approach may be Cisco's acquisition strategy in the late 1990s. Often, it took a small equity stake in a target firm and became more informed about the company and its management. After learning as much as it could about the target, it then made a decision about whether to acquire the firm outright. For a discussion of Cisco's acquisition strategy, see C. Holloway, S. Wheelwright, and N. Tempest. (1998). "Cisco Systems, Inc.: Acquisition Integration for Manufacturing," Stanford Business School Case No. OIT-26.

31. One issue with adopting a "real options" approach may be that managers become susceptible to the sunk-cost effect. In other words, having made a series of irrecoverable small investments in a course of action that may not be panning out, they may not be able to "cut their losses." Instead, they may become concerned that they will "waste" their prior investments if they do not proceed, and they find themselves "throwing good money after bad." Staw and Ross. (1989): p. 216.

32. See Janis. (1989); Hammond, Keeney, and Raiffa. (1999).

33. D. Nadler. (1998). "Leading executive teams." In D. Nadler, J. Spencer, and Associates (eds). *Executive Teams*. p. 3–20. San Francisco: Jossey-Bass. p. 18.

34. Eisenhardt. (1989). p. 572.

35. For studies linking procedural fairness to trust in the leader, see Korsgaard, Schweiger, and Sapienza. (1995); R. Folger and M. Konovsky. (1989). "Effects of procedural and distributive justice on reactions to pay raise decisions," *Academy of Management Journal*. p. 32: 115–130; D. McFarlin and P. Sweeney. (1992). "Distributive and procedural justice as predictors of satisfaction with personal and organizational outcomes," *Academy of Management Journal*. 35: p. 626–637.

36. This account of the Mann Gulch fire draws on several sources: N. Maclean. (1972). *Young Men and Fire*. Chicago: University of Chicago Press; K. Weick. (1993). "The collapse of sensemaking in organizations: The Mann Gulch disaster," *Administrative Science Quarterly*. 38: p. 628–652; M. Useem. (1998). *The Leader-ship Moment: Nine Stories of Triumph and Disaster and Their Lessons for Us All*. New York: Times Business. Drawing on these sources, as well as the official investigation report and other accounts, I have written a case study about the Mann Gulch fire. See M. Roberto and E. Ferlins. (2003). "Fire at Mann Gulch," Harvard Business School Case No. 304-089.

37. Maclean. (1972). p. 74.

38. Ibid. p. 95.

39. Useem. (1998). p. 55.

40. Maclean. (1972). p. 40.

41. Ibid. p. 64.

42. Useem. (1998). p. 56.

43. Ambrose. (1970). p. 324-325.

Chapter 9 Endnotes

1. M. Loeb. (1995). "Marshall Loeb on leadership: Ten steps to effective leader-ship," Speech at the Minnesota Center for Corporate Responsibility. June 21, 1995.

2. "Growing worker confusion about corporate goals complicates recovery, Watson Wyatt WorkUSA study finds," Watson Wyatt. Press Release. September 9, 2002.

3. "Growing worker confusion about corporate goals complicates recovery, Watson Wyatt WorkUSA study finds," Watson Wyatt. Press Release. September 9, 2002.

4. "Declining employee confidence in corporate leadership threatens Canadian competitiveness, Watson Wyatt Survey Finds," Watson Wyatt. Press Release. October 21, 2002.

5. S. Cauldron. (2002). "Where have all the leaders gone?," *Workforce Management*. December: p. 29.

6. J. Collins. (2001). *Good to Great: Why Some Companies Make the Leap…and Others Don't*. New York: Harper Business. My colleague Rakesh Khurana also has written about the perils that firms face when they pursue charismatic CEOs

in the executive search process. See R. Khurana. (2002). "The curse of the superstar CEO," *Harvard Business Review*. 80(9): p. 60–65.

7. J. Reingold. (2003). "Still angry after all these years," *Fast Company*. 75: p. 89.

8. T. Peters. (2001). "Rule #3: Leadership is confusing as hell," *Fast Company*. Issue 44. p. 124–135.

9. For instance, see R. Tannebaum and W. Schmidt. (1958). "How to choose a leadership pattern," *Harvard Business Review*. 36(2): p. 95–101; V. Vroom and P. Yetton. (1973). *Leadership and Decision Making*. Pittsburgh: University of Pittsburgh Press.

10. Collins. (2001).

11. R. Heifetz. (1994). *Leadership Without Easy Answers*. Cambridge, MA: Belknap Press. p. 251.

12. W. Bennis. (1997). "The secrets of great groups," *Leader to Leader*. 3: p. 29.

13. Heifetz. (1994). p. 2.

14. Nadler. (1998). p. 16.

15. Karl Weick has described how individuals engage in sense making. That is, they try to make meaning of previous actions that they have undertaken. An individual's sense-making process naturally will be constrained by prior life experiences, mental models, etc. Therefore, a leader needs to be wary of relying too heavily on his particular interpretation of a given situation. Others may have made sense of a particular event in a different way. See K. Weick. (1995). *Sensemaking in Organizations*. Thousand Oaks, CA: Sage.

16. For more on this topic, see Edmondson, Roberto, et al. (2005).

17. Breashears's intuition served him well in this circumstance. Scholars define intuition as pattern recognition based upon experience. In this case, Breashears had many years of experience on Everest, and he spotted a pattern, a set of signals, which reminded him of past instances of looming risk with regard to weather conditions. For more on intuition, see Klein. (1999) and Klein. (2003).

18. Boukreev and Dewalt. (1997). p. 120.

19. D. Breashears. Remarks to Harvard Business School class. February 24, 2003.

20. For more on teaching by the case method, see L. Barnes, C. R. Christensen, and A. Hansen. (1994). *Teaching and the Case Method*. Third edition. Boston: Harvard Business School Press.

INDEX

A

affective conflict, 20-22, 115-116
  after decisions
    reflection, 131-133
    repair of damaged feelings, 133
    telling as classic stories, 134-135
  before debates
    ground rules, 119-120
    mutual respect, 122
    role playing, 120-122
  during debates
    redescription, 128-129
    reframing debates, 124-127
    revisitation, 130-131
  managing, 117-118
  versus cognitive conflict, 117
Ager, Mark, 165-167, 176, 183-186
All-Star Sports, 150, 162
  fair decision-making processes, 176
    misalignment problems, 188
Allen, Woody, 111
Allison, Graham, 10
Ambrose, Stephen, 196, 219
analogy reasoning, 155-157
Apollo 13 mission, 178-179
Army (U.S.), 131
Ashforth, Blake, 182

B

Ball, George, 104
Barrett, Don, 150, 162
  fair decision-making processes, 176
  misalignment problems, 188
Bay of Pigs, 3-4, 229
  CIA involvement, 30
  decision-making processes, 29-30, 35, 55
    groups, 74
    legitimate processes, 187
Beaujolais, Roger, 66
Beidleman, Ned, 17-19
Belichick, Bill, 95
Bennis, Warren, 227
Beth Israel Deaconess Medical Center
    (BIDMC), xviii, 119-120, 141-142
  closure, sustaining in decision
    making, 215
  culture of yes, 147-148
  fair decision-making processes,
    176-179, 190-191
Black Hawk helicopters (U.S.) shot
    down, 69-71, 76
Bohmer, Richard, xviii, 75
Boisjoly, Roger, 125-126
Bonaparte, Napoleon, 143
Bossidy, Larry, 207
Boston Red Sox, xiii
Boukreev, Anatoli, 18
Breashears, David, 231-233
Brooks, Mel, 111-112
Burns, Monique, 122-123
Bush, George W., 50, 53

C

Caesar, Sid, 111-112, 137
Cain, Leroy, 65
candor, lack of
  Columbia accident, 63-67
  General Electric, 59-61
  hard barriers, 67-83
  signals, 60-61
  systemic problem, 62
Capital One, 159
Castro, Fidel, 3, 29
Caufield, Steven, 119
  managerial levers use, 91-93
    U.S. Navy vessels, design/construction contract, 87-91
Central Intelligence Agency (CIA), 30
CEOs, critical decisions, 9-10
Challenger 1986 accident, xviii
  affective conflict, 125
  parallels to *Columbia* accident, 66
Chamberlain, Lloyd, 156
charade of consultation, 170-171
Charan, Ram, 144, 148, 163
Children's Hospital and Clinics, Minneapolis, 42
  language systems, 78
Chrysler, 159
Churchill, Winston, 131
CIA (Central Intelligence Agency), 30
closure in decision making, 195-198
  building trust and credibility, 216-219
  decision mode, 212-215
  divergent and convergent thinking, 198-202
  small wins, 202-205
    outcome-oriented, 206, 209-212
    process-oriented, 206-209
  sustaining closure, 215-216
Coca-Cola Company, formula change, 3-4, 42
cognitive conflict, 20-22, 116
  versus affective conflict, 117
Collins, Jim, 225
Colts, Indianapolis, 95
Columbia Accident Investigation Board, xviii, 65, 69, 80
  efficiency crowding out debate, 106
Columbia space shuttle 2003 accident, xviii, 3

decision-making processes, 36
efficiency crowding out debate, 106
lack of NASA's candor and dissent, 62-67
language systems, 78
structural barriers to candid communication, 69
communication, 229
  as managerial lever, 34, 43-48
    U.S. Navy vessels, contract competition, 91-94
composition as managerial lever, 34-40, 229
  U.S. Navy vessels, contract competition, 91-93
conceptual models, 99-100
conflict in decision making
  affective conflict, 20-22, 115-117
  building trust and credibility, 216-219
  challenges
    cognitive biases, 23-24
    cognitive rigidity, 24
    defensive routines by management, 25-26
    in-groups versus out-groups, 25
    leadership style, 23
  closure, 195-198
    decision mode, 212-215
    sustaining closure, 215-216
  cognitive conflict, 20-22, 116-117
  convergent and divergent thinking, 198-202
  debate diagnosis, 111-114
  fair and legitimate processes, 192-193
  management
    after decisions, 131-133
    before debates, 119-122
    during debates, 124-131
    telling as classic stories, 134-135
  small wins, 202-205
    outcome-oriented, 206-212
    process-oriented, 206-209
  Your Show of Shows, 111-112, 137
consensus in decision making
  conflicts, 192-193
  effects, 8
  fair processes, 168-176
    implementation, 176-179

lack of, 165-167

legitimate processes, 179-182, 185-188

misalignment problems, 188-189

teaching fair and legitimate processes, 189-191

content-centric learning, 54

context as managerial lever, 34, 40-43, 229

U.S. Navy vessels, contract competition, 91-93

control as managerial lever, 34, 48-54, 229

U.S. Navy vessels, contract competition, 91-93

convergent thinking, 198-202

Corning Incorporated, 214

Coy, Craig, 80

Cruise, Tom, 76

Cuban missile crisis, 229-230

decision-making bodies, 74

decision-making processes, 30-33, 38, 53-54

legitimate decision-making processes, 188

point-to-point communication, 105

cultural barriers to candid communication, 67, 75- 83

culture of maybe, 151-154

culture of no, 144-147, 154

versus Devil's Advocacy, 145-146

culture of yes, 147-151, 154

D

Daimler Benz, 179, 181

Daimler-Chrysler merger, 180

de Bono, Edward, 44

Deal, Duane, 106

debate stimulation, 94-95

conceptual models, 99-100

Devil's Advocacy, 100-101

Dialectical Inquiry, 100-101

leadership pitfalls, 103

efficiency crowding out debate, 105-106

encouraging entrenchment and polarization, 106

hub-and-spoke model, 104-105

misuse of Devil's Advocacy, 103-104

striving for false precision, 107-108

mental simulation, 97-99

point-counterpoint method, 101-102

practice of methods beneficial, 108-110

role playing, 95-97

U.S. Navy vessels, contract competition, 88-91

managerial levers use, 91-93

Debris Assessment Team, *Columbia* space shuttle accident, 64, 69

decision frames, 49

decision-making effectiveness, xiv

decision-making myths, 8

critical decisions

as cognitive endeavors, 11-12

by CEO, 9-10

by managers, 14

by managers after analysis, 12-13

by top management teams, 10-11

lone warrior myth, 226-228

versus reality, 8-9, 14-15

decision-making process

winning U.S. Navy vessels contract, 88-91

managerial levers use, 91-93

decision-making processes, xv

absence of candor

Columbia accident, 63-67

hard barriers, 67-75

soft barriers, 67, 75-83

systemic problem, 62

absence of dissent, 15-16

Bay of Pigs, 29-30, 35, 55

decision-making bodies, 74

legitimate decision-making processes, 187

challenges

cognitive biases, 23-24

cognitive rigidity, 24

defensive routines by management, 25-26

in-groups versus out-groups, 25

leadership style, 23

right decision versus right process, 26-27

cognitive and affective conflict, 20-22

Cuban missile crisis, 30, 32-33, 38, 53-54

decision-making bodies, 74

legitimate decision-making processes, 188

point-to-point communication, 105

decision mode, 212-215

Kennedy's Ex Comm, 30, 32-33

Mount Everest 1996 tragedy,

poor decisions, 16-19

role of leaders, xv

Devil's Advocacy, 45-47, 94

leadership pitfalls, 103-104

practice beneficial, 108

variants, 100-101

versus culture of no, 145-146

Dialectical Inquiry, 45-47, 94, 173

practice beneficial, 108

variants, 100-101

Digital Equipment Corporation (DEC), 161-162

decision-making bodies, 74

dissent in decision making

absence of candor

Columbia accident, 63-67

hard barriers, 67-75

soft barriers, 67, 75-83

systemic problem, 62

absence of dissent, 15-16

challenges

cognitive biases, 23-24

cognitive rigidity, 24

defensive routines by management, 25-26

in-groups versus out-groups, 25

leadership style, 23

Mount Everest 1996 tragedy, 16-19

perils, 20-22

Dittemore, Ron, 64

divergent thinking, conflicts in decision making, 198-202

Dodge, Wagner, 217-218

Dougherty, Kevin, 99-100

role playing, 121

Drucker, Peter, 127, 234

E

Edmondson, Amy, xviii

affective conflict, 126

closure by leaders of decision-making process, 53

collective problem solving and learning simulation, 42

patterns of participation and involvement, 51

status differences in candid communication, 75

effective listening, 174-175

80/20 rule, 128-129

Eisenhardt, Kathleen, 37-38, 52

closure in decision making, confidants, 215

process-oriented small wins, 207

scenario planning, 98

Eisenhower, Dwight, 195-200, 209, 215, 219

Electronic Arts, 101-102

affective conflict, 117

Emerson Electric, 109

repair of damaged feelings, 133

Enron, 77

Epstein, Theo, xiii

Ex Comm (Executive Committee of the National Security Council), 30-35

F

F-15 fighter jet pilots (U.S), shooting Black Hawk helicopters, 69-71, 76

fair decision-making processes, 168

conflicts, 192-193

definition, 168-171

implementation, 176-179

leadership role, 172-176

teaching good processes, 189-191

misalignment problems, 188-189

unanimity, lack of, 165-167

Farson, Richard, 42

Feldman, Martha, 181

Fenton, Ben, 124

Fischer, Scott, 3-4, 8

poor decisions, 16

Fisher, Roger, 120

Fisher, Scott, 231-232

Ford Motor Company, 13

Forest Service (U.S.), 78

Mann Gulch, Montana, forest fire, 217-218

Fortune magazine, 224

Foster, Richard, 74
4 C's, 229
free exchange approach to
    communication, 44

G

Gang of Nine, 204-209
Gardner, Howard, 128
Garvin, David, xviii, 131, 54
Gas Pipeline, 77
Gelbart, Larry, 111, 137
General Dynamics, 160
General Electric
    best practices initiative, 159
    debate, 108
    Jack Welch as CEO, 14
    lack of candor, 59-61
    reduction of hierarchy layers at GE, 68
George, Alexander, 72, 102
Gersick, Connie, 120
Gerstner, Louis, 144-145, 226
Gibbs, Barrie, 182
Gillette, 226
Glawson, James, 98
Goizueta, Roberto, 4, 42
Grayson. Leslie, 98
Grove, Andrew, 20, 96, 176

H

Hackman, Richard, 120
Hagerty, Robert, 101
Halberstam, David, 30
Hall, Rob, 3-4, 8, 231-232
    poor decisions, 16-19
Ham, Linda, 63-65
Hambrick, Donald, 10
hard barriers to candor, 67-75
Hardy, George, 125
Harris, Andy, 18
Harvard Business School, 233-235
Heifetz, Ronald, 226-228
Hewlett-Packard, 159
Honeywell International, 207
Houghton, Jamie, 214
Huard, Damon, 95
hub-and-spoke model, 104-105

I

Iacocca, Lee, 13
IBM
    culture of no, 144-145
    decision-making bodies, 74
IMAX film expedition, 231
imitation of best practices, 158-160
in-family events, 78
indecisiveness, 143-144
    accelerating decision making, 155
        adopting rules of thumb, 157-158
        *failure to solve underlying
        problems, 160*
        imitating best practices, 158-160
        reasoning by analogy, 155, 157
    culture of maybe, 151-154
    culture of no, 144-147, 154
        versus Devil's Advocacy, 146
    culture of yes, 147-151, 154
        *Beth Israel Deaconess Medical
        Center, 141-142*
    origins of indecisive cultures, 161-163
Indianapolis Colts, 95
Intel, 176
iterative process of divergence and
    convergence, 199-202

J – K

Janis, Irving, 104
Jet Corp, 184
Johnson, Lyndon, 103-105

Kassner, Bruce, 100
Kennedy, President John F.
    Bay of Pigs, 4, 229-230
        decision-making bodies, 74
        *decision-making processes, 29-30,
        35, 55, 187*
    Cuban missile crisis, 229-230
        decision-making bodies, 74
        *decision-making processes,
        30-33, 38, 53-54, 188*
        point-to-point communication, 105
    Ex Comm, 30-35
Kennedy, Robert, 31, 38
Keyes, Ralph, 42

Keystone, 184
Kim, W. Chan, 192
Kimberly-Clark, 226
Klein, Gary, 97-98
Knight, Chuck, 108-109
    repair of damaged feelings, 133
Korean conflict, 156
Korsgaard, Audrey, 172
Kourey, Mike, 107
Krakauer, Jon, 8, 18
Kranz, Gene, 178-179

L

leaders' roles
    decision-making processes, xv
    forms of taking charge, 228-230
    lone warrior myth, 226-228
    virtues of effective leaders, 225-226
leadership
    closure in contentious decisions,
        195-198
        building trust and credibility,
            216-219
        decision mode, 212-215
        divergent and convergent thinking,
            198-202
        outcome-oriented small wins,
            206, 209-212
        process-oriented small wins, 206-209
        small wins, 202-205
        sustaining closure, 215-216
    conflicts in decision making, 192-193
    fair decision-making processes, 172-176
        implementation, 176-179
        teaching processes, 189-191
    leadership emphasis, 224-225
    leadership style, 23
    leadership with restraint, 230-233
    legitimate decision-making processes,
        179-181
        destroying legitimacy, 182, 185-186
        misalignment problems, 188-189
        preserving legitimacy, 186-188
        procedural legitimacy, 181-182
        teaching processes, 189-191
Lee, Paul, 102
Lepper, Mark, 113

Levy, Paul, xviii, 119-120
    Beth Israel Deaconess Medical Center
        culture of yes, 147-148
        lack of action, 142
    conflict management, 135
    decision making
        fair processes, 176-191
        sustaining closure, 215
Liebman, Max, 112
Light, Paul, 207
listening effectively, 174-175
Loeb, Marshall, 224
Logan Airport, 81
lone warrior myth, 226-228
Lord, Charles, 113

M

managerial levers
    communication, 34, 43-48, 94
    composition, 34-40
    context, 34, 40-43
    control, 34, 48-54
    U.S. Navy vessels, design/construction
        contract competition, 91-93
Mann Gulch, Montana, forest fire,
    217-218
Manning, Peyton, 95
March, James, 181
Marshall Space Center, 125
Martinez, Pedro, xiii-xiv
Massport, 80-81
Mauborgne, Renee, 192
May, Ernest, 156
May, Randy, 69-73, 77
McArthur, Dean John, 234
McDermott International, 80
McMillan, Bruce, 117
McNamara, Robert, 13
mental simulation, 98-99
Mercedes subsidiary, Daimler Benz, 180
Mets, New York, xiii
Minaya, Omar, xiii
Minnesota Center for Corporate
    Responsibility, 224
misalignment problems in fair and
    legitimate decision making,
    188-189

Mission Management Team, *Columbia* space shuttle, 63
  efficiency crowding out debate, 106
Mockler, Colman, 226
Moore, Gordon, 96
Morath, Julie, 42
  language systems at Children's Hospital, 78
Mount Everest 1996 tragedy, 3-4, 8, 231-232
  poor decisions, 16
Moyers, Bill, 104
Moynihan, Patrick, 207
Mulloy, Larry, 126
Munich analogy, 156
Myers-Briggs, 123

N

Nadler, David, 214, 229
NASA
  Apollo 13 mission, 178-179
  Columbia space shuttle accident, xviii, 3
  decision-making processes, 36
  efficiency crowding out debate, 106
  lack of candor and dissent, 62-67
  language systems, 78
  structural barriers to candid communication, 69
  space shuttle program
    framed as operational, 79
    lack of candid communication, 82
Navy (U.S.) vessels, contract competition, 87-91
  managerial levers use, 91-93
Neustadt, Richard, 156, 196
New England Patriots, 95
New Leaders for New Schools, 122
New York Mets, xiii

O

O'Neill, Tip, 205
Olsen, Ken, 161-162
out-of-family events, 78
outcome-oriented small wins, 206, 209-212

P

Parcells, Bill, 23
Pareto principle, 128-129

Patriots, New England , 95
Peters, Tom, 225-226
Pfeffer, Jeffrey, 147
Pisano, Gary, 75
point-counterpoint communication system, 101-102
point-to-point communication system, 105
Polycom, 101, 107
pre-mortems, 98-99
procedural legitimacy, 181-182
process-centric learning, 55
process-oriented small wins, 206-209

Q – R

Quick Market Intelligence, 159
Quinn, James Bryan, 10

Raben, Charles, 136
Rau, John, 156
Reagan, Ronald, 204
Rechner, Paula, 108
Red Sox, Boston, xiii
redescription, 128-129
reflection, 131-133
reframing debates, 124-127
Reiner, Carl, 111
repair of damaged feelings, 133
revisitation, 130-131
Ride, Sally, 66
Rocha, Rodney, 63-66
role playing, 95-97
  affective conflict management, 120-122
Roosevelt, Franklin, 102
Ross, Lee, 113
Royal/Dutch Shell, 97
rules of thumb, 157-158
Rumsfeld, Donald, 72
Russo, Edward, 199

S

Sandberg, William, 108
Sapienza, Harry, 172
scenario planning, 97
Schein, Edgar, 81, 161
Schlesinger, Arthur, 30
  legitimate decision-making processes, 187

Schnur, Jon, 124

Schoemaker, Paul, 199

Schrempp, Jurgen, 179-182

Schweiger, David, 108, 172

September 11, 2001 terrorist attacks, 50, 53

   Logan Airport, 81

Simon, Neil, 111

Skilling, Jeffrey, 77

smart-talk trap, 147

Smith, Darwin, 226

Social Security 1983 reform, 204-209

soft barriers to candor, 67, 75-83

Sorensen, Theodore, 31, 38

Spencer, Janet, 136

Stertz, Bradley, 180

Storm King Mountain fire, 78

structural barriers to candid communication, 67-75

Sun Life Financial

   Canadian Group Insurance subsidiary, 99-100

   role playing, 121

Sutton, Robert, 147

T

Tennant, Mark, 123

Tetrault, Roger, 80

Thibault, John, 168

Thiokol, Morton, 125

Thomson, James, 103-104

Tichy, Noel, 5

Top Gun, 76

Truman, Harry, 156, 195

   sign, *The Buck Stops Here*, 9

Tyler, Tom, 169

U

U. S. Forest Service, 217-218

U.S. Army, 131

U.S. Black Hawk helicopters shot down, 69-71, 76

U.S. F-15 fighter jet pilots, shooting down of Black Hawk helicopters, 69-71, 76

U.S. Forest Service (USFS), 78

   Mann Gulch, Montana, forest fire, 217-218

U.S. Navy vessels, contract competition, 87-91

   managerial levers use, 91-93

Ulrich, Dave, 5

unanimity in decision making

conflicts, 192-193

   fair processes, 168-176

      implementation, 176-179

   lack of, 165-167

   legitimate processes, 179-182, 185-188

   misalignment problems, 188-189

   teaching fair and legitimate processes, 189-191

Ury, William, 120, 125

V

Vaughan, Diane, 66, 79

Venton, Andrew, 200-201

Vietnam, 105

Vlasic, Bill, 180

W

Wal-Mart, 159

Walker, Laurens, 168

Wang, Jim, 76

Watkins, Michael, 170

   closure by leaders of decision-making process, 53

   patterns of participation and involvement, 51

Weick, Karl, 203

Welch, Jack, 14, 226

   best practices initiative, 159

   debate, 108-109

   GE's lack of candor, 59

   GE's reduction of hierarchy layers, 68

Wholesale Trading, 77

Wickson, Eric, 69-73, 76

Widnall, Sheila, 69, 78

Workforce Management magazine, 225

World Series, 2004, xiii

Worldwide Studios, 102

Writers' Room (*Your Show of Shows*), conflicts, 112, 137

Wyatt, Watson, 224

X-Z

Xerox, decision-making bodies, 74

Your Show of Shows, 111, 137

ZTech, 184